OSC IB STUDY & REVISION GUIDES
FOR THE INTERNATIONAL BACCALAUREATE DIPLOMA PROGRAMME

History
Paper 2: The Cold War

Standard & Higher Level

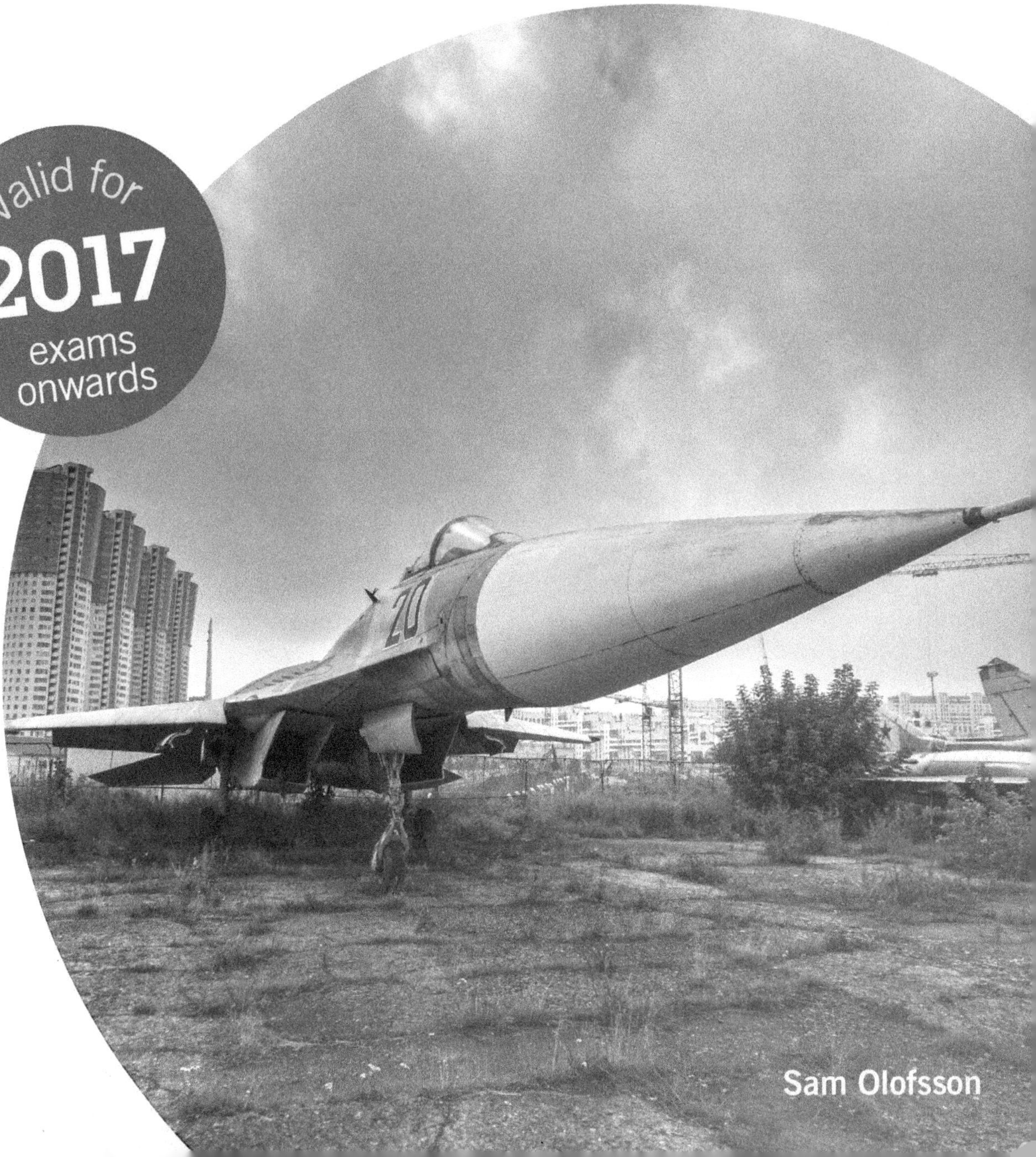

Valid for **2017** exams onwards

Sam Olofsson

OSC IB Study and Revision Guides
Published by OSC Publishing,
Belsyre Court, 57 Woodstock Road,
Oxford OX2 6HJ, UK

IB History Paper 2: Cold War
Standard & Higher Level
© 2017 Sam Olofsson

9781910689301

No part of this publication may be reproduced, stored in a retrieval system, or transmitted in any form or by any means, without the prior permission of the publishers.

PHOTOCOPYING ANY PAGES FROM THIS PUBLICATION IS PROHIBITED.

Sam Olofsson has asserted his right under the Copyright, Design and Patents Act 1988 to be identified as the author of this work.

The material in this Study and Revision Guide has been developed independently of the International Baccalaureate Organisation. OSC IB Study and Revision Guides are available in most major IB subject areas. Full details of all our current titles, prices and sample pages as well as future releases are available on our website.

How to order

Orders can be made via the website, e-mail, fax, phone or mail; contact numbers and addresses below.

OSC
Belsyre Court, 57 Woodstock Road
Oxford OX2 6HJ, UK
T : +44 (0) 1865 512802
F : +44 (0) 1865 512335
E : osc@osc-ib.com
W: osc-ib.com

Printed and bound by CPI Group (UK) Ltd, Croydon CR0 4YY
www.cpibooks.co.uk

Preface

I have had the pleasure of teaching IB history for over 20 years, mainly at Malmö Borgarskola in Sweden but also on revision courses in England and in the United States. It is my hope that this guide will give students the best possible help when preparing for their history exams.

My main aim is to encourage students to practise structuring essays. Each section of text is followed by a number of essay outlines. The idea is that students will first try to make their own outline and then compare it with mine. I have used this method with great success during my years as an IB teacher.

By the early 1990s, we thought we had put the Cold War behind us but in recent years, relations between the former antagonists have been very strained. What we must keep in mind about the Cold War period is that, while the superpowers were confronting each other on several issues, integration was increasing in Western Europe. The emergence of the EU is the most significant example of this. But history can unexpectedly take new paths. We are now living in a time of upheaval with events such as Brexit. Some may also see the US presidential elections in 2016 in this light. Commentators said that the "West" we have known since WWII, with cooperation and internationalization, now appears to be coming to an end. It is reasonable to assume that these events will one day become a new topic in the IB History syllabus, but it is only after we have distanced ourselves from these developments, that we can analyse them from a historical perspective—which is why the IB has its 10-year rule.

I currently divide my time between working at Malmö Borgarskola and as Secretary General of Star for Life, an organization that conducts education among 100,000 young people in Africa. My passion and my interest in education serves me in both these roles. This guide allows me to share some of the experience and knowledge I have acquired during more than two decades. Teaching history remains one of my greatest passions.

Sam Olofsson

Contents

Syllabus Relevance	6
How to Use This Study Guide	7
List of Essay Outlines	8
Essay Guidance	9
Credits/Acknowledgements	13

1. The Breakdown of the Grand Alliance and the Emergence of Superpower Rivalry in Europe and Asia (1943–1949) ... 14

Overview	14
Two Different Ideologies	15
Marxism-Leninism versus Liberalism and Market Economy, i.e., the Ideologies	16
Tension between the USSR and the US before WWII	17
In What Way Did WWII Contribute to the Cold War?	17
Events from WWII That Soured the Relationship between the US and the USSR	18
Casablanca, January 1943	19
The Cairo Conference, November 1943	19
The Tehran Conference, November and December 1943	19
Yalta, February 1945	19
Potsdam, July 1945	21
Historiography	21
1946: The Disintegration of the Wartime Alliance	24
1947: The Truman Doctrine—The Official Start of the Cold War?	26
1948: Rising Tension	27
Cold War Crisis 1: The Berlin Blockade 1948–1949	28
1949: The Formation of Two Germanys and NATO. China Turns to Communism	31

2. Korea, the US, the USSR and China: Superpower Relations (1947–1949), Containment, Peaceful Co-Existence, Sino-Soviet and Sino-US Relations, Détente ... 36

1950: The Cold War Ignites the Korean War	36
Cold War Crisis 2: North Korean Invasion of South Korea 1950	37
Impact and Significance of the 1950 Crisis	39
Impact and Significance of the Korean War	40
Two Cold War Leaders	45
The Cold War 1953–1964: Confrontation and Détente	48
Time for Détente (Lessening of Tension)? The New Russian Leadership after Stalin	48
The Eisenhower Administration and the New Look	49
The Non-Aligned Movement	50
Cold War Crisis 3: Hungary 1956	51
Impact and Significance of the Hungarian Uprising	53
Cold War Crisis 4: The Suez Crisis 1956	55

The Effects of the Suez Crisis	57
Cold War Crisis 5: Berlin 1958–1961	59
Impact and Significance of the Berlin Crisis	61
Cold War Crisis 6: The Cuban Missile Crisis 1962	65
Cold War Crisis 7: The Congo Crisis 1960–1964	72
The War in Indochina	75
Cold War Crisis 8: The Prague Spring 1968	78
Impact and Consequences of the Prague Spring	79

3. Détente 84
- Overview 84
- The Indochina and Vietnam Wars, 1946–1975 84
- The Indochina War, 1946–1954 84
- Course of Events 85
- How Did the Cold War Affect the Great Powers at Geneva? 85
- The Vietnam War 86
- How Did the Vietnam War Affect the 1970s? 88
- Why Was There a Period of Détente in the Late 1960s and 1970s? .. 90
- Examples of Détente 1968–1979 90
- Ostpolitik 91
- The Decline of Détente 92
- What Challenged Détente in the 1970s? The Middle East 92
- Africa 93
- The Emergence of the New Right 94
- Afghanistan 95
- To the USSR, Afghanistan Had Far-Reaching Consequences 95

4. The Coming of the Second Cold War and the Collapse of the USSR 99
- Overview 99
- The Background: Economic Stagnation during Brezhnev but an Increase of Military Spending 99
- Carter's policies 99
- 1979: A Turning Point 100
- Ronald Reagan and his Systematic Challenge 101
- Soviet Problems 102
- Gorbachev and the Fall of Communism 103
- Historiography 109

5. Germany, China, Vietnam and Cuba during the Cold War 117
- How was Germany Affected by the Cold War? 117
- How was China Affected by the Cold War? 118
- How was Vietnam Affected by the Cold War? 120
- How was Cuba Affected by the Cold War? 121

6. The Nuclear Arms Race and the Major Arms Agreement 123
- What were the Main Events in the Arms Race 1945–1991? 123

Further Reading 125

Syllabus Relevance

The syllabus is very specific regarding three areas that have to be covered:

1. 'The **impact of two leaders**, each chosen from a different region, on the course and development of the Cold War'.

2. 'The impact of **Cold War tensions on two countries** (excluding the USSR and the US)'.

3. 'Cold War crises case studies: detailed study of any **two Cold War crises from different regions:** examination and comparison of the causes, impact and significance of the two crises'.

Hence the guide will specifically cover these three areas. References to where these can be found in the book are below:

Cold War Crises
1. Berlin Blockade 1948–1949 ....[Page 28]
2. Korea 1950 ....[Page 37]
3. Hungary 1956 ....[Page 51]
4. The Suez Crisis 1956 ....[Page 55]
5. Berlin 1958–1961 ....[Page 59]
6. Cuban Missile Crisis 1962 ....[Page 65]
7. The Congo Crisis 1960–1964 ....[Page 72]
8. The Prague Spring 1968 ....[Page 78]

Cold War Leaders
1. Stalin ....[Page 45]
2. Truman ....[Page 46]
3. Eisenhower ....[Page 62]
4. Khrushchev ....[Page 77]
5. Reagan ....[Page 110]
6. Gorbachev ....[Page 111]

A Summary of How the Cold War Affected Different Countries from Different Regions
1. Germany ....[Page 117]
2. China ....[Page 118]
3. Vietnam ....[Page 120]
4. Cuba ....[Page 121]

How to Use This Study Guide

This guide will prepare you for Cold War questions in the IBDP History exam in Paper 2, covering the material you will study in Topic 12: The Cold War: Superpower Tensions and Rivalries. Some of the content could also be used when revising for Paper 3: Europe, particularly for Topic 17: Post-War Western and Northern Europe (1945–2000). The guide will hopefully provide you with relevant texts or summaries that will complement other sources available.

There is a method behind the writing, which I, from my experience, feel is very important to explain. I therefore recommend you to use the guide in the following way:

1. **Read** the text covering the topic (but not the essay outline which follows after).

2. Copy one essay template and try to answer the question by **writing down your main points** (not the details).

3. **Compare** your answer to the outline in the guide and assess the answers.

4. To read a guide and to write outlines does not prepare you fully for the exam. But when you think you know the main points of a topic, read your **textbook** which is much **more in-depth**.

An essay outline can, in many ways, be seen as an 'open document'. **There are always different interpretations and views and ways of structuring a question**. The aim of this guide is to show you possible yes and no arguments and topics to discuss.

My candidates have been trained to use this approach; i.e., to first study the topic in-depth and then put a lot of effort into trying to outline answers for essays. My experience is that the first five minutes used for an essay are of major importance. You need to:

- Read the question thoroughly and identify the command terms so that you understand what is required.
- Avoid the question if there are any terms you are unfamiliar with.
- Use some minutes to outline your essay before starting to write.

This is material which I have compiled after more than 20 years of IB teaching at Malmo Borgarskola, and revision courses at OSC in Oxford, Cambridge and Boston. Today I divide my time between teaching at Malmo Borgarskola—it is a passion—and working as Secretary General for Star for Life, an educational organisation reaching over 100,000 pupils in schools in Southern Africa.

I hope that this guide will provide you with the necessary historical knowledge as well as encourage you to write outlines for essays—I strongly recommend that you prepare in this way.

All the best of luck with your history studies!

Sam

List of Essay Outlines

1. To what extent was the Cold War a result of WWII? [Page 33]
2. 'The Cold War was a result of two conflicting ideologies'. To what extent do you agree with this statement? [Page 34]
3. Discuss how it's possible to explain the emergence of the Cold War by referring to events from the period 1945–1950. [Page 34]
4. To what extent had the policy of containment been successful in Europe and Asia between 1947 and 1950? [Page 35]
5. Compare and contrast the origins of two Cold War crises. (Berlin and Korea) [Page 43]
6. Discuss the outcomes of the Berlin crisis in 1948 and the Korean War. [Page 43]
7. Compare and contrast the impact and significance of two Cold War crises each chosen from a different region. (Berlin and Korea) [Page 44]
8. Compare and contrast the origins, impact and significance of two Cold War crises. (Korea 1950 and Hungary 1956) [Page 53]
9. Compare and contrast the origins of two Cold War crises. (The Korean War and the Suez crisis) [Page 58]
10. Compare and contrast the impact and significance of two Cold War crises each chosen from a different region. (The Korean War and the Suez crisis) [Page 58]
11. Examine how the Truman Doctrine and the policy of containment were implemented in the period 1947–1961. [Page 63]
12. Compare and contrast the Korean crisis of 1950 and the Congo crisis 1960–1961. [Page 74]
13. Why and with what results did the USSR place missiles in Cuba in 1962? [Page 81]
14. 'The Asian development of the Cold War was far more dangerous than European development'. With reference to events from the period 1945–1961, to what extent do you agree with this statement? [Page 81]
15. Compare and contrast the impact and significance of two Cold War crises each chosen from a different region. (Suez 1956 and Cuba 1962) [Page 82]
16. Discuss how the Vietnam War affected the Cold War. [Page 97]
17. Discuss why there was a period of détente in the 1970s. [Page 97]
18. Discuss why détente was brought to an end in the late 1970s. [Page 98]
19. To what extent did military expenditure lead to the collapse of the USSR? [Page 114]
20. To what extent did external pressure lead to the collapse of the Soviet system? [Page 114]
21. To what extent was Gorbachev responsible for the collapse of the Soviet system? [Page 115]
22. Examine the importance of détente in ending the Cold War. [Page 116]

Essay Guidance

> From the examination 2017, the essay questions will use five **command terms**:
>
> - **'Discuss'**
> - **'Examine'**
> - **'Evaluate'**
> - **'To what extent'** and
> - **'Compare and Contrast'**
>
> In **Paper 2**, the questions will be '**open**'; i.e., they will not refer to a specific topic. It will, however, be very difficult to ask questions about the Cold War and be totally 'open'—the question must be linked to something from that period.
>
> **Examples of two questions asking the same thing:**
>
> **Paper 2, i.e., an 'open' question:** *'A successful economic policy was essential for the maintenance of power by authoritarian leaders'. With reference **to one authoritarian leader**, to what extent do you agree with this statement?*
>
> A typical Paper 2 question will use the command terms (discuss, examine, evaluate, to what extent and compare and contrast) and then offer an opportunity to the candidate to choose his/her own example.
>
> **Paper 3** (asking the same question as above): *To what extent was a successful economic policy essential for Hitler to maintain his power?*
>
> You need to understand what each question requires in terms of structure.

1. **List questions, i.e., 'discuss', 'examine' and 'evaluate', you list the points you want to discuss:**

   Discuss the reasons for the Cold War.

   Go through the reasons for the Cold War and support each point with appropriate evidence. ('Discuss' could also be linked to a 'yes or no question'—see the text in point 2).

   Examine the impact of power vacuums in causing any 20th-century war.

   Account for, and examine critically showing the strengths and weaknesses of each point, how a power vacuum was important in causing war. You examine both the impact of the power vacuum and all other causes.

   Evaluate the success of the economic policies of one authoritarian leader.

   You shall weigh the strengths and the weaknesses of each point when explaining the leader's economic policies.

The questions ask you to examine and evaluate, i.e., to discuss critically all relevant points. It is not only a question of making a list of all the arguments. What you do additionally is assess each point in the question more critically, presenting both support and counter arguments to each point.

2. **'To what extent' questions**

   In this question you need to show arguments for 'to what extent it was' and arguments showing 'to what extent it was not'.

   Let's look at one example: *'The Asian development of the Cold War was far more dangerous than the European development'. With reference to events from the period 1945–1961, say to what extent you agree with this statement?*

   Show to what extent you **agree**, and to what extent you **don't agree**. Choose your own examples.

Author's Tip

Personally, I often advise students to write two lists. One describing 'yes' arguments, and one describing 'no' arguments. While some teachers may think this is too simplistic, my aim is to help students in preparing each question in the best way possible. It doesn't mean you have to slavishly follow the advice. But the guide and the outlines will show you all the possible arguments to use.

3. 'Compare and contrast the impact and significance of two Cold War crises each chosen from a different region.'

This is a typical Paper 2 question, i.e., you choose your own example. The question asks you to show the **similarities** and the **differences** between the two superpowers—**a comparison**. In many questions where you are asked to compare and contrast, the question is so extensive that you can only compare and contrast. You don't have enough time. **So go immediately to the similarities and after that to the differences, written in two parts of your essay. When you show the differences refer to both conflicts throughout your presentation.**

Overleaf are two templates for you to practise how to structure your essay.

Essay Template

Essay title to a 'to what extent', i.e., 'either/or question':
Introductory points:
1st main part:
2nd main part:
Conclusion:

Essay Template

| Essay title to a list question (i.e. discuss, examine and evaluate): |

| Introductory points: |

| Main part: |

| Conclusion: |

Credits/Acknowledgements

Chapter 1: *Karl Marx* — John Jabez Edwin Mayall (Photographer), International Institute of Social History in Amsterdam, Netherlands [Public domain], via Wikimedia Commons; *Vladimir Lenin* — Soyuzfoto (Photographer), Library of Congress (LC-USZ62-101877) [Public domain], via Wikimedia Commons; *'The Big Three' at Yalta* — Source: The National Archives (INF 14/447) [Public domain], via Wikimedia Commons; *Europe divided by the Iron Curtain* — Courtesy of Rickard Lundquist; *Franklin D. Roosevelt* — Source: The White House Historical Association Digital Library [Public domain]; *Joseph Stalin* — Yakov Yegorov (Illustrator), *Thirty Years of the Soviet State Calendar 1917–1947*, Foreign Languages Publishing (1947); *Stalin propaganda poster 'Beloved Stalin – fortune of the people'* — Unknown photographer [Public domain], via Wikimedia Commons; *Winston Churchill* — J. Russell & Sons (Photographer), Library of Congress (cph.3b12010) [public domain], via Wikimedia Commons; *Chiang Kai-shek, Franklin D. Roosevelt, and Churchill at the Cairo Conference in 1943* — Source: FDR Presidential Library & Museum (http://docs.fdrlibrary.marist.edu/images/photodb/09-1880a.gif) [Public domain]; *Harry S. Truman* — Greta Kempton (Photographer), Harry S. Truman Library [Public domain], via Wikimedia Commons.

Chapter 2: *Map of Korea* — Courtesy of Rickard Lundquist; *Georgy Malenkov* — Source: Dutch National Archives, The Hague, Dutch National Archives, The Hague, Fotocollectie Algemeen Nederlands Persbureau (ANEFO), 1945-1989 [https://creativecommons.org/licenses/by-sa/3.0/nl/deed.en]; *Nikita Krushchev* — Source: Bundesarchiv, Bild 183-B0628-0015-035 / Heinz Junge / CC-BY-SA 3.0 [CC BY-SA 3.0 de (http://creativecommons.org/licenses/by-sa/3.0/de/deed.en)], via Wikimedia Commons; *Dwight D Eisenhower* — Source: <http://www.history.navy.mil/photos/images/ac10000/ap16071.jpg> [public domain], via Wikimedia Commons; *John Foster Dulles* — Source: U.S. National Archives, number 306-PSC-60-15790 [public domain], via Wikimedia Commons; *John F Kennedy. White House, 7/11/1963* — National Archives Catalog (National Archives Identifier: 194255); *Cuban President Fidel Castro embracing Soviet Premier Nikita Khrushchev* — Superdominicano (Photographer) [http://creativecommons.org/licenses/by-sa/3.0/de/deed.en], via Wikimedia Commons; *US reconnaissance photograph from Cuba* — Source: National Archives and Records Administration (National Archives Identifier: 193933) [Public domain], via Wikimedia Commons; *ExComm meeting 29 October 1962* — Cecil Stoughton (Photographer), Presidential Library and Museum [Public domain]; *Portrait of Chairman Mao at the Tiananmen Gate* — Diego Delso (Photographer) [https://creativecommons.org/licenses/by-sa/3.0/nl/deed.en], via Wikimedia Commons.

Chapter 3: *Ho Chi Minh* — Source: Báo Cà Mau [Public domain], via Wikimedia Commons; *Lyndon B Johnson* — Elizabeth Shoumatoff (Artist), The White House Historical Association [Public domain]; *Leonid Ilich Brezhnev* — By Post of the Soviet Union, Ye. Aniskin (Designer), Andrei Sdobnikov (Scanned and processed image) [Public domain], via Wikimedia Commons; *Richard Nixon* — Source: The White House Historical Association [Public domain]; *President Nixon meets Mao Tse-tung on 29/02/1972* — Source: U.S. National Archives and Records (National Archives Identifier: 194759) [Public domain], via Wikimedia Commons; *Jimmy Carter* — Library of Congress (cph.3b52090) [Public domain], via Wikimedia Commons.

Chapter 4: *Ronald Reagan* — Source: dodmedia.osd.mil (ID: DASC9003096) [Public domain], via Wikimedia Commons; *Mikhail Gorbachev* — Source: White House Photo Office [Public domain], via Wikimedia Commons; *Eduard Shevardnadze* — R. D. Ward (Photographer) [Public domain], via Wikimedia Commons; *Ronald Reagan and Mikhail Gorbachev* — Source: Ronald Reagan Presidential Library (C31982-11) [Public domain], via Wikimedia Commons.

1. The Breakdown of the Grand Alliance and the Emergence of Superpower Rivalry in Europe and Asia (1943–1949)

> **Author's tip**
> Use these margins to write notes.

Figure 1.1: Iron Curtain after 1948[1]

Note: When Churchill talked about an Iron Curtain from Stettin in the Baltic to Trieste in the Adriatic in 1946, he didn't realise that the eastern zone of Germany would be within the Eastern Bloc and that Yugoslavia was outside the Eastern Bloc after 1948. If you study the map it is possible to find Churchill's Iron Curtain, i.e., Stettin to Trieste. This map above shows the Iron Curtain after 1948.

Overview

As we mentioned in the preface, the early years of the Cold War are of major importance when you study the whole topic. Trying to find an explanation for the Cold War implies that you need to be able to answer the questions:

> **Author's Tip**
> Don't use the Cold War as an example of a 'war' in an open question. It is, per definition, not a 'war'!

1. What was the Cold War?
2. When did it start?
3. How would you explain the different ideologies?
4. How important were events before and during WWII?
5. Who was responsible for the Cold War?

Ideologically, the USSR and the US represented two fundamentally different systems. There had already been major problems during the war and the alliance was more a result of a necessity to fight a mutual enemy than an expression of genuine understanding. It is clear that the US came out of the war as an economic superpower with access to nuclear weapons, while the USSR was in ruins.

---

[1] Courtesy of Rickard Lundkvist

As soon as the enemy, or enemies, i.e., Germany and Japan, were defeated, problems started to arise. Some historians argue that the Cold War started in July 1945, at the **Potsdam Conference**. Others argue that the dropping of the **atomic bomb** in August 1945 was the actual start of the Cold War, as the Americans didn't inform their ally, the USSR, about the bomb. Between 1945 and 1948, Stalin violated his promises to allow **free elections in Eastern Europe**. Together with the restart of the Civil War in China, this development alarmed the Americans. In 1947, President Truman announced his **Truman Doctrine**, a commitment initially made for Greece and Turkey, but soon extended globally. It was the most significant change of US foreign policy in the 20th century and isolationism was replaced by a commitment to fight communism globally. It has been seen as the official start of the Cold War. It was followed by the **Marshall Plan**, a US pledge to support the Western democracies economically.

Germany was the main trouble spot in Europe. Berlin was located in the Russian controlled Eastern zone, i.e., a capitalist island in a communist area. In 1948, Stalin tried to solve this problem by cutting off all land routes from the Western zones. It resulted in a one-year **airlift** with supplies from the West. It was now obvious that it was impossible to unite the different zones. The year after, two independent German states were announced. This year, 1949, also resulted in two major blows to the US: **China**, the most populous state in the world, became a communist state and the Russians exploded their first atomic bomb.

In 1950, North Korea attacked South Korea. After having 'lost' Eastern Europe to communism in 1945–1948, and watch China become a communist state in 1949, the Americans decided to turn the Cold War into a 'hot' war. The Korean War lasted from 1950 to 1953 and it was not until Stalin died in 1953 and Eisenhower replaced Truman, that it was possible to seek new positions. In 1953, both the US and the USSR had hydrogen bombs and a nuclear arms race had begun.

The first part of the Cold War, i.e., 1945–1953, turned two allies into enemies in a global conflict. The two superpowers had gone from cautious optimism in 1945 to a fierce struggle for world domination.

> To answer questions about the origins of the Cold War it will help you to know:
> 1. How WWII affected East-West relations.
> 2. The main differences in their ideologies.
> 3. The main events between 1943 and 1949.
> 4. The historiography.

Two Different Ideologies

Figure 1.2: Karl Marx

Figure 1.3: Vladimir Lenin

The Cold War can be defined as a state of permanent hostility between two systems and this conflict could never be allowed to erupt into a 'hot war' or armed conflict due to the fear of a nuclear war. This war could be fought by different means, i.e., not necessarily armed conflicts. It could be that one 'client state' (ally or satellite) was fighting a war against one of the superpowers, as in Korea, but it is worth noticing that there was no major armed confrontation between the USSR and the US between the years 1945 and 1989.

The term 'Cold War' had first been used in the 14th century to describe hostilities between Christians and Muslims. But it was an American journalist, Walter Lippmann, who started to use the term to describe the relations between the US and the USSR after 1945.

Adolf Hitler also realised what the future would bring. In his 'Testament' written in April 1945, he wrote:

> "With the defeat of the Reich...there will remain in the world only two great powers capable of confronting each other: the United States and Soviet Russia. The laws of both history and geography will compel these two powers to a trial of strength, either *military* or in the fields of *economics* and *ideology*." [2]

Marxism-Leninism versus Liberalism and Market Economy, i.e., the Ideologies

A. The Economy

In broad terms, a **communist society** or Marxism-Leninism rejects private capitalism and private companies and the state controls the means of production. To achieve an equal society, the state plans how resources are used and how the result of the production is distributed. State control of the means of production is a necessary prerequisite in creating an equal and classless society. Common ownership will guarantee both equality and wealth. In Soviet Russia, it led to a nationalisation of both land and companies, without compensation to the previous owners.

A worker in a capitalist society is exploited by the capitalists. Consequently, a true Marxist wants to liberate oppressed workers in other countries. The rejection of private capitalism and a desire to 'liberate' oppressed workers in other countries terrified conservative politicians in Western countries. The ruling classes should tremble according to Marx.

In a **capitalist system** private ownership and private companies are cornerstones of the society. Competition and a free market produce wealth, and government intervention is normally seen as a negative thing. Even though some state intervention may be acceptable to secure a free market, it is entrepreneurship, trade etc. that will guarantee prosperous economic development. The Americans wanted free trade between states to endorse economic growth and ship products to the consumers. This policy was referred to as an '**open door policy**'. From a Russian point of view, this was only a new form of imperialism. By creating economic dependence, the political life of each country would later be controlled. The American demand for 'equal rights' was a demand for economic conquest.

B. Political Life

In the USSR, the Communist Party represented the interests of the working class and the masses, so consequently there was no need for other parties. Soviet Russia was a **single-party state** and by representing the interest of the masses, it was claimed to be democratic.

In a Western society, the existence of a political opposition in a **multi-party system**, is meant to guarantee a democratic system. The people are offered the opportunity to replace the government in times of election. Freedom of speech, and association, freedom of the press, and free elections are essential in preserving a true democratic system. Whereas a single-party system is considered non-democratic as it does not offer the same opportunity to replace the government with an election. The USSR, however, accused the Western democracies of being non-democratic by allowing richer classes to influence political parties and media in the West.

C. Religion

In a communist society, religion was regarded as a means for richer classes to control and oppress the poorer classes. A Russian Marxist was, by definition, an atheist (someone who doesn't believe in any God or religion).

> **Author's Tip**
>
> You need to be able to discuss the importance of ideology as one reason for the Cold War. You should be able to explain the ideologies of the two superpowers. Let's do that by investigating four vital areas within society.

---

[2] Gaddis, J. L., *We Now Know: Rethinking Cold War History* (Oxford: Oxford University Press, 1997) p. 1.

Even though religion and the state are formally separated in the US constitution, it is clear that there is a strong Christian evangelical tradition and that religious groups are of major importance in political life. Atheism and 'Godless communism' scared many Americans during the Cold War.

D. Civil Rights

Both systems claimed that they were democratic and blamed the other side for not respecting democratic rights. Soviet Russia claimed that it exercised the '**dictatorship of the proletariat**', i.e., a transitional stage before a classless society, communism, was achieved. During this 'dictatorship' the majority exercised control over the minority. Some restrictions concerning civil rights (like freedom of speech and assembly) had to be temporarily imposed. This minority was the old elite and was now prevented from interfering and controlling political life. By restricting freedom of speech for a minority, a more democratic society was established.

After this period everyone would realise the benefit of socialism and the final stage, a communist classless society, would be accomplished. The USSR blamed the Western democracies for being non-democratic by allowing richer capitalists to influence the media.

In the US, freedom of speech, the press, assembly and worship are seen as major building blocks in their democratic society and are guaranteed in the constitution. The Americans clearly rejected the Soviet view of a Western society dominated by a few capitalists. In contrast, communist societies controlling the press and imprisoning political opponents were seen as brutal dictatorships.

The two systems opposed each other in every vital ideological aspect, i.e., the economy, political life, religion and civil rights. It is also important to mention that these two systems wanted to expand due to different reasons:

- To a communist, expansion meant that workers would be liberated from capitalist oppression.
- To a Western liberalist, expansion would bring prosperity and what they believed to be genuine civil rights.

Tension between the USSR and the US before WWII

It is possible to trace the origins of this conflict to the very foundation of the Bolshevik state in Russia in 1917. The new Bolshevik regime strongly believed that in order to survive it had to stimulate revolutions in other countries, i.e., a **world revolution**. The early development in the Weimar Republic can be seen against this background. The Comintern (the Communist International) was set up to promote this development in 1919. From 1918 to 1921, the new Russian regime had to fight a **civil war** against the White forces, made up of different groups opposing the new regime. The Whites were supported by Western powers fighting in WWI. The Western powers claimed that they wanted to re-open the Eastern front after the Bolshevik regime had signed the Treaty of Brest-Litovsk. The Western powers continued the fight against the new regime in Russia, even after the war had ended. It was now clear to the Bolsheviks that capitalists were not prepared to accept a state based on Marxist ideology. After leaving Russia, the intervention was replaced by an economic embargo and it was not until 1933 that the US and the USSR established diplomatic relations. There was no major difference to Stalin between the capitalist states and to him it was only a confirmation of his worst fears when France and Britain did nothing to prevent Hitler's expansion in the mid-1930s. The **Munich agreement** in 1938 forced Stalin to turn to his arch enemy Adolf Hitler, when signing the **Non-Aggression Pact** in August 1939. From a Western point of view, Stalin had clearly shown that he was a ruthless dictator by signing a pact with another ruthless dictator, which enabled Hitler to attack Poland.

In What Way Did WWII Contribute to the Cold War?

The outcome of the war had a major importance for the development of the Cold War. Remember that officially the two superpowers were allies during the war:

1. The war resulted in **two superpowers** with totally opposing ideologies. After WWII we start to use the term 'superpower' instead of a 'great power'.
2. One of these superpowers had a **nuclear monopoly**. The atomic age had a profound effect on international relations. This is covered in the next section.

3. **The USSR had suffered enormously** from WWII. Twenty-five million people were killed, 1,700 cities and 70,000 villages were in ruins, 70% of their industries and 60% of the transportation facilities were destroyed. It can clearly be questioned if it is correct to describe the USSR as a 'superpower' after the war.

4. **The US had experienced a wartime economic boom**. The industrial output of the US grew by 90% between 1940 and 1944. Taking this into consideration, and the fact that the Americans had a **nuclear monopoly**, it can be argued that the Americans have never been as strong as they were just after the war. On the other hand, industrialists and politicians were worried that the end of the war would bring an end to this development. International trade and an 'open-door' policy would compensate for the loss of war production.

5. **Germany.** Germany did not exist politically and economically when the war ended. There was an enormous **power vacuum** in the centre of Europe which is one major reason for the Cold War. Decisions were made at Yalta and Potsdam in 1945 to divide Germany into 'zones of occupation' (see below) and that there should be a Western zone in Berlin, totally surrounded by the Russian zone. This would later create a lot of problems.

6. **The Red Army had liberated and controlled most of Eastern Europe**. How would Stalin use this control? In 1945, he claimed: *"Whoever occupies a territory also imposes on it his own social system. Everyone imposes his own system as far as his army has power to do so. It cannot be otherwise."*[3] In 1944, Stalin and Churchill had concluded the **Percentages Agreement** concerning influence in South-East Europe (the Balkans). The ratios for Britain and the USSR were: Romania 10:90, Greece 90:10, Bulgaria 25:75, Hungary 25:75, and Yugoslavia 50:50. Notice that it didn't involve Poland and Czechoslovakia. Churchill later claimed in his memoirs: *"[We] were only dealing with immediate wartime arrangements."*[4] Was this the case or did he only try to justify his actions? And what was Stalin's interpretation?

Did You Know?

'Indochina' refers to Vietnam, Laos and Cambodia.

7. During the war, Japan occupied **Korea, China and Indochina**. In 1943, Churchill and Roosevelt had issued the Cairo Declaration: *"Japan will also be expelled from all other territories taken by violence and greed…Korea **shall become free and independent**."*[5] This commitment was confirmed by the USSR, Britain and the US at Potsdam. It was stated that *"The terms of the Cairo Declaration shall be carried out."*[6]

Both Korea and Vietnam should be temporarily divided and later unified. Would it work? Would the Civil War in China restart? Like Europe, there was clearly a **power vacuum** in Asia after the Japanese surrender.

Events from WWII That Soured the Relationship between the US and the USSR

1. Even though the US and the USSR had been allies during WWII, there were reasons for distrust, not only from a political and ideological point of view. The USSR had signed the **Nazi-Soviet Pact** in 1939 enabling Hitler to start the war. The question of a **Second Front** in Europe had divided the allies. Stalin wanted help to ease the burden of the Red Army after the German invasion in 1941. It was not until 1944 that the Western powers finally invaded France and opened a real 'Second Front' in Europe. Was it a deliberate move to let the USSR bleed to death? Stalin concluded that for every American who was killed, 90 Russians died.

2. The War ended with the Americans dropping an A-bomb on **Hiroshima** and **Nagasaki**. The USSR had promised the Americans to join them in defeating Japan at Yalta. Now the Americans dropped the bomb without informing their major ally only two days before the Russian attack. Historians have argued that it was the last battle of WWII and the first battle of the Cold War.

Finally, let us emphasise the wartime conferences which were of major importance. Some of the decisions at these conferences have been partly covered above, but are listed here for the sake of completeness:

---

[3] McCauley, M., *Origins of the Cold War 1941–1949* (Harlow: Longman, 1995) p. 117.
[4] McCauley, M., *Origins of the Cold War 1941–1949*, p. 117.
[5] http://avalon.law.yale.edu <Accessed 5 January 2017>
[6] http://avalon.law.yale.edu <Accessed 5 January 2017>

Casablanca, January 1943

1. The US and Britain would demand an **unconditional surrender** of the enemies. The meeting took place between Churchill and Roosevelt, i.e., Stalin did not attend.

2. When North Africa had been liberated, America and Britain would open a **front in Europe**. Italy was seen as the main alternative. American and British war efforts should be coordinated.

The Cairo Conference, November 1943

This meeting took place between Roosevelt, Churchill and Chiang Kai-shek from China to discuss the war against Japan and the future of Asia.

In the Cairo Declaration it was stated that:

1. The war against Japan should be continued until there was an **unconditional surrender**.

2. Japan should **leave all conquered territories** (this included Korea and Indochina).

The Tehran Conference, November and December 1943

Many of the issues later decided in detail at Yalta and Potsdam in 1945, were discussed at this conference. The main questions when **The Big Three** met were:

1. The opening of a second front in Western Europe, i.e., **Operation Overlord**, in northern France, should be executed in May 1944

2. That the USSR should support her allies in defeating **Japan**

3. The future of **Germany**

4. The establishment of the **United Nations**

5. The future of the **Baltic States and Poland.**

Yalta, February 1945

1. **Poland:** It was moved 300 km to the West. A compromise was reached over the future government when Stalin promised that some members of the London government (pro-Western) should join the Lublin government (pro-Soviet). 'The Declaration of Liberated Europe' was signed by Stalin promising free elections in Eastern Europe.

2. **Japan:** Stalin promised to help the Americans in defeating Japan and to declare war 2–3 months after the war had ended in Europe.

3. **United Nations:** A renewed attempt towards collective security was agreed upon and Molotov would attend the first meeting at San Francisco in April 1945.

4. **Germany:** It should be de-Nazified and was divided into four zones of occupation, i.e., an American, Russian, British and French zone. Berlin was also divided into different zones and the result was a Western zone within the Eastern zone. The establishment of zones of occupation had been decided at a series of conferences and the French zone was added at Yalta. The Berlin solution was probably Stalin's worst mistake because the Berlin problem would later cause major problems to the USSR. The Berlin Wall would later be the symbol of Soviet control of Eastern Europe. Germany should be governed by an Allied Control Council with veto rights for each power. The reparation issue was not solved but handed over to a Reparation Commission.

Yalta is normally considered as a 'success'. Agreements were made over Germany, Japan, Poland and the United Nations.

Figure 1.4: 'The Big Three' at Yalta

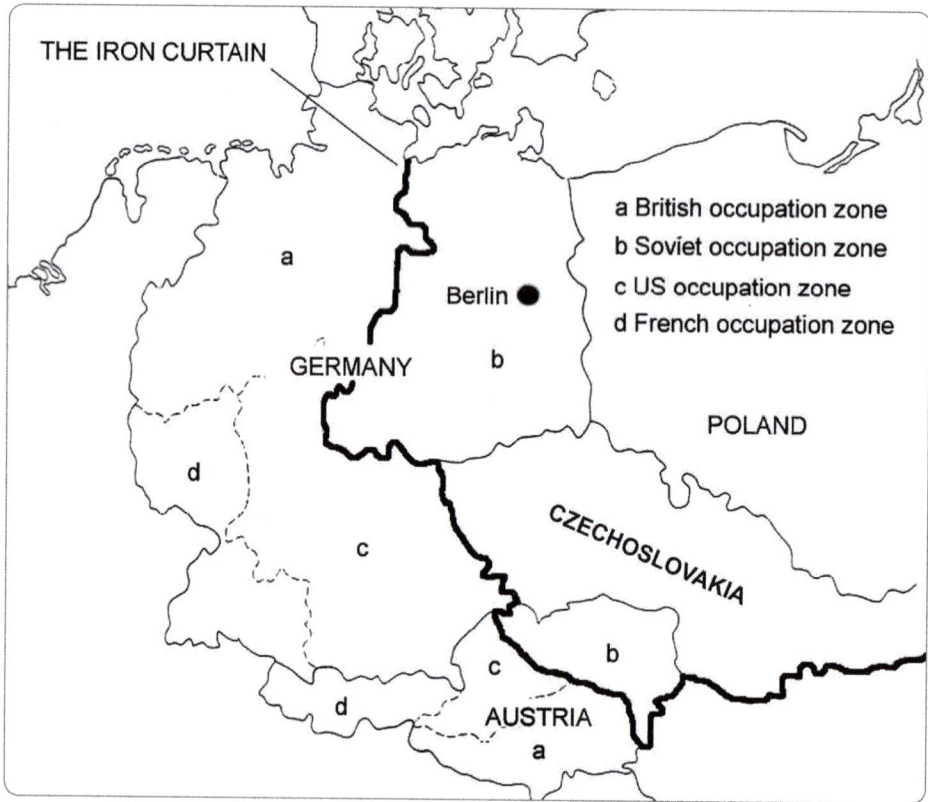

Figure 1.5: Europe divided by the Iron Curtain

Potsdam, July 1945

1. **Germany:** The zonal division of Germany was finally confirmed in the 'Potsdam Protocol on Germany'. No final agreement was reached over reparations. Russia demanded $20 billion from Germany, which was rejected by the Western powers. Russia was left to take what it could from their zone of occupation and to get some reparation from the Western zones.

2. **Eastern Europe:** Western leaders were deeply shocked over developments in Eastern Europe. There were 'sharp exchanges' and the West claimed that Stalin didn't follow the spirit of the **Declaration of Liberated Europe.**

3. **Japan:** The Potsdam Proclamation called for Japan's unconditional surrender: *"The alternative for Japan is prompt and utter destruction,"*[7] according to the Potsdam Proclamation.

   Truman knew at Potsdam that the bomb would work and wanted to end the conflict on his own terms. Stalin was prepared to take part in the defeat of Japan and did not desire a quick Japanese surrender.

4. **Vietnam and Korea:** In Asia, Japan had occupied **Korea, China and Indochina**. In 1943, Churchill and Roosevelt had issued the Cairo Declaration: *"Japan will also be expelled from all other territories taken with violence and greed... **Korea shall become free and independent**."*[8] At Potsdam this commitment was confirmed by the USSR, Britain and the US. It was stated that *"The terms of the Cairo Declaration shall be carried out."*[9] Agreements were made to divide the countries temporarily and then unify them later.

Key Point

Potsdam July 1945: The war had now ended in Europe but Japan did not surrender until August 1945.

Did You Know?

Potsdam is normally described as a failure filled with disputes. Some historians even see the Potsdam meeting as the start of the Cold War.

> **Author's notes:** A final assessment of the importance of events of WWII on the Cold War will be covered later when we have studied the events between 1945 and 1950. It is difficult to remember and to separate different events from the Yalta and Potsdam conferences. But without any doubt it can be **concluded that some of the decisions made at Yalta and Potsdam would play a major role in the Cold War** later. Especially:
> - The German solution with Berlin would lead to two Berlin crises (1948 and 1958) and the erection of the Wall in 1961.
> - The division of Korea and Vietnam would later lead to the two worst armed conflicts during the Cold War.

Historiography

Before describing developments that took place after the war, we would like to introduce some of the major interpretations concerning responsibility for the Cold War.

The Orthodox view: Stalin and the **ideology of Marxism-Leninism** were responsible for the Cold War. To Americans it was in the nature of communist ideology to attempt to spread the ideal of communism. Marxist-Leninism was an expansionist, aggressive force formally claiming that the aim was to 'liberate the masses' from capitalism. Throughout his whole career, Stalin had clearly shown that he tolerated no rivals. His policy in Eastern Europe after the war is a very good example. Not only did he violate his promises from Yalta in the **Declaration of Liberated Europe** promising *"free elections of Governments responsive to the will of the people and to facilitate where necessary the holding of such elections"*[10]; he also introduced and imposed a brutal political control of **Eastern Europe**, executing many of his political opponents. These states should have been seen as independent sovereign states, but they were soon referred to as Soviet 'satellites'. Arthur Schlesinger writes: *"Leninism and totalitarianism created a structure of thought and behaviour which made post-war collaboration between Russia and America inherently impossible."*[11]

---

[7] http://avalon.law.yale.edu <Accessed 5 January 2017>
[8] http://avalon.law.yale.edu <Accessed 5 January 2017>
[9] http://avalon.law.yale.edu <Accessed 5 January 2017>
[10] http://avalon.law.yale.edu <Accessed 5 January 2017>
[11] McCauley, M., *Origins of the Cold War 1941–1949*, p. 108.

It is interesting to notice that Stalin's responsibility for the Cold War has survived the opening of Soviet archives in the mid-1980s. John Lewis **Gaddis** writes in '*We Now Know': Rethinking the Cold War*: "*I think the 'new' history is bringing us back to an old answer: that as long as Stalin was running the Soviet Union a Cold War was unavoidable.*"[12]

The Revisionist view: This view emerged from mainly American historians in the late 1960s. The US didn't realise how weak the Soviet Union was after WWII and how much stronger the Americans were. Russia had suffered enormously during WWII, while the Americans not only experienced **an economic boom**; they also had a **nuclear monopoly**. Stalin realised Russia's weaknesses and his desire to control Eastern Europe was mainly a defensive move to protect the USSR. How did the Americans use their superiority? They issued the **Truman Doctrine** giving them a right to intervene everywhere. The US tried to impose its ideals on other people and American values of liberty and free markets should be applied worldwide. After WWII the Americans had the military power to enforce their will—and consequently tried to do this. With the Marshall Plan and their economic **open door policy** they tried to control countries by economic dependence. Old-fashioned colonialism had never been popular in the US due to the simple fact that the US had once been a British colony. But with this new form of imperialism, where economic dependence would be exploited politically, there was no need for traditional formal political control. It was referred to by the Russians as 'dollar-imperialism'. William Appleman Williams writes: "*It was the decision of the United States to employ its new and awesome power in keeping with the traditional Open Door Policy which crystallized the Cold War.*"[13]

The Post-Revisionist view: With access to new archives a new school of post revisionist historians emerged in the late 1970s. The Cold War was a result of mutual misunderstandings and overreactions due to **fear** from both sides. The Americans didn't really understand the USSR's need for security against the West and her need for buffer states and how their strength and 'open-door policy' affected the USSR.

The Russians didn't fully realise how their policy in Eastern Europe affected opinions in the West.

It is also clear that the development of nuclear weapons and the different ideologies of the two countries resulted in a lot of mutual misunderstandings and fear. Defensive measures by one power were often seen as offensive by the other power. This was met by further measures and a dangerous cycle of action and reaction came into being. The outcome, especially if we take into account the development of nuclear weapons, was less security for both sides. This is called the **security dilemma**. The post-revisionist historians argue that it was more **miscalculations** and fear by both which created the Cold War. Melvyn Leffler writes: "*The Kremlin was so totalitarian and repressive. US officials intelligently decided to rebuild Western Europe…. These actions were of decisive importance in fuelling the Cold War…. Western Europe required security guarantees, not the extensive armaments that America wanted it to have.*"[14]

The 'Realpolitik' School: It has its roots in Bismarck's Germany. According to this school some politicians tend to ignore their ideology when dealing with other states, as long as it is to their benefit. When discussing the Cold War it is clear that 'ideology' is a key word. It is therefore useful to be aware of the Realpolitik School which **dismisses the idea of the importance of ideology**. Ideology is only an additional weapon deliberately used by the superpowers to rally the support of the nation. It is a propaganda tool and a mask used to get support while trying to fulfil their state interests. Economic pressure, military power and ideology were means used to achieve an aim. It is clear that both superpowers used ideological arguments to get support from their nations. Could it be that American politicians talked about 'Godless communism' when in fact they wanted access to a new and important market? Or did Stalin and the Soviet leaders depict a hostile and dangerous surrounding capitalist world threatening the USSR just to get support for traditional Russian expansion, this time in Europe? Richard Nixon was a well-known anti-communist who was prepared to cooperate with

Author's Tip

Make sure that you can explain the arguments of these four schools.

---

[12] Gaddis, J. L., '*We Now Know': Rethinking Cold War History* (Oxford: Oxford University Press, 1997), p. 292.
[13] McCauley, M., *Origins of the Cold War 1941–1949*, p. 110.
[14] McCauley, M., *Origins of the Cold War 1941–1949*, p. 111.

both the USSR and China, as long as the US gained from this cooperation. Historians believing in the Realpolitik school would downgrade the importance of ideology in explaining the origins of the Cold War and argue that other reasons were behind this conflict.

Figure 1.6: Franklin D. Roosevelt

What were the post-war aims of Roosevelt?

- **The world should be open to free trade, i.e., the 'open door policy'**. To promote this development, the Americans stood behind the creation of two important institutions at the Bretton Woods conference in 1944: the World Bank and the International Monetary Fund.
- **To promote peace and international co-operation**. The idea to make a second attempt with collective security, the United Nations, was Roosevelt's idea.
- The Americans rejected the idea of **'spheres of influence'**, i.e., that one state should indirectly be controlled by an outside power. **National self-determination** (the right to decide in which state a population shall belong), **democratic institutions** and civil rights were cherished by the Americans. The British colonial empire had no strong support in the US which would become obvious in 1946, when Churchill made his Iron Curtain Speech. (A revisionist historian would however question this point arguing that the Americans were looking for their own kind of domination. A new form of economic imperialism derived from their economic domination.)
- To continue to maintain **relations that were as good as possible with the USSR.**

Stalin's Post-War Aims

Figure 1.7: Joseph Stalin

Figure 1.8: Stalin propaganda poster 'Beloved Stalin fortune of the people'

Critical Thinking

Is it possible to trace the origins of the Cold War in these aims? Were they conflicting?

- Stalin realised that the USSR was severely weakened after the war and that **American aid** could be beneficial to the USSR. The Russians had received aid through the 'lend-lease' agreement during the war and wanted to continue this co-operation.
- Russian **security**, i.e., controlling states in Eastern Europe which should be seen as a Russian sphere of influence.
- To prevent a **German recovery**. This aim would be clearly visible in the future in Germany.
- To **regain territories** that had been lost after WWI.

1946: The Disintegration of the Wartime Alliance

Economic hardship in Western Europe after the war and electoral successes of the communist parties in Italy and France deeply worried political leaders in the West. Tension also rose over the development in **Eastern Europe**. Harassment, terror and rigged elections produced communist single-party rule in countries like Bulgaria, Romania, Poland and Hungary in 1946–1947. It was a clear violation of the Declaration of Liberated Europe. Western leaders saw the development in Eastern Europe as a first step in taking control of the countries in the West. An attempt to put nuclear weapons under UN control, the **Baruch Plan**, was vetoed by the USSR. The plan would not only prevent the Russians from continuing to develop their own nuclear weapons, it would also bring UN inspectors to the USSR. From a US point of view there was a very problematic development in Asia:

In **China**, the **Civil War** had restarted and south of China, in **Vietnam**, a full-scale war between the French and Vietnamese Communists and Nationalists, Vietminh, started in 1946—the **Indochina War**.

In 1946, we can see signs of a changing attitude in the West that would progressively lead to the introduction of the Truman Doctrine in 1947:

1. In February George **Kennan**, a diplomat at the US Embassy in Moscow, wrote his **Long Telegram**. It was a report written for the State Department and it was widely circulated within US bureaucracy and provided the intellectual basis for the '**doctrine of containment**'. A public version of the Long Telegram was published in a famous article in Foreign Affairs in July 1947, called 'the X article'. Kennan stated that no long-term co-operation was possible with the Soviet regime and that communism must be contained within its present borders. The USSR was aggressive, expansionist and hostile and described by Kennan as *"World Communism is like malignant parasite which feeds only on diseased tissue."*[15]

    Kennan's Long Telegram influenced Washington to a major extent and is a very important background factor behind the policy of 'containment' and the Truman Doctrine issued in 1947. It is, however, important to notice that Kennan himself questioned Truman's emphasis on military containment. In his memoirs he writes that he *"considered containment as primarily political and economic,"* according to Crockatt.[16]

2. In March, the British ex-premier **Winston Churchill** gave his **Iron Curtain Speech** at Fulton in the US.

> "From Stettin in the Baltic to Trieste in the Adriatic an iron curtain has descended across the Continent. Behind that line lie all the capitals of the ancient states of Central and Eastern Europe. Warsaw, Berlin, Prague, Vienna, Budapest, Belgrade, Bucharest and Sofia; all these famous cities and the populations around them lie in what I must call the Soviet sphere."

---

[15] Hanhimäki, J. M. and Westad, O. A., eds., *The Cold War: A History in Documents and Eyewitness Accounts*, (Oxford: Oxford University Press, 2003) p. 111.
[16] Crockatt, R., *The Fifty Years War: The United States and the Soviet Union in world politics*, 1941–1991 (London: Routledge, 1995) p. 74.

Figure 1.9: Winston Churchill

Figure 1.10: Chiang Kai-shek, Franklin D. Roosevelt, and Churchill at the Cairo Conference in 1943

The speech appealed for a **renewal of the Anglo-American alliance** as a means of deterring Soviet expansionism. Churchill continued his speech:

"If the population of the English-speaking Commonwealth be added to that of the United States, with all that such cooperation implies in the air, on the sea, all over the globe, and in science and in industry, and in moral force…. there will be an overwhelming assurance of security." [17]

Revisionist historians argue that it was now that **Stalin** definitely decided to 'satellite' Eastern Europe. He saw it as a major threat to Soviet security and **answered** in a speech:

"Mr. Churchill begins to set war loose, also by a racial theory, maintaining that only nations speaking the English language are fully valuable nations, called upon to decide the destiny of the entire world." [18]

Churchill's speech, which must be today described as 'famous', was initially met with suspicion in the US. US opinion was not yet prepared to regard the USSR as an implacable enemy and many Americans suspected that Churchill simply tried to get US assistance to maintain the power of the British Empire worldwide. At the time Britain suffered from an economic crisis and problems in India, Greece and Palestine. It is also clear that the speech did have a major impact on US opinion and contributed to the new policy in 1947.

3. In September, the **US Secretary of State, Byrnes,** announced in his **Stuttgart Speech** that the US supported a revival of Germany politically and economically. *"The German people…should now be given the primary responsibility for the running of their own affairs."*[19]

It was clear that Germany constituted a major problem to the occupation forces. In May the US had suspended **reparation** deliveries from their zone to the Russians, which was seen as a violation of the Potsdam agreement. Both France and the USSR had good reasons to fear a German recovery. **The Allied Control Council**, which had been set up to govern Germany, never worked due to the **veto power** of each occupational force. In 1946, it was apparent that the US and Britain had realised that a recovery of Europe was dependent on a German recovery. It was against this background that Byrnes made his speech in September. In 1946, Germany was divided into two hostile camps and each side now started to encourage the revival of German political parties. On 1 January 1947, the British and the US zones were merged into one zone, Bizonia. By now it was possible to foresee that there would be two German states in the future. It was something that Stalin had never realised during the war, accepting West Berlin as a capitalist island in the Eastern zone.

---

[17] McCauley, M., *Origins of the Cold War 1941–1949*, p. 131.
[18] McCauley, M., *Origins of the Cold War 1941–1949*, p. 132.
[19] McCauley, M., *Origins of the Cold War 1941–1949*, p. 133.

1947: The Truman Doctrine—The Official Start of the Cold War?

Figure 1.11: Harry S. Truman

In 1947, the US adopted a policy of **containment**, influenced by George Kennan. The aim was to prevent the spread of communism beyond its present borders, i.e., to contain it within its existing borders. The Americans calculated that they were the strongest country in the world both economically and militarily. By adopting a more active role, they would not only be able to prevent a further expansion of communism, they would also strengthen the 'free world'. Members of the Truman administration, who still believed in some kind of dialogue with the Russians, were eased out of office. One important change was that Byrnes was replaced as Secretary of State (foreign minister) by general **George Marshall**.

The immediate reason for the Truman Doctrine was that in February Britain informed the US that they could no longer support **Greece and Turkey** economically. Britain had traditionally supported allies in the Eastern Mediterranean against Russian expansion. In 1946, there was a civil war in Greece where the government was fighting a communist-led insurgency. Stalin had announced that he wanted a revision of a treaty from 1936 that had put the **Straits of Constantinople** (Istanbul) under Turkish control. He wanted international control of this important waterway and delivered a strong note demanding this in the summer of 1946.

Truman knew that in order to win over a **US Congress** dominated by **Republicans**, his arguments had to be convincing: "*At the present moment in world history nearly every nation must choose between alternative ways of life,*" Truman argued. Some historians claim that he exaggerated the threat from communism when he delivered his speech to the Congress. It is clear that it was a historic moment. The US role of **isolationism towards world politics** was now, definitely, going to be replaced by an **active role.** This is the most important turning point in US foreign policy in the 20th century. Initially, his request for money was only intended for Greece and Turkey but it was soon extended globally and would lead to armed conflicts in both Korea and Vietnam. Truman said:

> "One way of life is based upon the will of the majority….The second way of life is based upon the will of a minority. It relies upon terror and oppression…it must be the policy of the United States to support peoples who are resisting attempted subjugation by armed minorities or by outside pressures." [20]

---

[20] McCauley, M., *Origins of the Cold War 1941–1949*, p. 138.

'**Outside pressures**' was of course Moscow, even though Stalin had remained neutral in the civil war in Greece. The Congress granted Truman $250 million to Greece and an additional $150 million to Turkey. Using this help for military needs the communist insurgents were eventually defeated. It was clear that the Turkish government was far from democratic but there would be many more examples in the future where it was more important to be anti-communist than democratic. The US also reorganised its administration. In the **National Security Act** (NSC) from 1947, the War and Navy Department were merged into a new Defense Department and the Central Intelligence Agency (**CIA**) was created.

In June of the same year the Secretary of State George Marshall announced his **Marshall Plan**. This massive economic help for European reconstruction was initially offered to most European countries, even the communist states. But it was soon rejected by the USSR and her satellites. From a Russian point of view, this type of new economic imperialism and dependence had to be turned down. Marshall however stated in his speech: "*Our policy is directed not against any country or doctrine, but against hunger, poverty, desperation and chaos.*"[21]

The reasons for this 'act of humanity' have been widely discussed by historians. There were probably several reasons:

- Marshall had been in Europe in early 1947 and was appalled at the economic and social situation in Europe. **Help** was definitely **needed**.
- **Political reasons: Hunger and poverty were a perfect breeding ground for communism**. The French Communist Party belonged to the coalition government in the country and the Italian Communist Party was also very strong. There was a risk that some Western democracies would turn to communism. That Western Europe should be 'lost to communism' was unacceptable. The Marshall Plan would bind the states in Europe to the US, not just only economically but also politically.
- An economic slump or Western Europe turning to communism would deprive the Americans of one **important economic market**. The US would benefit from a prosperous Europe.

Truman was able to pass the Marshall Plan through Congress in 1948. He was assisted by a communist takeover in Czechoslovakia the same year (see 1948). The effect of the Marshall Plan is normally considered as **successful** and led to massive industrial growth with a GNP growth in Europe of around 15–25% annually. Financial stability returned. Politically the development in 1947 was a **major turning point**. It was now clear that the US would play an active world role and it is hardly surprising that **Stalin now tightened his grip in Eastern Europe**. The successor of Comintern, the international communist organisation, was formed in 1947 and renamed as **Cominform**. The aim was to control and organise communist activities outside the USSR. Non-Communists were expelled from the Hungarian government and developments in both Czechoslovakia and Yugoslavia in 1948 are hardly surprising. The Soviet deputy foreign minister Andrei Vyshinsky said in a speech in the UN in September 1947:

> "The so-called Truman Doctrine and the Marshall Plan are particularly glaring examples of the manner in which the principles of the United Nations are violated….It is becoming more and more evident to everyone that the implementation of the Marshall plan will mean placing European countries under the economic and political control of the United States and the direct interference by the latter in the internal affairs of these countries."[22]

1948: Rising Tension

The establishment of communist rule in Eastern Europe followed a general pattern. The Red Army had liberated the countries from Nazi control and immediately introduced a policy of denazification. Communists who had been educated in the USSR and were loyal to Stalin soon took leading positions within their national parties. Left-wing parties were pressured by the Communists to join them in '**Popular Fronts**' and they soon dominated national provisional governments by controlling key posts such as **Ministers of Justice, Interior** (controlling the police) etc. By controlling the judicial and repressive systems of the state, the Communists were able to **rig elections**, i.e., to ensure communist

---

[21] McCauley, M., *Origins of the Cold War 1941–1949*, p. 137.
[22] Hanhimäki, J. M. and Westad, O. A., eds., *The Cold War: A History in Documents and Eyewitness Accounts*, p. 126.

victories. Political opponents were harassed or simply made to disappear. Between September 1947 and February 1948 all non-Communists were purged from the governments in Czechoslovakia, Bulgaria, Romania and Hungary.

Once the political system was controlled, a **Sovietisation of other aspects of life like economy, culture, land distribution and media could proceed.** Formally these satellites retained their full independence but they were controlled by the USSR. There were two major exceptions in Eastern Europe: Yugoslavia and Czechoslovakia.

There are many examples from Eastern Europe showing this. In Poland, the Peasant Party refused to join the Democratic Front which was requested by the Communists. The party was subjected to harassment and terror and elections in 1947 were manipulated. The communist controlled 'electoral bloc' got more than 90% support in the elections. In Hungary, the leader of the Smallholders party Béla Kovács, and other representatives from his party, were arrested by Soviet troops in 1947. In Romania the Communists and their allies got 372 out of 414 seats in the elections in 1946. The results had been falsified. In Bulgaria, the Fatherland Front secured 90% of the votes at elections in 1945 and used terror and coercion against the political opposition.

Yugoslavia had been liberated from Nazi control by Yugoslav partisans under the leadership of Josip Broz **Tito**—and not by the Russian Red Army. After the war Stalin tried to impose his plans for economic development in Yugoslavia, i.e., to concentrate on heavy industry. Tito resisted this policy and took his own initiatives to form a custom union with Bulgaria and Hungary. Stalin could not allow this form of 'national communism' and withdrew his economic and military advisers from Yugoslavia. In June 1948, Yugoslavia was expelled from Cominform, the international communist organisation, accused of 'bourgeois nationalism'. The Eastern Bloc now announced an economic blockade and broke off diplomatic relations. **Yugoslavia was now expelled from the Eastern Bloc**, but Tito and his regime had considerable national support. It was also important that they didn't share a border with the USSR. The US offered considerable financial assistance. The outcome of this crisis led to the creation of a **non-aligned**, non-Stalinist, **communist state**. But it also led to a major purge of '**national communists**' in Russian satellite states. The Yugoslav example should not be copied.

Czechoslovakia had been liberated from Nazi occupation by the Red Army. But there was much stronger support for communism in Czechoslovakia compared to other satellites due to 'the ghost of Munich'. The betrayal by the Western democracies in 1938 had not been forgotten. Communists secured 38% support in free elections in 1946 and joined a coalition with non-communist parties. In 1947, the country suffered from an economic crisis and the Communist Party feared that this would affect its chances at the elections in 1948. After disputes within the government regarding nationalisation of industries and land reform, non-communist ministers resigned. The Prime Minister formed a new National Front government with only Communists and reliable supporters. When elections eventually took place, the Communists won 237 of 300 seats in parliament and soon **all other parties were dissolved**. The only country in the Eastern Bloc with a genuine multi-party system had now been transformed to a communist single-party state

In the West and in the US, this confirmed the view of the 'hardliners'. The **coup in Czechoslovakia** helped the US government to pass the Marshall Plan through Congress.

Cold War Crisis 1: The Berlin Blockade 1948–1949

On 23 June 1948, the Russians cut off all land links to West Berlin. The city was a capitalist island or enclave surrounded by the Russian controlled Eastern zone. 2.5 million West Berliners were now cut off from coal, food and other supplies. **It was the first Cold War crisis in Europe during the Cold War.**

A. What were the underlying reasons for this conflict?

1. The two superpowers had **conflicting aims concerning Germany**.

    a) Stalin and the Soviet Union feared a **Germany recovery**. In order to promote Soviet security, Germany had to remain weak. The Soviet buffer system in Eastern Europe would then be more effective.

Author's Tip

The development in Eastern Europe is of major importance if you want to support the 'orthodox view'. It was claimed that Stalin violated the Declaration of Liberated Europe. You must be able to give some examples showing this, when explaining the 'orthodox school'.

b) Stalin also thought that it was possible that the US would leave Germany after the war, which could result in a Soviet takeover.

c) On the other hand, the US had realised that a German recovery was important for two reasons: (1) it would generate growth in Europe, (2) it would **prevent the spread of communism in Europe**.

2. By 1948, Stalin had realised that the Berlin solution from Yalta and Potsdam, a capitalist enclave in a Soviet controlled area, was extremely problematic if Germany were to remain divided. Germans living in the Eastern zone just had to cross a street and they were in the West. With Marshall aid pouring into West Berlin, there would be economic pressure as well. There were to be elections in October 1948, and West Berlin's economic development was seen as a problem in the East. Stalin had not realised that the division of Germany might be permanent but in 1948 this outcome was seen to be likely. **The Berlin problem must be solved**.

The crisis in steps:

1946
In September 1946, the **US Secretary of State, Byrnes,** announced in his **Stuttgart Speech** that the US supported a political and economic revival of Germany.

1947
In 1947, the **Truman Doctrine** was announced. The US would play an active role globally to defend Western democracies against 'outside pressures', i.e., against communism.

The same year the **Marshall Plan** was announced. In the Soviet Union, it was seen as a US attempt to control European states economically and politically.

In January 1947, the US and Britain joined their two zones into one. Later that year the French also joined.

In December 1947, the US, Britain and France met at the **London Conference** to discuss a future German state—without the USSR.

1948
In February 1948, the Western powers proposed a new four-power currency. The Soviets rejected this proposal.

In March 1948, at the London Conference, Britain, France and the US announced their intention for a unification of the Western zones and the establishment of a **West German government**.

The Western powers announced that the **currency reform** would be implemented in the Western zones, including Berlin, from June 1948. If the German economy were to recover, it needed a stable currency. The Soviets had however debased the Reichsmark by mass printing money. The Soviets rejected Western plans for a reform and the currency reform was the formal reason for the blockade, i.e., the currency reform was a Western violation of the wartime agreements.

The USSR cut off all water-, road- and railroad links to West Berlin in June 1948. **The Soviets offered to drop the blockade if the currency reform was withdrawn**. 2.5 million inhabitants were suddenly without food and coal. To support the population of Berlin was very symbolic. This was the year after Truman had promised to 'defend democracy' in the Truman Doctrine. Many in the West feared the blockade could be followed by an invasion of the Western zones. There were 98,000 American troops in West Germany in March 1948 and 1.5 million Soviet military forces in the Soviet sector that surrounded Berlin. It should be noted that the ground routes had never formally been negotiated at Potsdam, but air space had been discussed. On 30 November 1945, they had agreed in writing that there would be three 20-mile-wide air corridors providing free access to Berlin. To shoot down a US unarmed cargo aircraft filled with humanitarian aid was not an easy decision. On 1 July, the US and Britain organised a massive airlift to supply the population with necessary supplies.

There were other alternatives discussed to solve the crisis. One was to respond with military means, which could of course provoke a major clash. Others suggested taking the issue to the UN. Truman chose to take direct action with the airlift, which probably surprised Stalin. It was a very problematic operation taking into account adverse weather conditions and that the two airports were surrounded by apartment buildings. The very scale of the operation was so extensive that the Soviets thought it was impossible. Planes landed every three minutes during a 10-month period and provided the city with 2,326,406 tonnes of supplies on 278,228 flights. During 323 days this 'Operation Vittles' supplied Berlin with goods until the blockade was lifted in May 1949.

B. Impact and significance

1. To the US it was a propaganda triumph. They had been prepared to protect the population in West Berlin against brute force and inhumanity from the Soviets. Communism had been contained.

2. After this conflict it was impossible to cooperate over Germany. It led to the creation of the **Federal Republic of Germany** (FRG) on 23 May 1949. Konrad Adenauer was elected West Germany's first Chancellor. As a response the **German Democratic Republic** (GDR) was formed in October of the same year. It can be argued that this development most likely would have taken place without the Berlin crisis, but the crisis made it absolutely inevitable. West Germany was proclaimed the same month as the airlift ended. Both states were organised according to the blocs to which they belonged.

3. In March 1948, the UK, France, Belgium, the Netherlands and Luxembourg had signed the Treaty of Brussels. The aim was to prevent the spread of communism. In September, after the blockade had started, it was expanded with a mutual defence agreement. This would lead to the establishment, in April 1949, of the North Atlantic Treaty Organization (NATO). It was a full military alliance, i.e., an attack on one was to be considered as an attack on all. West Germany should be protected. An alliance between the Western powers would "*keep the Russians out, the Germans down and the Americans in.*"[23] **NATO** was a major commitment to the Americans. It was the first treaty signed with a European state since 1778, when they had signed an alliance with France. The significance of the Truman Doctrine, or the new world role played by the Americans was now obvious. Twelve states joined the organisation when it was founded: United States, Canada, Britain, France, Belgium, Netherlands, Luxemburg, Italy, Portugal, Denmark, Norway and Iceland. West Germany was not a formal member but the territory would be protected by the alliance. Greece and Turkey were added in 1951. It was a full military alliance and according to article 5, "*an armed attack against one or more … be considered an attack on them all*"[24] and would be met by armed force. A joint NATO command to co-ordinate the defence of the territories was also formed.

4. With the crisis it was clear that the USSR had to accept the special status of **West Berlin as a part of the West**. The special status of Berlin, as the only place where armed soldiers from the two superpowers stood face to face, would remain.

5. The most significant result of the crisis was that it resulted in a definite establishment of two blocs in Europe. Some have argued that it 'drew the line' in the Cold War in Europe. As a consequence of this a **substantial military build-up** followed and that the US was more committed than ever to make their contribution.

The historian Bell concludes: "*The significance of the Berlin crisis 1948–49 cannot be overstated […] it was a turning point in international affairs […] The psychological foundations of a western alliance were laid in this time…*"[25]

---

[23] Edwards, O., *The USA and the Cold War 1945-63* (London: Hodder & Stoughton Educational, 1992) p. 50.
[24] Edwards, O., *The USA and the Cold War 1945-63*, p. 50.
[25] Bell, P. M. H. and Gilbert, M., *The World Since 1945: An International History* (London: Arnold, 2001) p. 94.

1949: The Formation of Two Germanys and NATO. China Turns to Communism

The formation of NATO was seen as a major escalation by Stalin and the USSR but he could find comfort in the fact that the Russians exploded their first **atomic bomb** in the same year. Molotov, the Foreign Minister concluded: "…*the imperialist camp has lost thereby one of its most powerful means of blackmailing peoples*".[26] In China, Mao's communist forces could proclaim the foundation of The People's Republic of **China** in October. The most populous state in the world had now turned to communism and to the Americans this new China was another state controlled by Moscow. Truman was accused of the 'loss of China'.

Student Activities

We have outlined the most important part of the Cold War from the examiners' point of view. This can be concluded by studying how questions are set in exams. Questions about how the Cold War started, The Truman Doctrine, containment and the Korean War are frequent in IB exams. What is very important is to use this knowledge to structure your essay answer. The questions about the origins of the Cold War do not normally require an ability to write one full essay about the Truman Doctrine or any other event from the period. You need to use events from the period 1945–1950 to answer such a question and to form an argument. So if we should simplify what we have done so far, **you are expected to know:**

Key information:

- **The consequences of WWII including the Yalta and Potsdam conferences**
- The **ideologies** and to be able to explain them
- The main interpretations, i.e., **historiography**.

1946

- The Civil War in China had re-started
- The Indochina war started
- Kennan's Long Telegram
- Churchill's Iron Curtain Speech
- Byrnes's Stuttgart Speech
- The development in Eastern Europe 1945–1948.

1947

- The Truman Doctrine and the policy of containment
- The Marshall Plan.

1948

- Yugoslavia
- The coup in Czechoslovakia
- The Berlin Airlift.

1949

- The establishment of two separate German states
- NATO
- The Russian A-bomb
- China turns to communism.

Key Point

Some historians have argued that the Berlin Airlift drew the line in Cold War Europe and that the Korean War would do the same in Asia in the early 50s.

---

[26] Ball, S. J., *The Cold War: An International History 1947–1991* (London: Arnold, 1998) p. 17.

This brings us to the question how or why did the Cold War start? It brings us to an important issue, namely, when did it start? Officially there is no formal starting point, even if many historians refer to the Truman Doctrine. We have earlier defined the Cold War as a state of permanent hostile relations between the two camps, which could not be allowed to become 'hot' due to the existence of nuclear weapons i.e. the Cold War started in 1945 or later. It has been argued that:

- The Cold War can be traced back to the Russian Civil War in 1918–1921 when the White forces were supported by the Western powers.

- Did it start at the Potsdam conference? There were heated arguments over developments in Eastern Europe. No agreement was made over reparations and Truman, who was informed about the existence of the Atomic Bomb during the conference, did not properly inform Stalin, only the British.

- Was it the dropping of the bomb on the 6 August 1945 that started the Cold War? The USSR meant to attack Japan on the 8th but was not informed by the Americans that they were going to use the bomb. 'It was the last battle of WWII but the first battle of the Cold War'. The use of the bomb and post-war discussions about how to share nuclear technology deeply affected Stalin.

- How much attention should be paid to the Iron Curtain Speech? After all, Churchill was an ex-leader when he made the speech and it was met with suspicion by many Americans. On the other hand, it had a major impact on US opinion and on Stalin. Some historians have argued that Stalin tightened his grip on Eastern Europe after the speech, which deeply affected the West.

- With the Truman Doctrine in 1947 the US officially declared a new role to meet what they perceived as the challenge of communism. The Marshall Plan was seen as 'dollar imperialism'.

1 The Breakdown of the Grand Alliance and the Emergence of Superpower Rivalry in Europe and Asia (1943–1949)

We shall now outline some typical exam questions on the origins of the Cold War:

1. To what extent was the Cold War a result of WWII?
2. 'The Cold War was a result of two conflicting ideologies'. To what extent do you agree with this statement?
3. Discuss how it is possible to explain the emergence of the Cold War by referring to events from the period 1945–1950?
4. To what extent had the policy of containment been successful in Europe and Asia 1947–1950?

We will provide you with some outlines with suggested answer points. There is never a 'final' answer to these types of questions and we think it might be useful to do the following:

1. Study the question. What does it require? What kind of question is it?
2. Write down your suggested answer points (use the essay plan templates).
3. Study our model answer and compare it with your own. It may be that you have used another approach that is just as relevant. The important thing is to assess and compare the answers.

Make an attempt to answer this question and compare your answer with the outline below and on the following pages.

Exercise 1: To what extent was the Cold War a result of WWII?

(Elaborate the reasons why the Cold War was a consequence of WWII then offer a counter argument stating it had nothing to do with the war.)

Yes, it was a result of the war (elaborate on the following points):

1. The war resulted in two victorious and dominant superpowers with totally different ideologies.
2. One had a nuclear monopoly and had used the bomb without informing her ally. The atomic bomb made a 'hot' war impossible, hence brought the 'Cold War'.
3. The USSR had suffered enormously from the war while the US emerged stronger than ever. The question of a 'second front' during the war had soured relations.
4. The Red Army controlled Eastern Europe, which would have a major significance in post-war Europe.
5. Germany did not exist politically and militarily. There was a power vacuum in the heart of Europe. Decisions during the war had resulted in Germany being divided into zones of occupation, Berlin was to have a western zone and there should be a ruling Allied Control Council with veto rights assigned to each occupying power.
6. In Asia, Japan had surrendered and control had to be re-established in Korea, China and Indochina.

No, the Cold War was not a result of the war:

1. Tension had already surfaced during the Russian Civil War 1918–1921 and it took years until the Americans recognised the USSR. Their relations had always been hostile, which was expected.
2. Write about how fundamentally different these two systems were from an ideological point of view. It is likely that there would have been tension between these two systems even without the war. Neither believed in a peaceful co-existence. **This is the most important point in Part II.**
3. You could put yourself in the shoes of an orthodox historian by arguing that a Marxist Leninist system would challenge the free world even without WWII. This was inevitable due to the USSR's wish to 'liberate' oppressed workers in capitalist countries. Lenin had argued that clashes between the Soviet Republic and bourgeois states were inevitable.
4. You can use arguments from a revisionist historian. The Open Door policy aimed at dominating other countries economically and this kind of 'dollar imperialism' cannot be purely seen as a result of the war and it would of course provoke the USSR.
5. To post-revisionist historians, 'fear' is one key explanation of the Cold War and one reason for this fear was of course nuclear weapons. The construction of nuclear weapons had started before the war and it cannot be argued that nuclear weapons were a result of WWII. It is clear that the existence of nuclear weapons in the future would cause tension and this cannot be seen as a WWII phenomenon.

Conclusion: It is difficult to totally ignore the importance of ideology during the Cold War. But it is also possible to argue that the results of the war in combination with the ideologies played a role. It can also be argued that ideology was of no importance to a politician like Stalin, thereby supporting the Realpolitik school.

1. The Breakdown of the Grand Alliance and the Emergence of Superpower Rivalry in Europe and Asia (1943–1949)

Exercise 2: 'The Cold War was a result of two conflicting ideologies.' To what extent do you agree with this statement?

(You have to define and show the importance of their ideologies in the first part of the essay and argue that the problems were not due to ideological difference, in the second part.)

Yes, ideology was important:

1. **Explain Marxism Leninism** (the economy, political life, religion and civil rights) and its desire to expand into other countries. What a communist perceived as the 'dictatorship of the proletariat' was seen by Western observers as a ruthless and totalitarian form of government with single party rule, planned economy and atheism.

2. **Explain capitalism, market economy** (the economy, political life, religion and civil rights) **and the 'open door policy'** and its desire to expand into other markets.

   Use examples illustrating how each side perceived the 'other side'.

   For example, what the Americans thought about Russian policy in **Eastern Europe** and in **Asia**. They were horrified over the fact that political opposition was harassed, land and industries had been nationalised without compensation, etc. You can write a lot here.

   What did the USSR think about the **Marshall Plan** and the **Truman Doctrine**? Why was it so important to revive Germany? Show how they were coloured by their ideologies.

No, it was not an ideological conflict:

1. Explain the 'Realpolitik school', which claims that powers may act out of reasons other than ideology but use ideology to disguise their real intentions or simply as a means of getting support.

2. Even if ideology was important, some historians emphasise the importance of WWII. The differences of the ideologies existed before 1939, but why did relations collapse after the war? The war created a unique situation where these two superpowers achieved world domination and powers like Germany and Japan were totally destroyed. This situation led to a contest for power globally.

3. It is interesting to notice that the Americans were prepared to support non-democratic regimes like Tito in Yugoslavia, Syngman Rhee in Korea, Batista in Cuba and Diem in Vietnam, whose most important qualifications were that they opposed Moscow. How much attention shall be paid to ideology?

4. Stalin's expansion into Eastern Europe deeply worried the Western powers. But had this expansion anything to do with communist ideology or was it caused by security reasons or a traditional Russian desire to dominate surrounding countries?

Conclusion: It is difficult to totally ignore the importance of ideology during the Cold War. But it is also possible to argue that the results of the war in combination with the ideologies played a role. It can also be argued that ideology was of no importance to a politician like Stalin, thereby supporting the Realpolitik school.

Exercise 3: Discuss how it's possible to explain the emergence of the Cold War by referring to events from the period 1945–1950

(This can be approached in several ways. It is a list question and it is possible to go through the question by writing a chronological account. There is a risk that this will become a narrative account which will not score well. We recommend you use the different schools of interpretation again. It will enable you to write a more analytical essay. **It is however very important to support each school by referring to different events.***)*

- Describe the **'orthodox view'** and explain Marxism-Leninism from an ideological point of view. Use examples from the period that will strengthen your argument. Possible points to cover: the **Russian policy in Eastern Europe versus commitments made at Yalta**, the policy in Germany where an economic unity was blocked, the **Berlin airlift, the coup in Czechoslovakia**, Comintern and developments in **China, Korea and Vietnam**.

- A **revisionist historian** would describe this period by explaining how strong the Americans actually were after the war, both economically and militarily. This strength was used to achieve world domination. It is possible to strengthen this view by referring to the dropping of the **A-bomb**, policies in Germany, the **Truman Doctrine** leading to support for Greece and Turkey; and perhaps most importantly, the **Marshall Plan** providing for **'dollar imperialism'** and an 'Open Door policy'. US policies in Asia, such as in Korea, and support for the French in Indochina are also possible points to use. The US also misinterpreted Stalin's foreign policy. They thought that his driving force was an expansionist communist ideology and not national security.

- A **post-revisionist historian** would describe the emergence of the Cold War as a result of mutual misunderstandings and fear. The Americans didn't understand that Stalin's aims in Eastern Europe were mainly defensive and that he genuinely feared US military and economic strength. Instead they issued the Truman Doctrine aiming at world domination. Stalin was probably not fully aware of how his brutal policies in the satellites affected politicians in the West. It is also clear that with so fundamentally different systems combined with the development of weapons of mass destruction, a lot of fear and misunderstandings were inevitable. Both sides must bear responsibility.

Conclusion: Summarise your main points and emphasise what you think is important. But notice that the question doesn't explicitly ask you to make your own 'final judgement'.

Exercise 4: To what extent had the policy of Containment been successful in Europe and Asia between 1947 and 1950?

(Write one part of the essay claiming that it had been successful and a second part showing failures. Note that you must explain the term containment at the beginning of the essay.)

It is always important to define difficult words in the question. 'Containment' needs to be defined. **Containment** was the US policy that was adopted by President Truman in his Truman Doctrine in 1947 by which the US attempted **to prevent further Soviet or communist expansion** beyond territories occupied in 1945. No long-term co-operation with the USSR was possible and George Kennan provided the intellectual basis in his Long Telegram from 1946. By supporting the 'free world' economically through the Marshall Plan in Europe and economic aid to Japan, the expansion of communism would be prevented.

Successes:

1. The Marshall Plan led to a substantial economic recovery in Western Europe and it is believable that conditions which bred left-wing support were receding as a result of this. The communist parties in both Italy and France lost some of their substantial support in elections in the late 1940s.
2. This was probably most obvious in the western part of Germany, which went through a remarkable economic recovery. Germany became a democratic and economically stable country bordering the Eastern Bloc. A pro-Western Germany was without any doubt essential for the survival of Western Europe as a part of the 'West'. The conservative Christian Democrats and Konrad Adenauer were victorious in free elections.
3. The Berlin airlift must be described as a 'victory'. The Americans had been able to support 2.5 million Germans and this support had turned the population pro-American.
4. The support for Greece and Turkey enabled these two countries to remain within the Western camp. (Both joined NATO in 1951.) The Communists had been defeated in the civil war in Greece.
5. The building up of a strong Western military alliance, NATO, under American leadership, strengthened the West.
6. In the late 1940s, the Americans successfully started to build up Japan as an ally in Asia and a bulwark against communism.
7. South-Korea was given support and protection in 1950, when the north attacked.

Failures:

1. The US build up of Western Europe was a threat from Stalin's point of view, and he strengthened his control of the satellites. The Czech coup in 1948 and a purge against 'national communists' can partly be seen as a response to the build up in Western Europe and these counter actions were not 'successful' from an American point of view.
2. The 'loss' of China was a major failure. The most populous state in the world turned to communism and signed a Sino-Soviet Friendship Treaty in 1950. The Nationalists in China had received economic aid after 1945, yet they lost the Civil War.
3. In 1950, the Korean War started. Even if it was too early to assess the final outcome of this conflict in 1950, it was clear that the Americans were facing an expansionist enemy. At the end of 1950, Communist-controlled China also attacked the UN forces in Korea.
4. In Vietnam, the French were fighting a difficult war against communist guerrillas who were not easily defeated. The US had now started siding with an unpopular colonial ruler and feared a domino reaction throughout South-East Asia.

Conclusion: Summarise the successes and the failures. It is possible to conclude that containment had been more successful in Europe than in Asia.

2. Korea, the US, the USSR and China: Superpower Relations (1947–1949), Containment, Peaceful Co-Existence, Sino-Soviet and Sino-US Relations, Détente

The Truman Doctrine in 1947 and the Berlin crisis in 1948 had a major impact on the continuation of the Cold War. We shall now study how Cold War tension spread to Asia.

1950: The Cold War Ignites the Korean War

Figure 2.1: Map of Korea

In early 1950, The National Security Council (NSC) delivered a classified report to the Truman administration known as the **NSC-68** report. It stated, "*Soviet efforts are now directed towards the domination of the Eurasian land mass*"[27] and **recommended a massive US build-up of both conventional and nuclear arms**. It can be seen as a response to an expected increase in Russian aggression as a nuclear power and to the 'loss' of China. It was not enough to have a dominant economy. The US needed to be militarily superior to meet the challenge of communism. The US should develop a hydrogen bomb. The problem was that this policy would require **higher taxes**, i.e., it would cause domestic problems for Truman. In June, North Korea suddenly attacked South Korea and this is considered as a turning point in

---

[27] See https://history.state.gov/historicaldocuments/frus1950v01/d85 <Accessed 4 January 2016>

the Cold War. It was assumed that Stalin had ordered Kim to attack and Soviet aggression would follow in other countries, the Domino Theory. The recommendations of NSC-68 were now implemented and US defence spending went from $13 billion in 1950 to $50 billion within a few years. The Russian A-bomb, the 'loss' of China and the Korean War provided senator Joseph McCarthy with ammunition for his witch-hunt in the US in the early 1950s.

> Why is this 'crisis' confined to only 1950? And if we write about the impact and consequences of the attack in 1950, should we describe events, which happened years later, as an 'impact' of the crisis in 1950?
>
> **Some advice from the IB Curriculum manager:** *"A Cold War crisis should be a flashpoint that involves a clear escalation in Cold War tension."* It is not necessary that the superpowers were directly involved but there needs to be involvement *"of some kind."* Focus should be more on how the crisis involved superpower relations than the events that took place. It is also stated that *"…it is better if it's more sharply focused on a shorter time period. So for example, rather than using 'the Korean War', it would be better to use 'The North Korean invasion of South Korea' (1950) as the crisis. Then the focus can be on the invasion and the US/USSR reaction, rather than just treating it in exactly the same way as you would if you were doing the whole Korean War as an example of a 20th century war."* This leads us to describe 'impact and consequences' with a narrower time frame. So the Korean War will be described as:
>
> 1. Firstly, there will be writing about the causes, impact and consequences of only the invasion and the events in 1950, with the focus mentioned above. This to be used as an **example of a 'crisis' in Topic 12 Paper 2: The Cold War.**
> 2. Secondly, the text will continue with the whole war and its impact and consequences, so the Korean war can be used as an **example of a 'war' in Topic 11 Paper 2: 'Causes and effects of 20th century wars'.**
>
> So the Korean War can be used in two topics in Paper 2.

Cold War Crisis 2: North Korean Invasion of South Korea 1950

Japan had annexed Korea in 1910. At the Cairo Conference in 1943, it had been decided that the country should be independent when the war was over. This decision was confirmed at the Potsdam Conference and that the US should control territories south of the 38th Parallel and the USSR north of the Parallel—in order to promote a development where Korea would be able handle its own affairs. The idea of unification never materialised. In the North the Soviets installed a communist regime under the leadership of Kim Il-sung. In the South, the Americans installed Syngman Rhee, an anti-communist and authoritarian leader. Both were very nationalistic and wanted to unite the country under their rule. In 1948, there were elections for a National Assembly but only in the South, where Syngman Rhee was elected President. The same year two separate Korean states were established. The division was deeply resented by both sides and the population wanted a unified Korea. In late 1948, Soviet troops left the North and in early 1949, American troops left the South. This development reminds us of the development in Germany—no co-operation was possible.

Kim Il-sung met Stalin in May 1949 and again in April 1950, in both occasions suggested that the North should invade the South. While Stalin had rejected the idea in 1949, he was more positive at the meeting in 1950. There were a number of reasons why this decision was made:

A. Why did Kim want to attack the South?

1. Kim can be seen as a Korean nationalist who wanted to unite his country, which had been **controlled by the Japanese between 1910 and 1945**, and then divided after the war. The Korean War can also be seen as a **civil war** where Kim Il-sung and Syngman Rhee wanted to **unite** their country. There had been constant border disputes between the two countries before the attack.

2. **Ideologically** he had reasons for 'liberating' the South from capitalism.

3. It can be argued that he **didn't expect the US** to support the South. The US Secretary of State, Dean Acheson held a speech in January that defined what should be considered as being within the US '**defence perimeter**'. Neither Korea nor Taiwan were included.

4. **Both US and Russian troops had left** Korea but Stalin had provided Kim with arms. In June 1950 alone, the USSR provided the North with 258 tanks, 178 warplanes and 1,600 artillery pieces.[27] Kim had strong reasons to believe in a brief conflict.

5. The CIA estimated that there were 600,000 active members in the Communist Party in the South, or 10% of the population. They would support the forces from the North.

B. Why did Stalin accept the attack?

1. Both Kim and perhaps Mao would become **dependent on the USSR**.

2. It would expand and strengthen **communism in Asia**. A united communist Korea would also make Russia's border more secure.

3. If Stalin had rejected it, **Kim might turn to Mao**.

4. Some have argued that it was a way to divert attention from Europe.

5. It was not expected that the US would defend the South. But if they did, it was not only negative. The attack would entice the US into a war.

On 25th June 1950, troops from the North crossed the 38th Parallel. On the same day the Americans brought the issue to the Security Council in the UN. The USSR did not attend the meeting. They were able to get support for a resolution of withdrawal. The Soviet boycott was due to the fact that communist China was not allowed to represent China in the UN—Taiwan was. The Korean War was technically a UN operation and 16 countries participated but it was mainly an American operation with 260,000 American troops compared to 35,000 men from other nations. These troops and the South Korean army were placed under US General Douglas MacArthur who was accountable to President Truman.

- In September the North had conquered the whole of South Korea except for the Southeast corner.

- In the same month, MacArthur launched a daring counter-attack from the sea just south of the 38th Parallel at **Inchon**—behind the enemy lines—in an attempt to cut off troops from the north.

- Soon the South was recaptured and Truman decided to cross the 38th Parallel to capture the North, to roll back the Communists. If this had succeeded it would be the first area to be 'liberated' from communist control.

- On 19 October, 300,000 **Chinese 'volunteers' crossed the Yalu river**, the border between Korea and China, and the Korean War had reached a critical point. In December, UN forces lost 11,000 men in two days and in one of these two days, the Americans lost 3,000 soldiers. Chinese casualties were far higher. The UN forces were pushed back across the 38th Parallel.

C. Why did the US support the South?

1. **The Truman Doctrine, the policy of containment, the NSC-68 report and the Domino Theory**, all indicated that the US must take action. We can also add the experiences from the 1930s where appeasement had failed and encouraged Hitler no make new moves. It was a question of credibility and according to Cold War beliefs, aggression from Communists was seen as a test of US determination to defend the free world.

2. Truman was under **domestic pressure** due to Eastern Europe's loss to communism between 1945 and 1948, the 'loss' of China and the Russian A-bomb in 1949.

3. The Cold War had clearly turned more global and **Asia** was now a trouble spot with Mao in China, problems in Korea and the French being embroiled in a full scale war against communist guerrillas in **Vietnam**. Truman said: "*If we stand up to them like we did in Greece three years ago, they won't take any next steps.*"[28]

D. Why did China support North Korea?

1. Mao and Kim had fought together in the Chinese civil war. It was a way of paying Kim back.
2. **Mao felt threatened** when the UN forces, dominated by Americans, were close to the Chinese border. This was 1950, only months after the Civil War had ended on the mainland. China saw it as very dangerous with US troops at Yalu river—it might spur a renewal of the Civil War with a possible US intervention.
3. Mao clearly wanted to play the role of **international communist leader**.

Impact and Significance of the 1950 Crisis
A. To the South and the North

Estimates will be described later about the total victims from the two Korean states. But from the beginning this was a 'total war' to these two states.

B. To the US

- By taking actions in Korea, Truman had shown that he was going to live up to his **Truman Doctrine and the idea of containment**. It was a very important signal both in the US and in the outside world.
- The UN had been ignored by the US during the Berlin Crisis. On the day the North attacked, Truman decided to bring this question to the **UN**. The US thereby declared that Korea should be considered as being within the **US defence perimeter—a new policy**.
- When the conflict started the US moved the Seventh Fleet into the **Taiwan Strait** to discourage the spread of military conflict in the region, i.e., to prevent a Chinese attack.
- The US started to support the French economically in **Indochina**.
- Chinese military intervention had major consequences and would affect **Sino-American relations** for decades.
- It was considered in the US that the attack from the North was carried out on direct orders from the USSR/Stalin. This had major consequences.
- Truman had been reluctant to implement the **NSC-68 recommendations**. The attack changed this and he signed it in **September 1950** and as a result defence spending tripled as a percentage of the gross domestic product between 1950 and 1953 (from 5% to 14.2%). The NSC68 recommendations became US policy.
- But finally we must emphasise how the war was carried out. After the attempt to conquer the North in October 1950 and when the Chinese entry finally led to a stalemate around the 38th Parallel again, **the US fought a limited war**. There was no question of conquering the North, atomic weapons were not used and the USSR and China should not necessarily be provoked.

C. To the USSR

- With both **North Korea and China** embroiled in a war against one of the superpowers, both states were **tied to the USSR**.
- The USSR was formally **neutral** during the war. While Stalin **limited** Soviet support, he asked Mao to support the North in the event of American participation, before the conflict started. He also asked Mao for armed support to the North when UN forces headed for the Yalu river in the autumn. Stalin limited Soviet support to arms, advisors and a few pilots.
- **Relations to the US** were very strained since the US believed that Stalin had ordered the attack.

---

[28] Edwards, O., *The USA and the Cold War 1945–63*, p. 68.

- The US was involved in an armed conflict while the USSR was neutral. The former Soviet foreign minister Andre Gromyko later admitted that the Soviet boycott of the meeting in the Security Council was a deliberate move to entice the US into the war.[29] If so, **Soviet policies dragged America into the war.**

D. To China

- The US decision to protect **Taiwan** was seen as interference in Chinese **internal affairs**. With the US fleet defending Taiwan it was impossible for mainland China to conquer and finish the Civil War.
- That 300,000 Chinese 'volunteers' attacked the UN forces was probably the most serious crisis during the whole Cold War. It would take decades to normalise the relation to the UN.
- **China gained reputation** from many smaller states in the Third World by defending a small nation against a superpower.
- By involving herself actively in the conflict she became closely **tied to the USSR.**

E. To the UN

- It was good that the UN had been able to take action. One of the main reasons for the failure of the League of Nations was that no actions had been taken when Japan had invaded nearby Manchuria in 1931.
- On the other hand, the organisation was seen as a 'tool of capitalism' by the communist camp.

Author's Tip

Important: If we go beyond 1950, facts can be used to describe a 'war' in topic 11.

The continuation of the war:

1. The Chinese forces soon pushed the UN forces across the 38th Parallel again and in 1951 a stalemate was established around the 38th Parallel.

2. Truman decided **to continue to 'limit'** his war aims, not to conquer the North. This was deeply resented by MacArthur who wanted to widen the conflict and he publicly criticised the President and called his 'limited' strategy a form of appeasement. MacArthur wanted to attack China and use soldiers from Taiwan against them. He also issued an unauthorised nuclear threat on China. In April 1951 Truman **dismissed MacArthur** who returned to the US, seen as a hero by many.

3. Peace talks began in July 1951 but the war dragged on for another two years around the 38th Parallel.

4. An **armistice** was not signed until **1953**, when Stalin had died and Eisenhower had succeeded Truman.

Impact and Significance of the Korean War

There are many different estimates in terms of the victims of the Korean War.

South and North Korea, 1950–1953:

1. **415,000 South Koreans** were killed and **500,000 in the North in 1950–1953** (2/3 of the population lived in the South)

2. Five million Koreans were homeless, and most of the infrastructure and industries were destroyed. To Korea it was a '**total war**'.

3. Politically the country remained **divided** and Kim imposed a Soviet style system in the North. In the South, Syngman Rhee established a right-wing dictatorship.

4. The hostilities between the two Koreas resulted in both countries using vast resources to arm themselves in the future. Resources which could have been used for other purposes.

---

[29] Lynch, M., *The People's Republic of China 1949–76* (London: Hodder Education, 2008) p. 88.

China:

1. The US made a pledge to defend Taiwan. The fact that China had entered the war, fighting UN/US troops, led to hostilities between the two countries that were not resolved until the 1970s. It **isolated China diplomatically** for years. US commitments in Asia after the war also threatened the security of China (see effects to the US).

2. It tied China to the USSR. In 1950 a Sino-Soviet Friendship Treaty was signed.

3. **China lost around 360,000 soldiers.** (difficult to estimate)

The USSR:

1. There were now two communist states in Asia—North Korea and China—closely **tied to the USSR.**

2. The most important consequence was that the war led to a far-reaching **military build-up** from both sides. In 1953, the USSR had built their first hydrogen bomb. It has been argued by many that the Russians could not bear the cost of this in the long term. The Korean War can be seen as a major starting point of a militarisation of the Cold War, which resulted in a larger proportion of the USSR's GNP being used for military expenditure.

3. Korea affected the Cold War in Europe. The US committed itself even more to the defence of Germany and Western Europe. This would lead to further commitments by the USSR. When Germany was made a full member of NATO in 1955. The USSR formed the Warsaw Pact. It was all a greater and more costly escalation.

The US:

1. **33,000 men were killed.**

2. It deeply affected public opinion in the US. It is no coincidence that Senator Joseph McCarthy started his witch-hunt for Communists in the US during these years.

3. The war was an important reason for the election of a Republican as US President after some 20 years. Eisenhower and his Secretary of State, John Foster Dulles, rejected containment and fighting 'limited wars'. They introduced a policy of possible 'massive retaliation'—the use of nuclear arms and 'roll-back'—a policy of 'liberating' communist-controlled areas.

4. As mentioned before, the **NSC-68 report was implemented** and a substantial increase in military expenditure took place. US expenditure rose from $13 billion to $50 billion per year during the war. It never dropped below $40 billions for the rest of the century. NATO was strengthened economically. Decisions were made to re-arm West Germany and let her contribute with troops, to become a full member. A peace treaty was concluded with Japan in 1951 and the country became the key in the US system of alliances in Asia. In 1954, the Americans created the **SEATO** (the South East Treaty Organization) made up by the US, France, Britain, Australia, New Zealand, the Philippines, Thailand and Pakistan, in an attempt to fight communism in Asia.

5. The US started supporting the French in their war in **Vietnam**. But it was not total support.

6. When the French withdrew from the war in 1954, the Americans were bearing 70% of the cost of the French Indochina War. But it was the Korean lesson that made Eisenhower introduce his New Look, a reluctance to fight limited wars in the Third World. Korea affected both Eisenhower and Kennedy in their Vietnam policy and their rejection of sending combat troops.

7. The US committed itself to protecting **Taiwan** from an attack by Communist-controlled China.

The UN:

1. The UN had shown that it could take action. One of the major reasons for the failure of the League of Nations had been the inability to take action against Japanese aggression in the same area, **Manchuria**, in 1931.

2. It was partly seen as a 'tool of capitalism' within the communist camp, which weakened its authority.

Some Concluding Remarks about the Significance of the Korean War

It is clear that the Korean War had a major impact on the Cold War. What had been declared or indicated in the Truman Doctrine from 1947 was now implemented. It marks a point where a major escalation took place. The Cold War had been made a 'hot war' which was fought by 'client states'. It is probably correct to conclude that the Chinese entry into the Korean War was one of the most critical moments of the Cold War. It has been argued that the Berlin Blockade 'drew the line' in Europe in that it resulted in two German states and the formation of NATO. **The Korean War had the same importance in Asia and led to major commitments from both sides, in Korea, to Japan, Taiwan, China and Vietnam.**

Student Activities

The Korean War can be used as an example in Topic 11 'Causes and Effects of 20th Century Wars' and in Topic 12 'The Cold War'. When studying the Cold War, the IB syllabus states that candidates shall undertake a detailed study of two Cold War crises from different regions and **examine and compare the causes, impact and significance** of the two crises. The syllabus states specifically that the attack of the North in 1950 can be used as an example of a 'crisis'—**but it should be limited to 1950**.

Let's make an attempt to answer essay questions. You will find a suggested answer plan to the question on the next page. But before reading it: try first to write your own outline and then compare the answers.

The first question relates to the syllabus asking for an analysis of two Cold War crises from two different regions. We have now outlined two such crises from two regions: The Berlin Crisis from 1948 to 1949 and the Korean War 1950. This gives us an opportunity to write an outline to a question about these two crises. **The syllabus specifically asks for a comparison of causes, impact and significance of the two crises.** A 'comparison' means that you show 'similarities' and 'differences'. A challenging question could be **'Compare and contrast the origins of two Cold War crises'**. A 'compare and contrast-question' is not easy. There are so many aspects to cover and try to do this and compare your answer with the outline, which follows.

Another question will be: **'Evaluate the impact upon the course of the Cold War of two crises, each chosen from a different region'**. In Paper 2, questions will be 'open', i.e., you choose your own examples. We now have the opportunity to choose Berlin and Korea. In this question asking for the 'course of the Cold War', we go beyond 1950.

Finally we make a comparison about the impact and significance: **'Compare and contrast the impact and significance of two Cold War crises each chosen from a different region'.** Again we have an opportunity to use Berlin and Korea, in this question limited to 1950 in Korea.

2. Korea, the US, the USSR and China: Superpower Relations (1947–1949)

Exercise 5: Compare and contrast the origins of two Cold War crises.

(Structure: show the similarities and the differences between the two crises. Use Berlin and Korea as examples.)

Similarities:

1. It was a **typical Cold War conflict where the two superpowers took actions in two client states.**
2. In both conflicts it can be argued that the communist side or **Stalin initiated the conflict**. The currency reform was just an excuse used by Stalin to finally settle the German or Berlin problem. Kim would never attack without Stalin's approval.
3. Both states remained divided as a result of the Cold War. The division was initially a result from the conferences during the war and the aim was to administrate the occupation. Taking into account that the superpowers had totally different aims in Germany and Korea, **the divisions were a very important reason for the crises.**
4. The Berlin Crisis in 1948 and the Korean Crisis 1950 were **both conflicts where Truman's new policies were tested. The Truman Doctrine** was based on the idea of containment, i.e., not to allow a further expansion of communism. If the Americans had remained inactive during those two tests, the new policy would be considered as worthless. By opening an airlift and by sending troops to Korea, Truman showed that he was going to live up to his declarations.
5. In both conflicts there were aspects which suggested that the superpowers were not fully prepared militarily when the conflicts started. Both Soviet and US troops had left Korean in June 1950 and the US did not have full protection of the western zones in Germany in 1948.
6. It can be argued that there was a '**Stalin miscalculation**' in both conflicts. He hoped to get full control of Berlin, which he didn't. He hoped that South Korea would be conquered, which didn't happen.

Differences:

1. The Korean War started with an **armed conflict**. The Berlin Crisis did not. So the very nature of the start of the conflict differed fundamentally.
2. **The aims also differed.** When the North attacked the South in 1950 the aim was to conquer the South. In Germany, Stalin's primary aim was to get a solution to the Berlin problem. If that was possible, Stalin would be happy with the West calling off the currency reform, but most likely he realised that they would not.
3. Truman decided not to involve the **UN** in Germany. The Americans brought the Korean question to the Security Council the very same day as the North attacked.
4. The Korean War has, by many, been described as a Civil War which did get outside support. Both Kim Il-sung and Syngman Rhee were Nationalists who wanted to unite their countries and there had been constant **border disputes in 1948 and 1949** killing thousands of Koreans. There were no such disputes in Germany.
5. Stalin had probably other aims than just conquering the South in Korea. An armed conflict would **tie both North Korea and China closer to the USSR**.
6. **Mao's involvement** in Korea had no equivalent in Germany. To Mao, it was a question of Chinese security when the Americans reached the Yalu river. But most likely, it also had to do with Mao's ambition to be an international leader.
7. Some have argued that Stalin saw a war in Korea as a conflict which would **divert attention** from Cold War tension in Europe.
8. By boycotting the meeting in the Security Council, Stalin tricked the US into the war in Korea.

Conclusion: Summarise the most important similarities and differences.

Exercise 6: Discuss the outcomes of the Berlin Crisis in 1948 and the Korean War.

(You cannot limit this to 1950—the question asks for the 'Korean War'.)

Impact of the Berlin Crisis 1948–1949:

1. It is normally considered that the Berlin Crisis **'drew the line'** of the Cold War in Europe, i.e., with this conflict both sides committed themselves fully to the conflict.
2. As a result, a number of European states including the US and Canada formed **NATO** in 1949. It was a full military alliance and West Germany was under NATO protection.
3. With the crisis Stalin and the USSR had to accept that parts of **Berlin belonged to the West,** with all future implications.
4. The idea of forming a separate and independent West German state had been discussed before the crisis. However, the crisis made it fully clear that no meaningful cooperation was possible. As a result **two German states** were formed in 1949. Both states were organised in line with the political block to which they belonged.
5. To the US the crisis was a **propaganda victory** and the president had lived up to his policy of containing communism.
6. The Berlin Crisis, together with other events during this period, convinced both sides that meaningful cooperation had been brought to an end. It led to a **major military build up**. It is interesting to study the size of the US army

1938	1945	1948	1951	1956
185,000	8,268,000	554,000	1,532,000	1,026,000

(Continued)

2. Korea, the US, the USSR and China: Superpower Relations (1947–1949)

Exercise 6: Discuss the outcomes of the Berlin Crisis in 1948 and the Korean War. *(Continued)*

With the advent of the Cold War we can see how the size of the US army has grown. Before the war it was only 185,000. In 1948, it has been reduced considerably. In the 1950s, we can see a new peace time situation with a much larger army, which is explained by the Cold War. Both the Berlin Crisis and Korea are normally considered as the events which made this possible. **The Truman Doctrine and NSC 68 recommendations could be implemented due to these two crises. The USSR also had to devote resources to the Cold War.**

Impact of the Korean War:

1. To Korea, the war was a disaster. Between 1950 and 1953, **415,000 South Koreans** were killed and **500,000 in the North** (2/3 of the population that lived in the South). Five million Koreans were homeless, and most of the infrastructure and industries were destroyed. The war resulted in a divided Korea.

2. This conflict '**drew the line**' in the Cold War in Asia and had a number of consequences to other states than Korea.

3. **China** was to some extent tied to the USSR. As a result of her involvement where she was fighting UN forces, she became **diplomatically isolated**. We believe that around 300,000 Chinese soldiers were killed.

4. The US started to support the **French in Vietnam in 1950**. She gave guarantees to defend **Taiwan**.

The US also started building up Japan and making the country a key ally in Asia. In 1954 the Americans created the **SEATO** (the South East Treaty Organization) made up by the US, France, Britain, Australia, New Zealand, the Philippines, Thailand and Pakistan, in an attempt to fight communism in Asia.

5. It can be argued that the Korean War also had **domestic consequences in the US**. It brought a Republican to power for the first time in 20 years and containment was replaced by a declared policy of a 'rollback' of communism (never materialised). The war deeply affected the opinion in the US and senator McCarthy attacked Washington for being 'soft on communism'.

6. The USSR war was also more committed to Asia. Both the regime in **North Korea and China were now more dependent on the USSR**. In 1950, China and the USSR signed a friendship treaty.

7. The Korean War had shown that the **UN** was able to take actions. This had not been the case when Japan had invaded Manchuria in 1931. In the communist camp the UN was seen as a 'tool of capitalism'.

Conclusion: Even though the nature of these two conflicts was very different, one was an armed conflict, the impact and significance are very similar: it 'drew the line' of the Cold War in two parts of the world. These two conflicts were of major importance for the development of the Cold War.

Exercise 7: Compare and contrast the impact and significance of two Cold War crises each chosen from a different region.

(Structure: Show the similarities and the differences. Use Berlin and Korea as your examples but it must be limited to 1948/1949 and 1950.)

Similarities:

1. Both these conflicts are normally considered as having a **profound effect** on the course of the Cold War. **In September 1950, Truman signed the NSC68 report.**

2. Both the **USSR and the US were the key drivers** and policymakers in these crises even though it took place in two other countries.

3. In both conflicts the superpowers **limited their actions,** i.e., didn't allow the conflicts to escalate into an armed conflict between the superpowers.

4. Taking into account why these crises actually started, nothing was achieved.

5. Both conflicts led to the superpowers committing themselves even more to their allies—many examples can be mentioned.

Differences:

1. The Korean War was an **armed conflict**, Berlin was not.

2. As a result of the crisis in Germany, **two German states and NATO** were formed in 1949.

3. In Korea, the **UN** was used as a tool. Truman chose not to use the UN in 1948.

4. With the Korean conflict came immediate commitments from the superpowers. Examples of this were the US support to the French in the **Indochina War and a US pledge to defend Taiwan**.

5. **China** involved herself militarily in Korea—nothing similar happened in Germany.

6. If Gromyko was right, **Stalin tricked the US into getting involved** in the war by boycotting the meeting at the Security Council. Stalin was definitely not planning for an armed conflict in Berlin.

7. The states involved in the two crises differed a lot. There was no similarity to the UN coalition and China in Berlin. That 300,000 Chinese soldiers attacked the UN/US was of course very serious.

Conclusion: Similarity: These two conflicts had both the superpowers as the drivers but in both they limited their actions to avoid a direct confrontation.

Difference: In Korea, the UN was involved and it led to an armed conflict. In Korea many states were directly involved, but was not the case in Berlin.

Two Cold War Leaders

The syllabus also asks how **different leaders from different regions affected the course and the development of the Cold War**. When 1953 had come to an end, we have the opportunity to assess two of the key figures in the Cold War, **Stalin and Truman**. The guide will present two summaries about their policies and contributions to the development of the Cold War:

Cold War Leader 1: Josef Stalin Secretary General and Soviet Leader, 1929–1953

The Soviet Union emerged from WWII as one of the two **superpowers**. It can of course be debated how much the USSR deserved this title, taking into account the enormous damage that had been caused by the war. But the USSR and the Red Army controlled Eastern Europe.

1945
At Yalta, in February 1945, Stalin committed himself to free elections in countries liberated from Nazi control. The **Declaration of Liberated Europe** was one achievement at Yalta. Others were that the USSR promised to join the UN and to help the US in defeating Japan. Agreements were also made about post-war Germany and the zonal division of the country. In July, when it was time for the Potsdam conference Western leaders accused the Soviets of violating the agreement made at Yalta over free elections and there were **sharp exchanges** over the development in countries controlled by the Red Army.

One major source of tension after the war was the future of Germany. While **Stalin feared a German recovery** and wanted to prevent this with all possible means, the US came to realise that a German recovery was vital for a working economy in Europe. Stalin also wanted control of countries in Eastern Europe, which traditionally had been used when the USSR had been attacked by Western powers.

1946
When Churchill delivered his Iron Curtain Speech in 1946, Stalin tightened his grip on Eastern Europe.

1947
The next year Truman issued his **Truman Doctrine** and **Marshall Aid**. Stalin saw this as an attempt to control countries economically, which would later lead to political control. The satellites in Eastern Europe were forced to reject American aid.

1948
In 1948, all states in Eastern Europe were under Soviet control except for Yugoslavia. Stalin could not allow this form of 'national communism' and withdrew his economic and military advisers and the country was expelled from Cominform, the international communist organisation, accused of 'bourgeois nationalism'. The Eastern Bloc now announced an economic blockade and broke off diplomatic relations, but Tito and his regime had considerable national support and didn't share a border with the USSR. The US offered considerable financial assistance. The outcome of this crisis led to the creation of a **non-aligned**, non-Stalinist, **communist state. Czechoslovakia** was another satellite. A coalition ruled the country including non-Communists. After disputes in the government over nationalisation of industries, the non-Communists resigned. When elections were held, the Communists won 237 of 300 seats in parliament and soon **all other parties were dissolved**. The only country in the Eastern Bloc with a genuine multi-party system had now been transformed to a communist single-party state.

The final crisis in 1948 was the Berlin Crisis. When it became obvious to Stalin that the Western powers were planning to form a separate West German state, and when a currency reform in the Western zone was announced, the Soviet Union closed off all land routes to West Berlin. The USSR needed to solve the Berlin problem where hundreds of thousands fled the Eastern zone every year. The US and Britain opened an airlift lasting 10 months which meant that Berlin and its 2.5 million inhabitants survived the blockade. Both the coup in Czechoslovakia and the **Berlin Blockade** were seen as proof of Soviet aggression

in the West. The next year a separate West German state was formed and NATO, a full military alliance made up by Western powers, was formed.

In 1950, North Korea attacked the South. We know today that Kim Il-sung pressed Stalin to finally approve the invasion. Kim had been armed by the USSR, and when the North attacked it was a major escalation, which Stalin, with his support and foreknowledge, was of course to some extent responsible for. Gromyko, the foreign minister, later admitted that the Soviet boycott of the UN was a trick to involve the US in a war in Asia while the USSR would remain neutral.

In conclusion: An **orthodox historian**, blaming Stalin and the USSR, would argue that Stalin and the USSR were responsible for the outbreak of the Cold War. Stalin had signed the Declaration of Liberated Europe, which he totally violated. All the states in Eastern Europe had communist single-party systems by 1948. It had also been impossible to co-operate with the Soviets in Germany and Stalin's aggressive policies had been seen in Yugoslavia, Czechoslovakia, Berlin and Korea.

A **revisionist historian**, emphasising the responsibility of the US, would argue that the USSR had suffered enormously during WWII. 1,700 cities and 60,000 villages were in ruins and 25 million Russians had been killed while the US had increased industrial output during the war with 90% and they had a nuclear monopoly. In this situation, Stalin's desire to control Eastern Europe was mainly defensive. He wanted control of these states since they had been used for attacks on the USSR. In this situation, the US issued the Truman Doctrine where they gave themselves the right to intervene anywhere. With the Marshal Aid Programme they wanted to control countries in Europe economically, which would lead to political control. It was a new form of imperialism, which was described as 'dollar imperialism'. It was the US, and not Stalin, who must bear responsibility for causing the Cold War.

Cold War Leader 2: Harry S. Truman US President, 1945–1953

Harry S. Truman became president of the US on 12 April 1945, when President Roosevelt passed away. He had hardly any experience of foreign policy and one of his first major undertakings was to participate in the **Potsdam Conference** in July 1945. The conference is normally considered as a failure and some have even described it as the start of the Cold War. There were heated arguments over Soviet policies in Eastern Europe. Some would argue that Truman was responsible for this. In 1946, he wrote to his Secretary of State James Byrnes: "*Unless Russia is faced with an iron fist and strong language another war is in the making. Only one language do they understand–'How many divisions have you?' I do not think we should play compromise any longer.*"[30]

During the conference Truman was informed that the **A-bomb** would work, but decided not to inform Stalin in spite of the fact that the Soviets had promised to support the Americans in defeating Japan. The dropping of the bomb has been seen as "*the last attack of World War II [and] the first attack in the Cold War.*"[31]

Truman's most important contribution to the Cold War was the introduction of the Truman Doctrine in 1947. In February 1946, George **Kennan**, a diplomat at the US Embassy in Moscow, had written his **Long Telegram**. It was a report written for the State Department and it was widely circulated within US bureaucracy and provided the intellectual basis for the '**doctrine of containment**'. Kennan stated that no long-term co-operation was possible with the Soviet regime and that communism must be contained within its present borders. His ideas provided the intellectual basis for the Truman Doctrine. With the introduction of the Truman Doctrine the US policy of **isolationism** was replaced by an **active world role. This is the most important turning point in US foreign policy in the 20th century**. Initially his request for money was only intended for Greece and Turkey but it was soon extended globally and would lead to both **Korea and Vietnam**. It is normally considered as the official start of the Cold War.

---

[30] See http://teachingamericanhistory.org/library/document/letter-to-james-byrnes/ <Accessed 4 January 2017>
[31] McWilliams, W. C. and Piotrowski, H., *The World Since 1945: A History of International Relations* (London: Lynne Rinnier Publishers, 1993) p. 20.

2. Korea, the US, the USSR and China: Superpower Relations (1947–1949)

1947

In June the same year, the Secretary of State George Marshall announced his **Marshall Plan**. This massive economic help for European reconstruction was initially offered to most European countries, even the communist states. But it was soon rejected by the USSR and her satellites. From a Soviet perspective this was seen as a type of new economic imperialism and dependence, which had to be turned down. Marshall however stated in his speech: "*Our policy is directed not against any country or doctrine, but against hunger, poverty, desperation and chaos.*"[32]

1948

When the problems with the divided Germany emerged after 1945, the Truman administration came to realise that it was necessary to **build up Germany** as a bulwark against communism. This was first announced by the Secretary of State James Byrnes in his Stuttgart speech in 1946. In March 1948, the US, Britain and France announced their willingness to establish a new currency in the Western zones and to form a West German government. In June, the Soviets cut off all land routes to West Berlin.

A total of 2.5 million inhabitants, fearing the Soviets, had to rely on US and British support through an airlift. For ten months to come, the **Berlin Airlift** provided the population in the Western zones of Berlin with necessary supplies. It became a propaganda success for the US. The Blockade convinced the West that a West German state had to be created.

1949

This took place in 1949. The same year NATO was formed. It was a full military alliance between a number of West European states including the US. The Berlin Airlift is normally considered as the **conflict which drew the line in the Cold War in Europe** and it led to a massive military build up.

1950

National Security Council Report 68 (**NSC-68**) was a top secret policy paper presented to Truman in April 1950. It recommended a substantial US military build up to handle the USSR. Today it is considered as a key strategic document outlining US policy during the Cold War. Truman was initially against it but with the North Korean attack on the South in June, Truman implemented the plan. This included the decision to develop the hydrogen bomb and became a key policy of the US. Truman signed it in September 1950.

1950

When **North Korea** attacked the South in June 1950 Truman and the US were able to get UN support to fight back the attack. The reason was that the USSR were boycotting the Security Council when the decision was taken. After having fought back the attack in the South the US led forces crossed the 38th Parallel to 'liberate' the North. In December 1950, China decided to intervene and China and the US were now involved in direct fighting. This is normally considered as one of the most dangerous escalations which took place during the Cold War, but it might be noted that after a while Truman **limited his aims**. It was enough to liberate the South.

If the Berlin Airlift had drawn the line concerning the Cold War in Europe, the Korean war did the same in Asia. US defence spending trebled during the last years with Truman as President. From 1950 to 1954, the Americans gradually increased their economic support to the French and in 1954, when France pulled out, the **Americans were paying** more than 70% of France's cost for the war. Japan was considered as a key ally in the region and the US committed itself to guarantee support for Taiwan in the event of an attack from 'red China'.

Key Point

It's interesting to study Truman, Stalin and the outbreak of the Cold War. Both of them would argue that they only responded to aggression from the other side.

In conclusion: An **orthodox historian** would describe Truman's policies between 1945 and 1953 as an attempt to defend the free world. He was responding to Soviet aggression. A **revisionist historian** would argue that Truman took advantage of US strength and nuclear monopoly **and** Soviet weakness, and with the Truman Doctrine and the Marshall plan he tried to establish the economic dependence of various countries, which would ultimately lead to political control. It was Truman's 'dollar-imperialism' which created the Cold War.

---

[32] McCauley, M., *Origins of the Cold War 1941–1949*, p. 137.

The Cold War 1953–1964: Confrontation and Détente

The continuation of the Cold War is very much influenced by the **death of Stalin** and the rise to power of Nikita **Khrushchev**. If Stalin had been more of a cautious planner, Khrushchev was much more **adventurous and difficult to predict**. Officially, he announced a new policy of **peaceful co-existence** with the capitalist West and started a de-Stalinisation process. But he soon involved the Red Army in crushing the Hungarian Uprising in 1956 and issued a Berlin ultimatum in 1958. Most fatal of all, he placed nuclear missiles on **Cuba**. While Stalin had tried to extend Soviet influence in neighbouring countries, Khrushchev intervened in areas like the Middle East and Central America.

The new US administration with President **Eisenhower and the Secretary of State, John Foster Dulles** were both fierce anti-Communists and publicly announced in their new foreign policy, known as the **New Look**, plans of **'massive retaliation', 'brinkmanship', 'rollback' of communism** and the necessity of **nuclear superiority**. But the practical outcome was that no real adventurous moves were taken: no support was given to the Hungarians and there was no major escalation in Vietnam.

The **nuclear arms race** escalated and even a space competition started during these years with costs that, with the benefit of hindsight, the Russians couldn't bear. There were also several attempts to establish a dialogue and the 1950s witnessed the first summits during the Cold War between the leaders of the super-powers. In 1961, the **Berlin Wall** was erected and the year after witnessed a very dangerous conflict over Cuba, **the Cuban Missile Crisis**. This crisis was one of many reasons for the Sino-Soviet split in the early 1960s. The outcome of the missile crisis led to a new period of relaxation and attempts to co-operate which were interrupted by two major conflicts: President Johnson's **escalation of the Vietnam war** and the **invasion of Czechoslovakia** by the Warsaw Pact in August 1968.

So the period of 1953–1969 can best be described as a period of **both** confrontation and détente.

Time for Détente (Lessening of Tension)? The New Russian Leadership after Stalin

Figure 2.3: Georgy Malenkov   *Figure 2.4: Nikita Krushchev*

> The policies of the new leadership in the USSR are the first signs of détente that we can see in the Cold War. But how much was this only rhetorical? We shall later assess if Khrushchev was a Cold Warrior.
>
> President Eisenhower on the other hand was not satisfied with 'containment'. He wanted to see a 'rollback' of communism. His policies would be tested in the 1950s and we shall also assess him from a Cold War perspective.

When Stalin died in 1953 there was no clear successor and a collective leadership emerged with Malenkov and Khrushchev as the most prominent leaders. In 1955, Malenkov was ousted by his rival Khrushchev. The new leadership opened up for new opportunities in the Cold War during the years 1953–1956:

- An armistice was finally signed in **Korea** in 1953.
- In 1954, a peace conference was arranged at **Geneva** to deal with the **Indochina War**, under the chairmanship of the USSR and Britain.
- In 1955, there was a Great power summit in Geneva between the USSR, the US, Britain and France. The leaders met for the first time since Potsdam 1945. The new and positive atmosphere was referred to as '**the spirit of Geneva**'.
- In 1955, the occupational forces of **Austria** decided to end the occupation and re-establish full independence of the country. This had not been possible in countries like Germany and Korea. Soviet troops were also withdrawn from Finland.
- Khrushchev started to **reduce the size of the Red Army** unilaterally (without the other side doing it).
- Khrushchev went to **Yugoslavia** in 1955, to heal the rift between the two states and to show that the USSR could accept the existence of a communist regime not totally controlled by Moscow, a clear break with Stalin's policies.
- In February 1956, Khrushchev gave a dramatic and important speech at a secret session of the 20th Party Congress, i.e., the '**Secret Speech**' in an attempt to promote 'de-Stalinisation' and liberalisation. It had far-reaching consequences as it started a de-Stalinisation process in the USSR. It can partly be seen as a **domestic political struggle** against old Stalinists like Molotov, but it had international implications as well. In **China**, Mao regarded the attack on Stalin's terror and the cult of personality as an indirect attack on his rule. Khrushchev also announced that there could be '**national roads to socialism**', i.e., an acceptance of 'national communism'. His new policy towards Tito in Yugoslavia implemented this change. In the same month, Khrushchev dissolved Cominform, the international communist organisation. Communist rule was soon questioned in two satellites in Eastern Europe, Poland and Hungary.
- Ideologically, Khrushchev announced a major departure from orthodox Marxism-Leninism by introducing the idea of **peaceful co-existence** with the capitalists.

> **Critical Thinking**
>
> Why do you think the Secret Speech is so important?

The Eisenhower Administration and the New Look

Figure 2.5: Dwight D. Eisenhower

Figure 2.6: John Foster Dulles

When Eisenhower became the first Republican president in 20 years, he had promised to end the Korean War. But there was no fundamental change in attitude towards communism and no positive response to the new policy in the Kremlin. Eisenhower introduced a new foreign policy which was referred to as **The New Look:**

- Communism should still be contained. Dulles even expressed the desire of a '**rollback**' of communist controlled areas i.e., a liberation of these areas from communism. Eisenhower supported it but clarified that it had to be achieved by peaceful means and no support was given in Germany in 1953, Poland and Hungary in 1956, when communism was challenged.

  Nuclear weapons were now regarded as weapons of first and not last resort. In practical terms this indicated a policy of **massive retaliation** against possible enemies, and less reliance on conventional forces and Truman's policy of fighting 'limited wars'. As both superpowers were nuclear powers it was a dangerous gamble and Dulles explained this policy of '**brinkmanship**' in a famous interview in 1956:

  > "The ability to get to the verge without getting into the war is the necessary art.… If you try to run away from it, if you are scared to go to the brink, you are lost." [33]

- The policy of containment continued by the formation of alliances directed against the Communists. In 1954, the South-East Asian Treaty Organization (**SEATO**) was created by the US, France, Britain, Australia, New Zealand, the Philippines, Thailand and Pakistan, with the main aim of preventing communist expansion in South East Asia. In 1955, the **Baghdad Pact** was formed between Britain, Iraq and later Iran and Pakistan with the aim of excluding the USSR from the Middle East. The US did not join for tactical reasons but stood behind the organisation. In Europe, Germany was offered full membership status in NATO in 1955, i.e., a decision to allow German troops again. **NATO in Europe, SEATO in Asia and the Baghdad Pact in the Middle East surrounded, or *contained* the USSR.**

Why did the US administration not respond to the new signals from the USSR?

- Eisenhower came to power during the war in **Korea** where the Americans had lost 33,000 soldiers due to attacks from two communist states: North Korea and China.
- In 1953, **McCarthy** was at the peak of his career and Eisenhower had won the presidential elections by attacking the Truman administration for being 'soft on communism'. It was not the right moment for an American 'thaw'.
- Both Eisenhower and Dulles were '**Cold Warriors**', i.e., strongly anti-Communists.
- Soviet signs of détente or a thaw were brief and interrupted in 1956 with the crises in **Hungary and the Suez**.

The Non-Aligned Movement

The process of decolonisation had resulted in a number of newly independent states in the Middle East, Asia and Africa. In 1954, the **Indian Prime Minister Nehru** made a speech discussing Sino (Chinese)-Indian relations. He declared five pillars which should be seen as a guide between the two nations. These pillars would later be the basis of what would be the **Non-Aligned Movement**. The principles were:

- Respect for territorial integrity
- Mutual non-aggression
- Mutual non-interference in domestic affairs
- Equality and mutual benefit
- Peaceful co-existence.

In 1955, some Asian and African states organised a meeting in **Bandung** in Indonesia. The aims were to promote **Afro-Asian economic and cultural cooperation and to oppose colonialism**. The meeting would play an important role in shaping a Third World identity. To oppose colonialism was

---

[33] Edwards, O., *The USA and the Cold War 1945–63*, p. 80.

in many ways equivalent to a desire to stay out of the Cold War. Twenty-nine states representing more than half of the world's population were present. The process of decolonisation had started and issues that were brought up were France's control of North Africa and the conflict between Indonesia and the Netherlands concerning New Guinea. The conference also supported *"the rights of the Arab people of the Palestine."* China played a very important role at the conference and her relations with other Asian powers were brought up. The Chinese Prime Minister Zhou Enlai successfully displayed a conciliatory role. One major issue that was brought up was whether Soviet control of Eastern Europe was comparable to Western colonialism. A declaration was made condemning *"colonialism in all of its manifestations."*[34] The conference called for redistribution of resources for the benefit of poorer states and supported Nehru's principles outlined in 1954.

As a result of the Bandung conference, the **Non-Aligned Movement was established in Belgrade, Yugoslavia in 1961**. The formation of the organisation was a result of a co-operation between Sukarno from Indonesia, Nasser from Egypt, Nehru from India, Nkrumah from Ghana and Tito from Yugoslavia. Twenty-five states participated. Three questions have dominated the organisation:

- Third World states and their relation to the superpowers, i.e., **Cold War issues**. The aim was to find a 'third way'. It is against this background we see Tito's deep involvement in the organisation.
- **Decolonisation:** The organisation had established itself as an important protest organisation against colonial rule both in Africa and in Asia.
- The third question which dominated later development was the question of a **new economic world order**; i.e., how resources should be transferred from richer to poorer countries.

Cold War questions tended to dominate the organisation in the early 1960s. In the 1970s, especially after the fourth summit in Algiers in 1973, economic issues and a new world order have dominated. **East-West relations** and conflicts had been replaced by the **North-South conflict**. Tito led the work with Cold War issues while Castro from Cuba was deeply involved in questions about a new economic order. The fact that Cuba, a close ally to the USSR, was deeply involved in the organisation was criticised by some member states. The movement was normally more pro-Soviet than pro-American. The Non-Aligned Movement **lacked economic, military and partly political power** and the member states were very divided.

The importance of the organisation as the **voice of the Third World** should not be neglected. When Soviet leaders discussed whether they should invade Afghanistan in 1979, the Foreign Minister Gromyko opposed the plan and argued: *"All the Non-Aligned countries will be against us."*[35] Many ideas, especially concerning a new economic world order, have been influential. The idea of a responsibility of richer countries towards the Third World is today widely accepted and the Non-Aligned Movement has been instrumental in this development. One example is the recommendations of the Brandt Commission in 1980.

Détente was interrupted by two crises in 1956.

Cold War Crisis 3: Hungary 1956

The Secret Speech started a dangerous political development which challenged Khrushchev's position. What did he say in his speech which gave the satellites this message? Khrushchev talked about how Stalin tried to overthrow Tito:

> "But this did not happen to Tito. No matter how much or how little Stalin shook, not only his little finger but everything else that he could shake, Tito did not fall. Why? The reason was that, in this instance of disagreement with [our] Yugoslav comrades, Tito had behind him a state and a people who had had a serious education in fighting for liberty and independence, *a people who gave support to its leaders.*

---

[34] http://digitalarchive.wilsoncenter.org/collection/16/bandung-conference-1955/2 <Accessed 5 January 2017>
[35] Rivero, D., *The Détente Deception: Soviet and Western Bloc Competition and the Subversion of Cold War Peace* (Maryland: Rowman & Littlefield) p. 81.

> We have carefully examined the case of Yugoslavia. *We have found a proper solution which is approved by the peoples of the Soviet Union and of Yugoslavia* as well as by the working masses of all the people's democracies and by all progressive humanity. *The liquidation of abnormal relationship* with Yugoslavia was done in the interest of the whole camp of socialism, in the interest of strengthening *peace in the whole world."* [36]

Would the USSR now respect a similar relationship with other satellites? Khrushchev's policy was being tested.

The first satellite to react to the Secret Speech was Poland. In June there were riots in **Poznan** and hundreds of workers were wounded by attacking security forces. The Russians and the government responded with a **reform programme and a policy of liberalisation**. Wladislaw Gomulka who had been imprisoned for years after Stalin's purge on 'national communists' in the late 1940s, was rehabilitated. Khrushchev and the **Russian Politburo** feared too far-reaching reforms in one of the satellites and **went to Poland unexpectedly** in an attempt to avoid a major political crisis. They realised that much had been set in motion by the Secret Speech. There were extremely tense negotiations and the Russians threatened to invade. Gomulka assured the Russian leadership that **no major alterations would be made to the Polish system**, i.e., a multi-party system would not be allowed and that Poland would still be a member of the Warsaw Pact and remain within the communist camp. But a form of 'national communism' had been accepted, collectivisation of agriculture was ended and the regime now sought better relations with the Catholic Church. Gomulka was appointed First Secretary but the Soviet bloc was still considered to be intact.

A more difficult test came only weeks after. In October, 50,000 students, inspired by the development in Poland, demonstrated against communist rule and Soviet control outside the Polish embassy in Budapest. Continuing disorder and political violence soon developed into a **Hungarian Uprising against Soviet rule**. The USSR accepted a new government led by Imre Nagy including two non-Communists. For a brief period the country went through reforms, political parties were formed, freedom of the press was introduced and political prisoners were released. Dulles made a speech and congratulated the Hungarians for challenging the Red Army. Radio Free Europe, financed by the US but not formally a part of the US government, promised US aid. On 27 October, a coalition government was formed.

On 30 October and 1 November, the Nagy government declared that they were **preparing to leave the Warsaw Pact, become a neutral country and allow free elections.** This was a critical moment for Khrushchev and Soviet control of the satellites.

If one satellite and Warsaw Pact member was allowed to leave, it was very likely that there would be a domino reaction within the Eastern Bloc. Probably the same development that we saw after Gorbachev's new policy was introduced in the late 1980s.

On 4 November, Soviet forces attacked Budapest and installed a new pro-Soviet government led by Janos Kadar. Imre Nagy was executed and 30,000 Hungarians and 7,000 Russian troops were killed in the uprising. 200,000 Hungarians fled their country and left a gulf of bitterness against Russian rule.

What were the reasons for the Hungarian crisis:

1. The **Secret Speech** brought hope to many in the satellites. The timing of the events in Poland and Hungary shows the significance of the speech.

2. The **solution of the Polish Crisis** inspired people in Hungary. A form of 'national communism' had been accepted by the USSR in Poland.

3. Soviet armed forces and Soviet control of the country was **resented by many**. This was the driving force behind the revolution.

---

[36] Khrushchev, N., *Khrushchev Remembers* (Boston: Little Brown and Company, 1972) p. 600.

4. The USSR finally decided to invade Hungary because the new government announced that a **multi-party system** would be introduced and that the country would **leave the Warsaw Pact**. This would mean an end of Soviet control and to Khrushchev, who surprisingly had delivered his Secret Speech, this was unacceptable for two reasons: (1) There was definitely a risk for a **domino reaction** in Eastern Europe. (2) There was a risk that **Khrushchev would not survive this as a leader of the USSR**. (With hindsight we know that there was an attempted coup against him the year after.)

Can we blame the US for the Hungarian Uprising? Eisenhower had outlined a policy of 'rollback'—this was the opportunity. We know that Radio Free Europe stated that the US and the world supported the Hungarians and promised support. The radio station was partly funded by the US government but independent is independent. So it cannot be seen as the voice of the US government. Most people in the administration remained silent even though the Secretary of States, J. F. Dulles, gave a speech claiming the importance of giving support to countries breaking free from Soviet control.

Critical Thinking

In what way had both Khrushchev's and Eisenhower's policies been tested in the Hungarian crisis?

Impact and Significance of the Hungarian Uprising

1. **The USSR's role as a model of communism was questioned** by many communist parties, especially in the West and communist parties in Western Europe lost support.

2. Khrushchev and the USSR had drawn a line showing what they could accept in Poland and Hungary. **A disintegration of the satellite system was not going to be tolerated**.

3. Domestically, Khrushchev's liberalisation after 1956 was questioned and there was an attempt to overthrow him by old Stalinists in 1957.

4. Eisenhower and **the US** had shown that they were not **prepared to risk a war** over territories within the Soviet **sphere of influence** and that an armed 'rollback' was no real alternative. **This is probably the most important outcome of the crisis**.

5. It definitely brought an end to the 'spirit of Geneva'.

6. Mao had been critical to the Secret Speech from the beginning. He concluded, which is correct, that the uprising in Hungary was a result of Khrushchev's speech. Mao blamed Khrushchev for the uprising and this issue was one of many behind the Sino-Soviet split.

Before looking at this outline, make your own attempt to answer the question.

Exercise 8: Compare and contrast the origins, impact and significance of two Cold War crises.

(Show the similarities and the differences. It is an open question and we will take Korea 1950 and Hungary 1956 as our examples. It's probably easier to find differences.)

Similarities: Origins

1. Both Korea and Hungary were rather small states but the crises became serious world crises because the outcome would decide to which bloc they would belong in the Cold War.
2. It can be argued that the Soviet side was more active in causing both crises (Stalin had approved Kim's plans and the USSR intervened in Hungary.).
3. Both conflicts can be seen as attempts to secure communist rule.
4. In both crises the Soviet Union believed that the US was not to use military means.
5. Both crises were Cold War crises but fought in client states.

Similarities: Impact and Consequences

1. In both crises, the superpowers limited their action to avoid direct confrontation. In Korea, the USSR was neutral and in Hungary the US didn't live up to her policy of 'rollback'.
2. Both crises were armed Cold War crises and affected opinions globally and to some extent they contributed to an escalation of the Cold War. Many examples can be given to show that both crises fuelled the Cold War: McCarthyism, support for Taiwan, NSC68 implementation (effects of Korea) and the spirit of Geneva was brought to an end with Hungary. (See below if the reactions to some extent differed.).

Differences: Origins

1. Korea started as an attack from one state against another, while Hungary started as a revolt from people in the country opposing Soviet control.

(Continued)

Exercise 8: Compare and contrast the origins, impact and significance of two Cold War crises. *(Continued)*

2. In Korea the North tried to conquer the South and in Hungary the USSR combatted 'counter revolutionaries' so that Hungary would remain in the communist camp.
3. South Korea was within a US sphere of influence. Hungary was within the Soviet sphere of influence.
4. The UN could take actions in Korea. The USSR blocked UN decisions about Hungary.
5. In Korea, Soviet actions were more in cover. It was, of course, not like that in Hungary.

Differences: Impact and Consequences

1. It was Korea which drew the line in the Cold War. In the US the NSC68 report was implemented. The Korean War was a turning point and Hungary was not.
2. The Korean conflict involved more than 15 states. Hungary did not. Even though international reactions were seen, the Hungarian Crisis compared to Korea did not cause such international involvement.
3. There was nothing like China attacking the UN in Hungary, with all its implications.
4. Korea quickly resulted in a number of commitments from the superpowers (China, Japan, Taiwan, Vietnam). We couldn't see the same in Hungary.
5. While Korea tied the USSR and China closer together, Hungary did not. Mao had disliked the Secret Speech from the beginning and they had different opinions on how to handle the crisis in Hungary. It contributed to the Sino-Soviet split.
6. It can be argued that the US lived up to her policies in Korea but not in Hungary, i.e., containment in Korea and no rollback in Hungary.
7. While it can be argued that the Korea War didn't solve the problem which had caused the conflict (one Korea) the USSR did achieve her aims in Hungary.
8. The Korean War was more devastating to Korea than the uprising in Hungary was to Hungary.
9. Hungary was a confirmation of the division of Europe after WWII. Korea cannot be seen in this light.

Conclusion: Both these conflicts were Cold War conflicts and world crises. In both conflicts, the USSR made attempts to secure full control for communist rule. But the reasons for the start, North Korea attacking the South and a Soviet military invention in a satellite, differed of course.

In Korea, the US lived up to her policy of containment, but the policy of rollback was ignored in Hungary. This led to there being no international support for the Hungarians and that the USSR, unlike in Korea, achieved her aims. Korea led to major international consequences, Hungary did not.

Cold War Crisis 4: The Suez Crisis 1956

> The Suez Crisis in 1957 gives us a crisis from a new region: The Middle East. It is a very interesting crisis. Initially both the US and the USSR stood on the same side: they both opposed the attack from Britain, France and Israel. As a consequence of the crisis, the USSR suddenly played a major role in this region, which was a departure from Stalin's **post-war foreign policy. The Suez Crisis is an example from the IB region 'Africa and the Middle East'**.

If we look at the Middle East in the mid-1950s we can conclude that there were four different but overlapping political conflicts:

1. **Britain and France** had traditionally dominated the region. They were in decline and **challenged** by regional leaders (the most important one was Nasser) and outside powers.
2. The two superpowers were now more active in the region making it a part of the **Cold War**.
3. There was a struggle between different Arab states for the **leadership in the Arab world**.
4. The fourth one was the **Arab-Israeli dispute** (Israel has been founded in 1948).

King Farouk of Egypt had been overthrown in an army coup in 1952. Soon **Gamal Abdel Nasser emerged as a new leader**. He was an **Arab nationalist** and opposed both the foundation of the state Israel and traditional Western domination in the Middle East. As an Egyptian leader he wanted full control of the Suez Canal. These aims and policies soon became a part of the Cold War. In 1953, the CIA evaluated Stalin's foreign policy. No attempts had been made to spread communism outside Eurasia. The CIA warned that **his successors might not be as cautious**. Khrushchev must be seen as more adventurous and when both Czech and Russian arms were sent to Egypt in 1955, it was the first Russian or communist arms agreement with a non-communist state. With Khrushchev the USSR embarked on a new foreign policy. The 'Third World' became a target area and even non-communist regimes, like Egypt, could be allies. This was new.

The situation in the Middle East was problematic to the US. Her NATO allies **Britain and France** had traditionally dominated the region which made them disliked in the eyes of Arab Nationalists like Nasser. US links to **Israel** were even more problematic. Nasser wanted a US arms deal, but refused to promise that the weapons should not be used against Israel. Nasser even supported armed raids killing Israeli civilians and this forced Eisenhower's hand—he could not sell US arms to be used in such actions.

France was facing a rebellion in Algeria and the National Liberation Front (FLN) rebels were given support from Egypt and Nasser. The rebellion was seen in a wider context of Arab nationalism in which Nasser was a key figure. To the French, this very problematic rebellion was secretly directed by the Soviet Union. Nasser could play off the superpowers in order to let them compete with each other, in attempts to buy his friendship.

- In 1955, Nasser made an **arms deal** with the USSR and one of Russia's satellites, Czechoslovakia and Soviet experts started to train the Egyptian army.
- In May 1956, Egypt recognised the communist regime in **China**. It was seen as a provocation by the West.
- Nasser also concluded an alliance between Egypt, Syria, Saudi Arabia and Yemen, against Israel.

Nasser's pro-communist attitude and anti-Western propaganda led to the US and Britain cancelling a loan which should finance the building of **the Aswan Dam**. With no Western support Egypt might turn to the USSR. This would probably only damage relations between Egypt and the USSR since the cost for the project would be difficult for the USSR to bear alone.

- **Nasser responded by a nationalisation of the Suez Canal**. The Canal was mainly owned by British and French stockholders but Nasser promised compensation. Control of the Canal would bring incomes to the Aswan Dam project.

Israel, Britain and France decided to invade Egypt in order to humiliate Nasser and replace him with a pro-Western leader. The decision to invade in 1956 was due to the following:

1. **Nasser** was an Arab Nationalist who **threatened British and French interests** in the Middle East.
2. The **oil** industry was one such important 'interest'. Two-third of Europe's oil was shipped through the Canal.
3. By accepting Soviet support, Nasser opened up for the USSR in the Middle East. Nasser's policies became a **Cold War issue**.
4. Nasser's anti-Western policies and the idea of an alliance of Arab states also **threatened Israeli** interests.
5. The French wanted to stop the flow of weapons from Egypt to **Algeria**.

On 26 October 1956, Israel invaded Egypt. The carefully drafted plan, denied by all three states, was that Israel should secure the Canal and then France and Britain should intervene to secure order and re-establish control of the canal zone. By humiliating Nasser one aim was to depose him. The invasion met worldwide opposition and worst of all, **opposition from both superpowers**. The US had been involved in discussions as to how to solve the crisis with Britain and France between July and October. The US had opposed an attack and the reasons were:

1. Eisenhower could not openly support what could be seen as a **colonial aggression**.
2. If the US had accepted the attack, and the USSR had been the only protector of an Arab state under attack, it **would give the USSR an upper hand in the Arab and Third World**.
3. When the attack was launched the **Hungarian revolt** had started. It was impossible to condemn Soviet aggression in Hungary, and defend British/French aggression in Egypt.

The attack caused uproar in Britain. The Labour opposition had been kept in the dark and during the period June–October, the public opinion had calmed down and was not expecting war at this point. But the international reaction was even more problematic. The Suez Crisis was in many ways unique: to some extent it was a Cold War conflict, but both superpowers supported Egypt and were taken by surprise when it started. To the US, trying to deal with Soviet aggression in Hungary, the Suez Crisis was impossible to defend. Vice President Richard Nixon said: "*We couldn't on the one hand, complain about the Soviets intervening in Hungary and, on the other hand, approve of the British and the French picking that particular time to intervene against Nasser.*"[37] To defend the attack would also provide Soviet propaganda with an advantage in the Third World. To the USSR, eager to replace Western dominance in the oil-rich Middle East, and to show herself a defender of countries in the Third World, the crisis was a golden opportunity.

The issue was brought to the Security Council in the UN by both the US and the USSR but Britain and France could veto all resolutions.

The Soviet reaction was even sterner. Prime Minister Nikolai Bulganin threatened to **intervene on the Egyptian side**, and to launch rocket attacks on Britain, France and Israel. Eisenhower feared a major escalation. The US could not remain neutral i**n a war between the USSR and two NATO allies**. The US had to use every possible means to end the conflict. The US refused to provide Britain and France with petroleum, in a situation where they were facing a Middle East embargo. The British economy suffered from the war and the British sought immediate assistance from the International Monetary Fund (IMF), but it was denied by the United States. Britain faced an economic crisis where the country would soon be unable to pay for import of food to feed the population. This **financial pressure** forced a solution. Britain surrendered to American demands and called the invasion off, without consulting the French. The French had to accept Britain's decision but were furious. Prime Minister Eden in Britain was forced to resign and a 74-year British presence in Egypt was brought to an end. The military assault on Egypt had been successful but the outcome confirmed Egyptian sovereignty and ownership of the Canal. To Britain and France it was a disaster. Especially the French who thought they had been betrayed by the leading state in NATO, the US.

---

[37] See https://www.marxists.org/archive/khrushchev/1956/02/24.htm <Accessed 5 January 2017>

When the crises were to be formally resolved, it was brought to the UN. For the first time, the General Assembly held an emergency session, and by using the Assembly it was impossible to block decisions through veto power. The UN had a template of sending peacekeeping troops and would from now on continue to do so in other crises in the world. The UN troops evacuated the area, separated troops and remained in the area as a peacekeeping unit.

The Effects of the Suez Crisis

- **Nasser's prestige** in the Arab world and the Third World increased and Arab nationalism grew in strength. The outcome of the crisis confirmed Egyptian sovereignty and ownership of the Canal.
- **Soviet influence in the Middle East grew** and it was Soviet money that financed the Aswan Dam.
- **The crisis was disastrous for the traditional British and French influence in the Arab world**. Some have argued that the crisis marks an end of the British Empire. Britain had to leave the Suez and Egypt after 74 years.
- This conflict can also be seen in the context of the decolonisation process. France and Britain had been the two leading colonial powers in the world and the humiliation in the Middle East gave strong impetus to the decolonisation process in the world.
- The Suez Canal was cut off and a pipeline from Iraq to the Mediterranean was also closed. This was a serious development for Europe and after the crisis the Japanese started to build super-tankers which went round the Cape of Good Hope. As a consequence, the crisis diminished the importance of the Canal. Few had realised this when it started.
- It diverted attention from the **Hungarian Uprising** from which the USSR benefited greatly.
- In January 1957, Eisenhower launched his '**Eisenhower Doctrine**' and the US Congress gave him the right to provide economic and military assistance to any Middle Eastern country threatened with armed aggression or internal subversion. As a result of this, the US intervened in Lebanon in July 1958.
- In July 1958, pro-Nasserite Iraqi army officers murdered the king and the Prime Minister in Iraq and withdrew the country from the pro-Western Baghdad Pact.
- In the late 1950s, **France started to move away from NATO**. A French politician, Pineau, concluded "*the main victim of the (Suez) affair was the Atlantic alliance…if our allies have abandoned us in difficult, even dramatic, circumstances; they would be capable of doing so again if Europe in its turn found itself in danger.*"[38] In 1966, the process ended when all French land and air forces were withdrawn from the NATO military command and with the removal of the NATO headquarters from France. France was still a member of NATO. The reasons for De Gaulle's independent foreign policy had several explanations but the Suez Crisis was not insignificant. The crisis also made the French realise that they needed nuclear weapons of their own.
- Many have argued that the Suez Crisis played a role in the process of integrating Europe. On the evening when Britain informed France that she was pulling out, the French foreign minister had a meeting with the German chancellor Adenauer. According to one account, Adenauer said: "*There remains to them* (i.e., France, Britain and Germany) *only one way of playing a decisive role in the world, that is to unite Europe… We have no time to waste; Europe will be your revenge.*"[39] The next year the **Treaty of Rome**, the founding treaty of the **European Economic Community**, was signed. The French did what they could to keep Britain out of the union as long as they could. Britain was still a close ally to the US and the Suez Crisis had shown that this Atlantic relation was more important to Britain than European co-operation. Britain was seen as America's Trojan horse.
- It was the UN which finally could send **peacekeeping forces** to the area. This was the first time the UN took such action. Lester B. Pearson, who would later become the Prime Minister of Canada, was awarded the Nobel Peace Prize in 1957 for his work of creating a mandate for a United Nations Peacekeeping Force.

Key Point

The Cold War had now turned to the Middle East which was an escalation and a departure from Stalinist foreign policy.

---

[38] Ball, S. J., *The Cold War: An International History 1947–1991*, p. 152.
[39] *The Economist*, 27 July 2006, p. 24.

Exercise 9: Compare and contrast the origins of two Cold War crises.

(Show the similarities and the differences. We choose the Korean War 1950 and the Suez Crisis 1956 as an example.)

Similarities:

1. Both conflicts started with an **armed attack** where **neither of the two superpowers were directly involved**.
2. Both conflicts started in what could be seen as **smaller countries**, but it was soon clear that the outcome would be of **major importance** to the Cold War.
3. Both conflicts gave an impression of being potentially very important and ran the risk that both superpowers could be directly involved.
4. Both conflicts involved close allies to the superpowers (China, Britain and France).
5. Both conflicts show that there were no geographical limits in the Cold War—it was global. (Stalin had been much more cautious.)

Differences:

1. The aims were **more limited in Egypt**. While the attacking powers would topple Nasser and take control of the Canal, the aim in Korea was initially to annex another state.
2. In Korea, the USSR had been a part of the preparation for the attack. **No such superpower involvement** could be seen in Egypt when planning the attack.
3. Many of the **aims in the two conflicts differed**. Kim wanted to unite his country. Stalin approved his plans for a variety of reasons. In Egypt there were many other reasons: to curb Arab nationalism, oil, Cold War reasons, control of the Canal, Nasser, Algeria, Israel's security and of course the desire of both Britain and France to maintain her influence in the region. (This point should be elaborated.)
4. The fact that two-third of Europe's **oil** went through the Canal and that the Middle East was so rich with oil, makes this conflict very special. (Egypt cannot however be seen as an oil producer of importance—it was the Canal which was so important for transporting the oil.)
5. In Korea, the UN could be used as a tool, while Britain and France could veto any decision in the Security Council in 1956. Consequently there was **no US coalition with active UN troops** in Egypt.
6. But the General Assembly in the UN held an emergency session when the resolution supporting a withdrawal of all forces was passed. It was the first time the Assembly was used in this way and it was decided that **UN forces** should be sent, under a **UN flag**, to implement the resolution. They would supervise the ceasefire with peacekeeping UN units. This was new and would be used many times in the future.
7. There was no **interference from another world crisis (Hungary)** influencing decisions when the Korean Crisis started.
8. The Suez Crisis can also be seen as a way of dealing with the revolt in **Algeria**.

Conclusion:

From the beginning most people realised that the outcome of the crises would be of major importance for the continuation of the Cold War. It is also worth noting that none of the superpowers were directly involved in the crises. But if we study the initial aims, why the conflict started from the beginning, it must be concluded that there are many differences (emphasise point 2 above).

Exercise 10: Compare and contrast the impact and significance of two Cold War crises each chosen from a different region.

(Show similarities and differences. We choose Korea 1951 and the Suez Crisis 1956 in the below example.)

Similarities:

1. Both conflicts confirm the **dominance of the two superpowers** in World affairs. Europe, excluding the USSR, is playing a secondary role.
2. Both conflicts would have a **major impact** from a Cold War perspective in each region. Both conflicts can be seen as **escalations** of the Cold War (one example is the NSC68 implementation).
3. Specific examples of 'major impact' were the US commitment to defend **Taiwan** in 1950 and support to the **French in Indochina**. The USSR stood firmly behind **North Korea and China**. In the Middle East, Eisenhower announced the '**Eisenhower Doctrine**' of 1957 where the US Congress gave him the right to provide economic and military assistance to any Middle Eastern country threatened with armed aggression or internal subversion. The Suez Crisis **opened up the Middle East for the USSR**. They would now finance the **Aswan Dam**.
4. Both conflicts boosted support for the **USSR in the Third World**. In Korea and in Egypt, Western powers were directly involved in armed conflicts against smaller nations.
5. In both conflicts the **UN** was involved. (The roles differed somewhat, which is explained below.)

Differences:

1. While Korea didn't really change the division of Asia from a Cold War perspective, the **Suez Crisis** resulted in many **new opportunities** in the Middle East to the USSR in particular.

2. The Suez Crisis did not strengthen **Atlantic cooperation**. Especially France felt betrayed by the US which partly explains France distancing itself from parts of NATO later.
3. On the other hand, the Suez Crisis spurred **European integration**. Germany gave strong support to the French during the crisis and in 1957 the European Economic Community was formed.
4. The Suez Crisis brought an end to an era. **Decolonisation gained much strength** and **British and French influence in the Middle East was ended**. Some even argue that this was the end of the British Empire in terms of international influence. Nothing similar could be seen in Korea.
5. The role of the UN was very different. In Korea it was used as a tool to fight back the attack from the North. In Suez it should implement the ceasefire and send peacekeeping forces. The UN organiser (the Canadian Lester Pearson) was awarded with the Nobel Peace Prize in 1957.
6. The Suez Crisis had a direct impact on the crisis in Hungary. Focus was in the Middle East and not in Hungary.
7. **Korea suffered** more in terms of destruction and causalities than Egypt did.
8. Nasser and Egypt came out as a clear victor from the Suez Crisis, nothing similar could be seen in Korea.
9. The Suez Crisis led to the Canal losing much of its importance as an oil supplier. It led to the Japanese starting to build super-tankers to go round the Cape.

Conclusion:

Both these crises were of major significance and affected both regions profoundly. Both superpowers committed themselves to different allies. One example is Truman's decision to implement the recommendations in the NSC68 report.

The Suez Crisis brought many changes. Britain and France lost most of their influence in the Middle East while the Soviet Union became a very important power in the region after 1956. It was a very clear departure from Stalin's foreign policy.

Atlantic co-operation was damaged through the Suez Crisis and Franco-American relations never recovered from this. On the other hand, co-operation in Europe gained from the crisis. The Suez Crisis was one building block in the European Union.

Cold War Crisis 5: Berlin 1958–1961

The next Cold War crisis according to the syllabus will be Berlin 1958–1961.
During this period there were actually two crises, one in 1958 and the second one in 1961, when the wall was erected. It is however also possible to see it as one on going crisis between 1958 and 1961.

Berlin would once more be a trouble spot in the late 1950s and early 1960s. The US poured money into West Berlin and soon the city was a **prosperous Western island** contrasting with the areas controlled by the USSR. The worst problem was that many young, educated East Germans fled their country through Berlin and it severely drained the resources of East Germany. It caused a 'brain drain'. Between 1949 and June 1961, **2,600,000 East Germans fled the country**, an average of more than 200,000 per year. The figures from the years when the wall was erected in 1961 were:

Year	1991
1957	261,622
1958	204,092
1959	143,917
1960	199,188
1961 (to 30 June)	103,159

Source: Taken from P. M. H. Bell, *The World since 1945: An International History*, Arnold, London 2001, p. 140.

A solution was needed because:

- The East German state would **collapse** if it continued.
- The difference between East and West Berlin, with its capitalist prosperity, was an **embarrassment** to the communist regime.
- There was no formal treaty where the two German states were fully recognised. Khrushchev wanted **both a treaty and a solution to the Berlin problem**. So Berlin was used as a tool to solve the German problem, which is often forgotten when the crisis is described.

Step 1: Khrushchev realised that something had to be done. On 10 November 1958, he made a speech and announced that the time had come to find a solution to the Berlin problem:

> "The time has obviously arrived for the signatories of the Potsdam Agreement to renounce the remnants of the occupation regime in Berlin, and thereby make it possible to create a normal situation in the capital of GDR. The USSR […] would hand over to the sovereign GDR the functions in Berlin." [40]

On 27 November, he followed up with a note to the Western Powers. **Khrushchev wanted a peace treaty where two German states would be fully recognised and that Berlin should be a free city without troops**. He declared the existing agreement on Berlin null and void and that all foreign troops should leave the city within six months and if no solution was reached the USSR would hand over the responsibility for Berlin to the German Democratic Republic. Khrushchev writes in his memoirs: "*We were simply asking the other side to acknowledge that two irreconcilable socio-political structures existed in Germany…*"[41]

This placed the West in a dilemma: if West Berlin remained as a 'free' city but the checkpoints would be handled by East Germans officials:

1. The West would be forced to **deal with a regime** they had promised West Germany not to accept or recognise.

2. The West Berliners also remembered the days of the Berlin Airlift in 1948. If the city was cut off in 1958, it would not be possible to support a much larger Berlin from the air.

3. **To accept Khrushchev's ultimatum** would be a devastating signal to other **allies**.

4. If the Western powers tried to enforce their rights there was always a risk for an **armed conflict**.

Khrushchev gave the Western powers a **six-month ultimatum**.

The Western powers were divided. Eisenhower saw a possibility of seeing East Germany as agents of the USSR, thus accepting East German control of the border. De Gaulle in France was in a phase of building the European Community and had already during the Suez Crisis established strong bonds with Adenauer in West Germany. Both were against any concessions to the USSR. To Adenauer a two-state German solution was unacceptable.

Step 2: Khrushchev did not press his point however. In 1959, he went to a much publicised visit to the US and was prepared to once again **postpone his Berlin ultimatum** until a Big Four summit meeting in Paris in May 1960. This summit collapsed on the very first day. In 1956, Eisenhower had authorised reconnaissance spy planes crossing Russian territories. They were out of range of Russian ground-to-air missiles. On 1 May 1960, a US plane was finally shot down by improved missiles and Khrushchev set up a trap. The Russians only announced that a plane had been shot down. The US now claimed it was a weather reconnaissance aircraft, assuming it had not been found. The problem was that the pilot Gary Powers survived and explained that he had not swallowed the cyanide capsule as he had been instructed to do. The Russians also had the wreckage of the aircraft and could later put it on display in Moscow with parts of the aircraft, the pilots equipment etc. The incident angered the Russians and Khrushchev demanded a full apology at the Paris summit. Eisenhower accepted full responsibility for this '**U-2 affair**', but refused to apologise and the Russians left the conference in anger. No solution to the Berlin problem was consequently achieved.

Step 3: In 1961, the US elected John F. Kennedy as president. Khrushchev and the Eastern Bloc wanted more than ever a solution to the Berlin problem due to the damaging number of refugees. Khrushchev wrote in his memoirs: "*I know there are people who claim that the East Germans are imprisoned in paradise and that the gates of the Socialist paradise are guarded by armed troops. I'm aware that defects exists…*"[42] When Kennedy met Khrushchev in **Vienna in June 1961**, he had experienced the fiasco at the **Bay of Pigs** the previous April (see 'the Cuban Missile Crisis') and couldn't abandon this outpost

---

[40] Williamson, D., *Europe and the Cold War 1945–91*, 2nd ed. (London: Hodder Murray, 2006) p. 123.
[41] Khrushchev, N., *Khrushchev Remembers*, p. 453.
[42] Khrushchev, N., *Khrushchev Remembers*, p. 456.

behind the Iron Curtain. Before the summit he said: "*I'll have to show him that we can be as tough as he is…*"⁴³ No solution was reached but **Khrushchev issued a second six-month ultimatum** concerning Berlin. Kennedy asked the Congress for more money to US defence.

Step 4: In August 1961, the uncertainty over Berlin became acute. On 12 August, 4,000 people fled the city and the day after the East German government started to erect the **Berlin Wall**, the very symbol of the Cold War. They did it because:

1. They needed a solution to the refugee crisis.

2. This would ease the tension to the US in the long run.

The days when the wall was erected were of course very tense. Shortly after there was a stand-off where tanks from both sides lined up along the border between the zones in Berlin. Khrushchev wrote in his memoirs:

> "The tanks and troops of both sides spent the night lined up facing each other across the border. It was late October and chilly." ⁴⁴

Impact and Significance of the Berlin Crisis

1. **Berlin ceased to be a major pressure point** in US-Soviet relations.

2. Khrushchev concluded: "*It was a great victory for us.*"⁴⁵ For the Russians **the problem of refugees was solved** but the propaganda value in terms of '**bad will**' should not be underestimated. The Berlin Wall became a symbol for communist oppression. In the Eastern Bloc it was however referred to 'the anti-fascist wall'.

3. The solution of the refugee problem was however important to the East German state and the USSR. With the Wall, Khrushchev concluded that **no peace treaty was needed**.

4. The crisis from 1958 to 1961 put a lot of pressure on **German-American relations**. This side of the crisis has many times been neglected. When Eisenhower publicly stated that he was not prepared to risk a war over Berlin and that the US was prepared to discuss Khrushchev's ultimatum in 1958, the Germans felt that the US was unwilling to defend them. It was France who stood aside Germany in this crisis. France on the other hand felt betrayed by the US after Suez–together this put a lot of strain on relations between the US and West Germany/France.

5. Officially, it gave an impression that Kennedy had survived his first test after the Bay of Pigs fiasco, no matter what Adenauer thought. West Berlin remained a 'free city'. Kennedy and the Americans had strong support from the West Berliners. In 1963, he went to Berlin and in one of the most well-known speeches from the Cold War declared:

> "Freedom is indivisible, and when one man is enslaved, all are not free. When all men are free, then we can look forward to that day when this city will be joined as one, and this country, and this great continent of Europe, in a peaceful and hopeful globe. When that day finally comes, and it will, the people of West Berlin can take sober satisfaction in the fact that they were in the front line for almost two decades.
>
> All free men, wherever they may live, are citizens of Berlin, and, therefore, as a free man, I take pride in the words "'Ich bin ein Berliner.'" ⁴⁶

---

[43] Edwards, O., *The USA and the Cold War 1945–63*, p. 114.
[44] Khrushchev, N., *Khrushchev Remembers*, p. 460.
[45] Ibid., p. 460.
[46] Hanhimäki, J. M. and Westad, O. A., eds., *The Cold War: A History in Documents and Eyewitness Accounts*, p. 331.

Cold War Leader 3: Dwight D. Eisenhower, President of the US, 1953–1961

In the beginning, Eisenhower took an even more aggressive stance against the USSR than Truman. We must be aware that in 1953, when Truman came to power, **McCarthy** was at the peak of his career and Eisenhower had won the presidential elections by attacking the Truman administration for being 'soft on communism'. Containment was no longer enough—there should be a rollback of communism. He became the first Republican president for 20 years and introduced a new foreign policy which was referred to as **The New Look**:

Communism should still be contained. His Secretary of State John Foster Dulles even expressed the desire of a '**rollback**' of communist-controlled areas, i.e., a liberation of these areas from communism. Eisenhower supported it but clarified that it had to be achieved by peaceful means.

Nuclear weapons were now regarded as weapons of first and not last resort. In practical terms this indicated a policy of **massive retaliation** against possible enemies, and less reliance on conventional forces and Truman's policy of fighting 'limited wars'. So nuclear weapons were produced and the size of the US army was reduced during the Eisenhower years (size of the US army/thousands):

1953	1954	1956	1960
1,534	1,405	1,026	871

Source: Taken from The Encyclopaedia of American Military.

In many ways, Eisenhower must be seen as a Cold Warrior, i.e., he was strongly anti-communist. Consequently a lot of alliances against communism were formed.

- In 1954, the South-East Asian Treaty Organization (**SEATO**) was created by the US, France, Britain, Australia, New Zealand, the Philippines, Thailand and Pakistan, with the main aim of preventing communist expansion in South-East Asia.
- In 1955, the **Baghdad Pact** was formed between Britain, Iraq and later Iran and Pakistan with the aim of excluding the USSR from the Middle East. The US did not join for tactical reasons but stood behind the organisation.
- In Europe, Germany was offered full membership status in NATO in 1955, i.e., a decision to allow German troops again.

But this new foreign policy and the idea of rollback would be tested:

- In 1953, there was a revolt in **East Berlin** against communist rule. **No US support** was given.
- In 1956, **Hungary** revolted against Soviet control. The US gave **no support** to the Hungarians.
- During the **Suez Crisis in 1956** the US refused to support her allies Britain, France and Israel. In fact they stood on **the same side as the USSR**.
- During the **Second Berlin Crisis in 1958** Eisenhower declared that he wanted to **avoid a war** over Berlin.

But there are many examples showing that he was a part of the Cold War:

1. In 1954, there was a *coup d'etat* in **Guatemala**. It was a covert operation carried out by the United States Central Intelligence Agency (CIA) which deposed the democratically elected Guatemalan President Jacobo Arbenz whom the US considered to be to leftist.

2. In 1956, Eisenhower had authorised reconnaissance **spy planes crossing Russian territories**.

3. Eisenhower committed the US to **defend Taiwan** during the Taiwan Strait Crises.

4. The US supported Diem in **Vietnam** after France had left. In 1954, it was Eisenhower who articulated the **Domino Theory**, when looking at communism in South-East Asia. If one country fell to communism it would lead to a domino reaction in Asia.

5. In 1957, the **Eisenhower Doctrine** was passed in Congress stating that the US would defend with arms any state in the Middle East threatened by communist aggression.

6. It was the Eisenhower administration which planned the **Bay of Pigs** invasion in Cuba.

2. Korea, the US, the USSR and China: Superpower Relations (1947–1949)

Cold Warrior or not, it is interesting to note the **Farewell Address to the Nation** from President Eisenhower on 17 January 1961. Eisenhower, the former General who had led D-day and had led his country during eight Cold War years said: "[…] *we must guard against the acquisition of unwarranted influence, whether sought or unsought,* **by the military–industrial complex**. *The potential for the disastrous rise of misplaced power* exists, and will persist. We must never let the weight of this combination **endanger our liberties** or democratic processes."[47]

Student Activities

Make an attempt to answer the question below. After you have written down your main points, compare them with the outline on the next page.

> **Exercise 11:** Examine how the Truman Doctrine and the policy of containment were implemented in the period 1947–1961?
>
> *(It is a list question. Go through chronologically how it was implemented and don't forget to define and explain the Truman Doctrine and the containment policy in the beginning.)*
>
> **Containment** was the US policy that was adopted by President Truman in his Truman Doctrine in 1947 by which the US attempted **to prevent further Soviet or communist expansion** beyond territories occupied in 1945. No long-term co-operation with the USSR was possible and the intellectual basis had been provided by George Kennan in his Long Telegram from 1946. By supporting the 'free world' mainly militarily but also economically, like the Marshall Plan in Europe and economic aid to Japan, the expansion of communism would be prevented. To prevent the expansion of communism resulted in the building of military alliances surrounding the Communists.
>
> **The Truman Doctrine** stated that it should be US policy to support nations who are fighting an internal or external communist threat. Initially intended only for Greece and Turkey but soon extended globally. Not only military means were used. Economical means, like the Marshall Plan, could be used.
>
> There is a lot of information so don't overwrite. Dealing with a question where you may know too many points requires that you emphasise your main points and briefly mention points of minor importance. The most important points are:
>
> 1. Help was given both to **Greece and Turkey** and they remained within the Western camp.
> 2. Truman was able to pass the Marshall Plan through the Congress in 1948. The effect of the Marshall Plan is normally considered as **successful** and led to a massive industrial growth with a GNP growth in Europe of around 15–25% annually.
> 3. From the late 1940s substantial aid was given to **Japan** to build a stronghold against communism in Asia.
> 4. Through the **Berlin Airlift** Berlin was saved from a communist takeover.
> 5. Germany was given both economic and political support. In 1949, the **independence of West Germany** was proclaimed and she received substantial economic aid.
> 6. In April 1949 **NATO** was founded. Twelve states joined the organisation and according to article 5, "*an armed attack against one or more …… be considered an attack on them all.*"[48] Germany became a full member in 1955.
> 7. In 1950, there was full support for **South Korea** when they were attacked by the North.
> 8. To achieve containment and to stop the expansion of communism the **NSC-68 report** was implemented from 1950. It led to a massive US military build-up.
> 9. Containment and the Truman Doctrine were now implemented in Asia. The US started to support the French in the **Indochina War** and support was also given to protect **Taiwan**. The build-up of Japan was strengthened.
> 10. With Eisenhower a partly new foreign policy was introduced called the 'New Look'. However, this policy was *in essence not different*. The aim was to prevent the spread of communism globally and to contain it. The talk about 'rollback' proved to be rhetorical.
> 11. In 1954, the South-East Asian Treaty Organization (**SEATO**) was created by the US, France, Britain, Australia, New Zealand, the Philippines, Thailand and Pakistan, with the main aim of preventing communist expansion in South-East Asia.
> 12. In 1954, CIA supported a coup in **Guatemala**.
> 13. In 1955, the **Baghdad Pact** was formed between Britain, Iraq and later Iran and Pakistan with the aim of excluding the USSR from the Middle East. The US didn't join this pact but unofficially clearly supported it.
> 14. In January 1957, Eisenhower launched his '**Eisenhower Doctrine**': the US Congress gave him the right to provide economic and military assistance to any Middle East country threatened with armed aggression or internal subversion. As a result of this the US intervened in Lebanon in July 1958.
> 15. **West Berlin survived 1958–1961**.
> 16. Trade embargo against **Cuba** and the Bay of Pigs in 1961. 15,000 US advisors in Vietnam.
>
> **Conclusion:** Summarise your main points.

---

[47] Hanhimäki, J. M. and Westad, O. A., eds., *The Cold War: A History in Documents and Eyewitness Accounts*, p. 291.
[48] Edwards, O., *The USA and the Cold War 1945–63*, p. 50.

Figure 2.7: John F Kennedy. White House, 7/11/1963

John F. Kennedy was elected US President in the 1960 elections after gaining a narrow margin over Richard Nixon. Kennedy had served on a torpedo boat during WWII and afterwards he wrote a bestseller about Britain's appeasement policy before the war, *Why England Slept*. His father, Joseph, had been US ambassador to Britain and an outspoken defender of appeasement. Appeasement was the policy where concessions were made to Hitler, to preserve peace. The lesson learned from appeasement was never to give in to a dictator. Would this affect Kennedy later?

As a young senator in the early 1950s and later as a presidential candidate, he was a dedicated anti-communist. He campaigned vigorously, **attacking the Eisenhower administration** for inadequate defence preparations and especially for allowing a '**missile gap**' to the Soviets. In 1961, Khrushchev boasted that "*The Soviet Union has the world's most powerful rocketry*"[49] which was not true. He also gave major shock to the Americans when the Soviets had launched the first Sputnik satellite into the space in 1957. Kennedy attacked Eisenhower for being "*second in space, second in missiles.*"[50] For a while the Americans were insecure about the size of the nuclear forces in the USSR. As late as 1961, the intelligence service was deeply divided on the question of the missile gap. In his inaugural speech he declared:

> "Let every nation know, whether it wishes us well or ill, that we shall pay any price, bear any burden, meet any hardship, oppose any foe to assure the survival and success of liberty." [51]

As US President he **increased military spending substantially on both nuclear and conventional forces** by 13% per year. It was the largest and fastest peacetime military build up in US history. Cuts in conventional forces made by Eisenhower were reversed by Kennedy. Military spending had reached its peak in 1953 when the Korean War ended but was partly reduced throughout the 1950s until Kennedy came to power. His new approach in foreign policy was referred to as a policy of '**flexible response**'. The reason behind this policy was that the **communist threat was considered to be more diverse**. Consequently the US must be able to fight a conventional war, a nuclear war with modern technology and to combat revolutionary movements in the Third World. Khrushchev had declared that the ultimate victory of communism would be achieved through '**national-liberation wars**' in the Third World and that he would support such wars whole-heartedly and without reservation. "*The front of the national-liberation movement are multiplying…front of struggle against US imperialism.*"[52] The main difference to Eisenhower's policies was less reliance on nuclear weapons. He also attached more emphasis on economic aid as part of a containment policy. This was especially important in the 1960s when the decolonisation process in Africa had started.

---

[49] Ball, S. J., *The Cold War: An International History 1947–1991*, p. 72.
[50] Lebow, R. N. and Stein, J. G., *We All Lost the Cold War* (New Jersey: Princeton University Press, 1994) p. 35.
[51] http://americanrhetoric.com/speeches/jfkinaugural.htm <Accessed 5 January 2017>
[52] Hanhimäki, J. M. and Westad, O. A., eds., *The Cold War*, p. 359.

Kennedy was not a traditional Democrat in his foreign and defence policies, especially if we compare him to the Republican Eisenhower. If we compare the two, Kennedy was the **hawk** and it was Kennedy who undertook a substantial build-up of the US defence system. The ex-general Eisenhower on the other hand had warned the US public of the growth of the 'military industrial complex' and in his farewell speech in 1961 he said:

> "This conjunction of an immense military establishment and a large arms industry is new in the American experience. The total influence—economic, political, even spiritual—is felt in every city…every office of the federal government. We must never let the weight of this combination endanger our liberties."[53]

It is very informative to study the size of the armies of the superpowers:

Active US Army personnel strength in thousands

1936:	**168**	1951:	1,532
1938:	185	1953:	1,534
1942:	3,076	1954:	1,405
1945:	**8,268**	**1956:**	**1,026**
1947:	991	1960:	871
1948:	554	**1969:**	**1,510**
1950:	**593**	1975:	781

Source: The Encyclopaedia of American Military.

The size of the Red Army dropped from 13 million during the war, to **3–5 million during the Cold War**, depending on different Western estimates. Khrushchev continued this reduction in the late 1950s and reduced the size of the Red Army from 3.6 to 2.4 million men. Even after this reduction Soviet conventional forces were far stronger than the US army, if we only count the number of soldiers.

There are several interesting things to notice about these figures. The size of the US army before WWII was smaller than the armies of most European states. Two things have been most discussed concerning Kennedy's foreign policy: the **Cuban Missile Crisis** and what his intentions in **Vietnam** were.

Cold War Crisis 6: The Cuban Missile Crisis 1962

Cuba was liberated from Spain in 1898 and soon a tradition of **US domination** developed, both politically and economically. The US had always seen Latin America as her sphere of influence. The **Monroe Doctrine** from 1823 stated that *"the American continents…are henceforth not be considered as subjects for future colonizations by any European power*[54]*"* i.e., any attempt by a European power to interfere in the New World was regarded by the US as an unfriendly act. Monroe also stated that *"Our policy in regard to Europe…is not to interfere in the internal concerns of any of its powers."*[55] This tradition of **isolationism** had been established by George Washington in his Farewell Address in 1796 when he advised the US *"to steer clear of permanent alliances with foreign nations."*[56] The development in America had also been quite peaceful in regards to 'wars', except for the US Civil War. Prior to the Second World War, the US army was smaller than the armies in many European states. President James Monroe's declaration in 1823 received little attention at the time but in 1904 **Theodore Roosevelt** announced that the US would interfere in any Latin American country guilty of **'chronic wrong-doing'**: *"Chronic wrongdoing, or an impotence which results in a general loosening of the ties of civilized society, may in America, as elsewhere, ultimately require intervention by some civilized nation, and in the Western Hemisphere the adherence of the United States to the Monroe Doctrine may force the United States, however reluctantly, in flagrant cases of such wrongdoing or impotence, to the exercise of an international police power."*[57]

Author's Tip

This is the first crisis we will study from America. As you will know by now, you have to compare crises from different regions.

---

[53] Hanhimäki, J. M. and Westad, O. A., eds., *The Cold War*, p. 291.
[54] http://avalon.law.yale.edu <Accessed 5 January 2017>
[55] http://avalon.law.yale.edu <Accessed 5 January 2017>
[56] http://avalon.law.yale.edu <Accessed 5 January 2017>
[57] http://en.wikiquote.org/wiki/Theodore_Roosevelt <Accessed 5 January 2017>

This extension has guided the US to justify intervention many times. In 1947, **the Rio Pact** was signed stating that *"the obligation of mutual assistance and common defence of the American Republics is essentially related to their democratic ideals* and that *an armed attack by any State against an American State shall be considered as an attack against all the American States."*[58] In 1948, **the Organization of the American States (OAS)** was formed and its charter stated that international communism was incompatible with American freedom. In 1954, the US and CIA had supported and organised a coup in **Guatemala** which led to the overthrow of a regime which had started a land-reform programme. In Guatemala, over half the population owned only 3% of the land but Eisenhower saw the land reform programme as a first step towards communism.

US domination in many areas also led to economic exploitation. This was the situation in Cuba where most of the economy was controlled by American companies. **Half of the land and most of the industry were owned by US companies**. Cuba was led by a right-wing and corrupt **military dictator, Batista**, with the support of the US. Havana was at the time a popular tourist resort infiltrated by US mafia.

Critical Thinking

Taking the tradition of isolationism in mind and the size of the US army before WWII: What were the effects of the Truman Doctrine, NATO, SEATO and the policies of containment, to the US?

- Fidel Castro was a young radical lawyer and a member of the reformist Cuban People's Party. Elections were scheduled for 1952 and Fidel wanted a seat in the House of Representatives. This year Batista carried out a coup which overthrew the government and the **elections were cancelled**.

- Castro now organised an armed opposition and in 1953 he led a suicidal attack on the **Moncada military barracks** with the intention of starting a general revolt, which failed. Castro was sentenced to 15 years imprisonment.

- He was released in 1955 and went to Mexico where Cuban exiles organised **the 26th of July Movement**. 26th of July was the day they had attacked the army barracks. The group declared that they wanted a radical social revolution but didn't declare themselves Communists.

- **In 1956, he returned** with 81 men and started to organise a guerrilla war against the Batista regime.

- After two years, in January 1959, Castro's units controlled the country. The **collapse of the regime** and its lack of support become clear considering the fact that Castro had 800 guerrillas and the Cuban army officially comprised 30,000 men. Batista fled the country. Castro went to the US in an attempt to get US support, both economically and politically. Eisenhower refused to meet him. Castro had started a **land reform programme and industries were nationalised** but he was still not an outspoken communist.

- In **1960**, foreign companies were nationalised step by step. In October the US responded with a **trade embargo**. The US was by far the most important market for Cuban sugar cane and the embargo was a serious threat to the new regime. In the same month all foreign companies were nationalised. **A trade agreement was signed with the USSR** and diplomatic relations.

Was it US actions which pushed Castro towards communism or was it a genuine ideological commitment?

Alternative I: Castro never declared that he was a communist when he seized power. He did so after the Americans started to attack his new regime. With a trade embargo and sabotage actions by the CIA, the Cuban revolution wouldn't be able to survive. From the beginning, Castro's regime and seizure of power was an attempt to achieve Cuban control of the country, a national liberation. With a US **trade embargo** there was no other alternative. **The US pushed Castro** to the USSR and left no options. In December 1961 he declared that he was a Marxist-Leninist, after the Bay of Pigs.

Alternative II: Castro was more than aware of what had happened in Guatemala in 1954. The Arbenz regime in Guatemala had been overthrown by the Americans only because they were suspected Communists. If Castro had declared himself a communist from an early stage, he knew that the Americans would never accept such a regime. Consequently **he disguised his beliefs for tactical reasons** in the early stage of the Cuban revolution. But there was no doubt that he was a communist from the beginning.

---

[58] http://avalon.law.yale.edu <Accessed 5 January 2017>

When Kennedy was elected president he inherited, from the previous administration, a plan from the CIA to attack Cuba with the help of Cuban exiles. The US trained the exiles, financed the operation and provided necessary equipment. The aim was for the attack, to spur a spontaneous revolt in Cuba. The plan was implemented at the **Bay of Pigs on 17 April 1961**: everything went wrong and the exiles were easily defeated by the Cuban army. No spontaneous revolt started and when the exiles ran into troubles, no support was given from the US navy. 1,179 Cuban exiles were captured and the US had to pay $53 million in baby food and medicine to get them released. Kennedy had to take full responsibility for this devastating fiasco. It was not a good start for this young and inexperienced president and Cuba became an obsession with him.

Fiasco notwithstanding, only three days after the Bay of Pigs he gave Castro a warning that the US government would not hesitate in meeting its primary obligations, the security of the nation. The trade embargo was maintained, the CIA continued with sabotage actions and there was strong political and military pressure from the US. In 1962, Robert Kennedy said: "*no time, money, effort—or manpower is to be spared and the budget was over $50 million a year.*"[59]

Miami was the largest CIA station in the world with 600 full-time CIA officers. The Bay of Pigs probably also taught the young president not to fully trust the army. This was a very valuable experience when dealing with the missile crisis in 1962.

In this situation Castro asked for further military support from the USSR. Khrushchev decided to place nuclear ballistic missiles on Cuba. Why did he do it?

Figure 2.8: Cuban President Fidel Castro embracing Soviet Premier Nikita Khrushchev

There were different reasons for the deployment of the missiles:

1. Khrushchev wanted to **protect the Cuban revolution**. The Foreign Minister explained the deployment as a result of "*the very sharp, aggressive stand of the* (Kennedy) *administration concerning the new Cuba.*"[60]

2. The US had 100 intercontinental ballistic missiles (ICBM) and 1,700 intercontinental bombers at the time. The USSR had only 50 ICBMs and 150 bombers. An intermediate range missile in

---

[59] Lebow, R. N. and Stein, J. G., *We All Lost the Cold War* (New Jersey: Princeton University Press, 1994), p. 25.
[60] Ibid, p. 30.

Cuba would reach major cities in the US and compensate for the lack of ICBMs. The USSR was planning to send 40 medium and intermediate-range missiles (IRBM) to Cuba which would almost double the Soviet nuclear strike capability. In practical terms, with the Cuban missiles, Khrushchev aimed to **reduce his nuclear inferiority** and save a sizeable amount of money for the USSR. The alternative, an expensive build-up of Russian ICBM missiles, was extremely costly. The strategic balance would be altered according to the formula IRBM + Cuba = ICBM. Khrushchev wrote in his memoirs: "*In addition to protecting Cuba, our missiles would have equalised what the West likes to call 'the balance of power'.*" [61]

3. The US had nuclear missiles in **Turkey**. Khrushchev wrote in his memoirs: "*The United States had already surrounded the Soviet Union with its own bomber bases and missiles. We knew that American missiles were aimed against us in Turkey.*"[62] Eisenhower had concluded in 1959, before the deployment of US missiles in Turkey: "*If Mexico or Cuba had been…began getting arms and missiles from them (the USSR), we would be bound to look on such developments with the gravest concern…. (and) take positive actions, even offensive military actions.*"[63]

4. A communist-controlled Cuba would provide the USSR with a springboard to spread communism to underdeveloped countries in Latin America. In the late 1950s, Khrushchev declared that the ultimate victory of communism would be achieved by war of liberations in the Third World.

5. He could claim that he wanted to protect a small state against a superpower. It would strengthen his position in the Third World (like in the Suez Crisis).

6. It would put him in a **bargaining position** with the US. 'Quid pro quo' i.e. 'something in return' was typical for the Cold War. Some kind of solution to the Berlin problem was one possible option. Khrushchev wrote in his memoirs: '*…if Russian blood was shed in Cuba, American blood would surely be shed in Germany*'.[64]

7. To show toughness to his critics in China and in his own country. Both his domestic and foreign policy were criticised in the Presidium, especially his agricultural policy, the Virgin Land Project, which had failed.

The crisis started when U2 spy-planes established evidence of Soviet medium range missile sites in Cuba on the 14 of October. **Why was this unacceptable to Kennedy**? After all, the Americans had the same type of weapons in Turkey.

1. The **Monroe Doctrine** stated that no interference from a European power in America would be tolerated. This policy had been further strengthened by Theodore Roosevelt and his declaration in 1904 of 'chronic wrong-doing' and the charter of the OAS and its rejection of communism. A communist Cuba protected by nuclear weapons by its ally, the USSR, was very difficult to accept. This was a **US sphere of influence**.

2. Kennedy had attacked Eisenhower for both a 'missile gap' and the 'loss' of Cuba. It was very difficult from a political point of view to accept a communist nuclear build-up so close to the US. An intermediate-range ballistic missile in Cuba would reach the US's major cities. **Politically this could not be tolerated**. From a strict security perspective the importance of this can be questioned. The Russians had 50 intercontinental ballistic missiles (ICBM) and some 150 intercontinental bombers and could destroy the US anyway. Robert McNamara, the Secretary of Defence concluded: "*A missile is a missile. It makes no difference whether you are killed by a missile fired from the Soviet Union or from Cuba.*" He also concluded: "*I don't think there is a military problem here […] this is a domestic, political problem.*"[65] There should be mid-term **election to the Congress** in November the same year. Another Cuban 'fiasco' would be devastating, politically to Kennedy and his Democratic Party. The Kennedy brothers even thought that if they had not

---

[61] Khrushchev, N., *Khrushchev Remembers*, p. 494.
[62] Khrushchev, N., *Khrushchev Remembers*, p. 493.
[63] Lebow, R. N. and Stein, J. G., *We All Lost the Cold War* (New Jersey: Princeton University Press, 1994), p. 43.
[64] Khrushchev, N., *Khrushchev Remembers*, p. 500.
[65] Lebow, R. N. and Stein, J. G., *We All Lost the Cold War* (New Jersey: Princeton University Press, 1994), p. 97.

reacted the President might run the risk of being impeached by the Republicans. The President told his brother on his way to an Ex Comm meeting: "*I would have been impeached.*"[66]

> You may see different terms describing medium-range missiles. The problem is that various terms are used by different countries; making definitions about medium range missiles is subjective and arbitrary.
> - **Medium-Range Ballistic Missile**, abbreviated **MRBM** is defined by the US Department of Defence as having a maximum range of 1,000–3,000 km, in other words a short-range missile.
> - **SS-** is an MRBM and what started the crisis when it was discovered on 14/10.
> - An **Intermediate-Range Ballistic Missile (IRBM)**, according to the US definition, is a ballistic missile with a range of 3,000–5,500 km and would reach the US west coast, i.e., a long-range missile. IRBM sites were discovered in October. It is doubtful if any IRBMs reached Cuba at any time but it was planned and sites **under construction** were discovered.

Figure 2.9: US reconnaissance photograph from Cuba

Figure 2.10: ExComm meeting 29 October 1962

14 Oct. **U2 spy-planes** established evidence of a Soviet medium-range missile base in Cuba.

16 Oct. The **ExComm**—a group of advisers was formed. **Possible solutions to the crisis:**
- Invasion, i.e., a direct confrontation with the Red Army.
- A 'surgical' air strike which could be followed by an invasion. It was turned down because an air strike would not destroy all missiles.
- A **blockade**, or a 'quarantine', i.e., a naval blockade to prevent the USSR from sending components for the missiles to Cuba. It would give time for a diplomatic solution but what would happen when the Russian ships met the US marines? Was it the start of World War III?

22 Oct. Kennedy gave a dramatic **TV speech** to the nation and announced the existence of nuclear weapons 90 miles away from Florida and the US **blockade**.

24 Oct. One of the most dramatic days, when the **Russian ships finally turned back**. The US Secretary of State Dean Rusk said: "*We were eyeball to eyeball, and I think the other fellow just blinked.*"[67]

26 Oct. Khrushchev sent Kennedy **a message** where he offered to withdraw the missiles if the US promised never to invade Cuba. The same day a US **U2 spy plane was shot down** over Cuba and the pilot was killed. Several advisers now recommended an assault on Cuba. What the Americans didn't know was that the nuclear weapons on Cuba were already operational and

---

[66] Ibid., p. 97.
[67] Ibid, p. 140.

that the Russian military commander had been authorised to use short- range tactical nuclear weapons in self-defence without consulting Moscow. This was a very critical day.

Khrushchev sent a **second message** prompting a deal that must include the removal of NATO missiles in **Turkey**. Robert Kennedy now secretly met the Russian ambassador Dobrynin and an agreement about the Turkish missiles was made, but it had to remain secret. Kennedy was aware that a removal required consultations within NATO and there was no time for that, a deal "*could break up the (NATO) Alliance by confirming European suspicions that we would sacrifice their security to protect our interests.*"[68] He was also not willing to officially admit that he had made such a commitment as a result of Soviet pressure.

Two days later, on the **28 October**, Khrushchev informed Kennedy via Radio Moscow that the USSR had accepted the terms. Castro had not been informed and refused a UN inspection of the dismantling of the missiles.

The solution of the crisis:
- The USSR would **remove the missiles**.
- A US pledge to **never invade Cuba**.
- US Jupiter missiles should be removed from Turkey. This was not made public.

Officially, **Kennedy gained** political favour from the crisis. He had made the Russians withdraw the missiles without a war. He had also been able to handle the internal pressure from warmongers, without starting a war. **Khrushchev** on the other hand was **criticised** not only in the USSR but by Mao in China. In 1964, he was forced to resign and even if according to the indictment against him it was mainly due to domestic reasons, the Cuban Crisis played a role. He was blamed for "*erratic leadership, of taking hasty and ill-considered actions.*"[69] The Red Army, already substantially reduced by Khrushchev, found the dismantling of the missiles in Cuba humiliating.

But there are several flaws in these conclusions. **Few or no one knew about the Turkish deal**. It is also clear that the US pledge to **never invade Cuba was a substantial victory to Khrushchev**. Kennedy's initial aim had been a withdrawal without any conditions. By placing missiles in Cuba, Khrushchev was able to secure the Cuban revolution and to remove missiles from Turkey. Another point worth considering is the responsibility for bringing the world to the verge of a nuclear war. It is generally believed by historians, still today, that this is the closest we have been to a nuclear war. Who was responsible for this? **Khrushchev** was responsible for the decision to place nuclear weapons on Cuba. Formally, it was the Presidium, the highest organ of the Communist Party in 1962 (it was the Politburo which was called Presidium between 1952 and 1966), which made the decision but it was Khrushchev's idea from the beginning and he was powerful enough to impose his will on the decision makers. He should have been aware of how serious this must have been to an American president. It was not only the tradition of the Monroe Doctrine. Central America and the Caribbean were under the **US sphere of influence** and it was a very dangerous game **to surprise your enemy with nuclear weapons in such an area**. Khrushchev wrote in his memoirs: "*I had the idea of installing missiles with nuclear warheads in Cuba without letting the United States find out that they were there until it was too late to do anything about them.*"[70] Cuba within a US sphere of influence was not comparable to Turkey. The Security adviser McGeorge Bundy said, "*we felt the same way you would feel if we put missiles in Finland.*"[71] The US had their suspicions and Kennedy warned Khrushchev before the crisis that the US would prevent the installation of Soviet nuclear weapons by whatever means might be necessary. Khrushchev had replied that "*we do not have any bases in Cuba*" and "*we do not intend to establish any.*"[72]

Kennedy on the other hand had put enormous pressure on Cuba with **the trade embargo, the Bay of Pigs invasion and sabotage in the Mongoose operation and this pressure was one of the main reasons for nuclear aid to Cuba**. In 1962, the US Senate had passed a resolution by 86-1, calling for the use of force, if necessary, to stop Cuban aggression and communist activities in the Western

---

[68] Ibid, p. 124.
[69] McCauley, M., *The Khrushchev Era 1953–1964* (Harlow: Longman, 1995) p. 83.
[70] Khrushchev, N., *Khrushchev Remembers*, p. 493.
[71] Lebow, R. N. and Stein, J. G., *We All Lost the Cold War* (New Jersey: Princeton University Press, 1994), p. 94.
[72] Ibid, p. 68.

hemisphere. It can also be argued that the US had no right to object to what the Russians were doing in Cuba due to the simple fact that they **were doing the same in Turkey**, or to use Khrushchev's own words: "*The Americans had surrounded our country with missile bases….now they would learn just what it feels like to have enemies' missiles pointing at you.*"[73] It can also be questioned if Soviet missiles in Cuba were a serious threat to US security and the real reason for Kennedy's actions. McNamara suggested that "*I don't think there is a military problem here… This is a domestic, political problem.*"[74] After his elections campaign attacking Eisenhower and after the Bay of Pigs, Kennedy couldn't afford to look like a **weak president**. The mid-term elections to the Congress in November played a role. A second Cuban fiasco would be devastating for the Democrats. This domestic political factor probably affected his decision-making.

The escalation of the crisis, the blockade and spy planes over Cuba, were Kennedy's decisions. It is a very strong case to argue that a **blockade** on international water against one state is illegal and that Kennedy was responsible for the crisis. Nuclear weapons were already in Cuba when Kennedy risked world peace by setting up this blockade.

Mikhail Gorbachev later concluded that both were to blame: "*The Cuban Missile crisis reminds me of two boys fighting in the schoolyard over who has the bigger stick.*"[75]

Historiography: Orthodox historians or traditionalists like Arthur Schlesinger Jr and insiders like Theodor Sorensen (i.e., pro-Kennedy), argue that the missiles were an intolerable provocation and that Kennedy responded due to a desire to defend **legitimate security needs**, to preserve **NATO** and show American **credibility**. The **quarantine was a successful** strategy and Kennedy was a skilful leader in times of crisis.

Revisionists like I. F. Stone and Ronald Steel argue that Kennedy, with his background attacking the Eisenhower administration for the loss of Cuba, risked a war over Cuba for **domestic political gains**. Confrontation would make it possible to get the missiles out before the November **elections**. But it was not only a question of electoral and political pressure. Kennedy also risked a **revolt from the military** and other hardliners in different departments. The **blockade was irresponsible** and Kennedy is seen as neurotic. The US also has to take the blame for the deployment of **missiles in Turkey** which led to the Cuban affair.

What were the consequences of the crisis?

1. The US was forced to tolerate a **communist state in the Caribbean**. But the US perception of Cuba being a communist threat against US domination in the region was not solved with the outcome of the crisis. The trade embargo was not lifted.
2. The time had come for a **more constructive dialogue**. The crisis had a profound sobering effect on the nuclear powers.
3. A **Test Ban Treaty** was signed in 1963 forbidding nuclear testing in the atmosphere.
4. A **Hot Line**, a direct telephone line, was established between the White House and the Kremlin.
5. **Khrushchev** was criticised not only by Mao in China but also in Moscow. In 1964, he was forced to resign. In Pravda he was criticised for being "*hare-brained*" and supporting "*wild schemes, half-baked conclusions and hasty decisions.*"[76] The Cuban Crisis was one factor behind his **dismissal**.
6. In a longer perspective it led to renewed **Soviet efforts to close the missile gap**. The consequence was an extensive and very expensive Soviet nuclear build-up which would have far-reaching consequences to the Soviet economy.

> The last point is often ignored. It is normally argued that the aftermath of the crisis led to a period of détente. This is true if we focus upon the immediate consequences. But it must be emphasised that the USSR leaders decided never to be humiliated again due to nuclear weakness. The USSR decided, partly as a consequence of the Cuban crisis, to close the only missile gap that existed, i.e., Soviet inferiority.

---

[73] Khrushchev, N., *Khrushchev Remembers*, p. 494.
[74] Lebow, R. N. and Stein, J. G., *We All Lost the Cold War* (New Jersey: Princeton University Press, 1994), p. 97.
[75] Ibid, p. 110.
[76] https://www.russianlife.com/stories/online-archive/nikita-khrushchev/ <Accessed 5 January 2017>

Let's study the nuclear balance after the crisis over a longer period:

		1964	1966	1968	1970	1972
US	ICBM	834	904	1,054	1,054	1,054
	SLBM	416	592	656	656	656
	ICB	630	630	545	550	455
USSR	ICBM	200	300	800	1,300	1,527
	SLBM	120	125	130	280	560
	ICB	190	200	150	150	140

ICBM = intercontinental ballistic missile; SLBM = submarine launched ballistic missile; ICB = intercontinental bombers

Source: Cold War to Détente by Brown/Mooney, p. 161.

By 1972, the Soviets had finally **closed the missile gap**, and even had an advantage. How much was this policy **a result of the Cuban Crisis**? It is of course a very difficult question to answer but many historians argue that this build-up was a result of the Cuban Crisis. What we do know for sure is that **the cost** of this programme was something that would severely affect Russian society.

The costs for the nuclear arms race were astronomical to both sides. In the 1980s, the US produced five nuclear warheads per day.[77] What was achieved from a security point of view? Gaddis writes:

> "McNamara insisted that a 17-1 advantage for the US in 1962 still translated into an effective nuclear parity because the prospect of only a few nuclear explosions on American soil would deter Washington from doing anything that might provoke them."[78]

Cold War Crisis 7: The Congo Crisis 1960–1964

After WWII, some European colonies in Africa and Asia began their path towards independence. In 1946, only 51 countries were represented in the United Nations versus the 193 of today, which to a major extent can be explained by this process of decolonisation.

No continent was spared from the Cold War:
- The Suez Crisis in the 1950 made it clear that the Cold War now also involved the Middle East as well.
- The Korean War and the Indochina War showed that Asia was a Cold War battle ground.
- The Congo Crisis in the early 1960 and the wars in Angola and Ethiopia in the 1970 clearly showed that Africa also was a focus of Cold War tension.

1. Congo was given **independence from Belgium in June 1960**. The country was led by **Prime Minister Patrice Lumumba and president Joseph Kasavubu.**

2. Only a few weeks after the independence the government ran into difficulties when the army mutinied against their Belgian officers. Acts of **violence** were committed against remaining Belgian and European residents and the Belgian government decided, against the will of the Congo government, to send **paratroopers** to protect the 100,000 European residents who lived in the country.

3. In the southern part of the country, in the **Katanga province**, a rival force led by Moise **Tshombe also challenged the government**. The province was incredibly rich in natural resources and Tshombe was soon supported by European investors and industrialists.

4. In this very problematic situation the Lumumba government appealed to the **UN**. The UN decided, in Resolution 143, **to send troops** to Congo to stabilise the situation. The resolution also made it clear that the UN would not take sides in the conflict. Lumumba's aim had been to get UN help in defeating Tshombe and his faction in the south.

---

[77] LaFeber, W., *America, Russia and the Cold War 1945–2006* (New York: McGraw-Hill Higher Education, 2002) p. 330.
[78] Williamson, D., *Europe and the Cold War 1945–91*, p. 170.

5. **Lumumba** accused the UN for siding with the Europeans or Western powers and **turned to the USSR for help**. Lumumba received massive military aid from the USSR and about a thousand Soviet technical advisers arrived within six weeks. Lumumba now launched an attack on Tshombe in the south which proved unsuccessful.

6. This caused major problems for the president and the army chief of staff, Mobutu. The Americans saw the Soviet activity as an attempt to spread communist influence in Congo. Mobutu came under great pressure. Western nations, which helped pay the soldiers' salaries, as well as Kasavubu and Mobutu's subordinates, favoured getting rid of the Soviet presence. Kasavubu's solution was to dismiss Lumumba.

7. The disintegration of the new state escalated when president **Kasavubu decided to remove Lumumba**. Lumumba had strong support in the eastern provinces and he was also reinstated by the parliament in the country. The USSR continued to support him with weapons. On 14 September **1960 Mobutu took control in a CIA-sponsored coup**. Lumumba was placed under house arrest and Kasavubu was kept as president. **Lumumba** was publicly beaten and forced to eat copies of his speeches. He **disappeared** and it has later been revealed that he was murdered the same day. **In 1961, four different groups claimed that they wanted to establish political control** of the country and it looked like the country was heading for a full-scale civil war.

8. Finally, the **UN** decided to pass a resolution which gave their forces the right to **use force**. In this situation three of four factions fighting for the control of Congo convened to form a new government under Cyrille Adoula. In August 1961 5,000 troops started an attack on Katanga and took full control of the province in 1963. Another rebellion led by Pierre Mulele was crushed between 1964 and 1965.

The UN had been able to take action but was criticised by many states, especially the USSR and Belgium. The UN Secretary General Dag Hammarskjöld died in a plane crash when he visited the region. Both superpowers had been involved in the crisis and it has been argued that the CIA was involved in the assassination of the pro-Soviet Lumumba. The CIA also supported Mobutu when he seized power in 1965. Mobutu ruled the country (renamed Zaire) between 1965 and 1996. His regime is normally described as both corrupt and brutal but he remained in power for such a long time due to the fact that he was supported by the US, which was very important during the Cold War. The fact that he finally lost power to the opposition leader Laurent Kabila in 1996 should also be seen in the light of the Cold War coming to an end. Western support evaporated and he was accused of corruption and human rights abuses.

Significance:

- The **UN had been able to use force** against civil disturbance, when asked to take actions by the legitimate government. The initial Resolution 143 stated that the UN should restore law and order and prevent the involvement of other countries—not take side in the conflict. But **UN forces finally crushed Tshombe's forces in the south**. The UN gained support from some states but was criticised by others. France, Belgium and the USSR refused to pay their agreed-upon costs which nearly bankrupted the UN.

- The Secretary General of the UN, Dag Hammarskjöld took an active role in dealing with the crisis—far from a bureaucrat in a powerless organisation.

- Both superpowers took active roles in the crisis, but the Soviet intervention was much more open. However, the support to Lumumba proved to be unsuccessful and the very outcome of the crisis was that **Mobutu seized power. He was considered anti-communist and pro-Western** (but he seized power in 1965 and the syllabus states that we shall study the period 1960–1961).

- The US acted more cautiously. They supported Lumumba's request to the UN in 1960, but couldn't accept that he later turned to the USSR for assistance. The US and CIA were probably involved in the assassination of Lumumba. No US troops were involved in the conflict but support was given to the UN in different ways.

- The Soviets didn't get a client state due to this crisis and their most important partner Lumumba was killed in 1961. In the long run the US did get it (1965). But Mobutu was brutal, corrupt and dictatorial. None of the two superpowers were satisfied with the outcome of the crisis.
- This crisis of course affected the region and contributed in bringing the Cold War to Africa.

Exercise 12: Compare and contrast the Korean Crisis 1950 and the Congo Crisis 1960–1961.

(Notice that the question does not specifically ask for origins or impact and significance, i.e., all aspects should be compared.)

Similarities:

1. Both crises started partly due to domestic and internal problems.
2. In both crises, the UN took an important role with combat troops. The involvement of the UN, not blocked by veto power, **was unique in these two conflicts**. We saw nothing similar in Berlin, Hungary, Czechoslovakia and Cuba, to mention a few other crises. Actions like these were normally blocked due to the veto power in the Security Council, during the Cold War.
3. The active involvement of the UN in both crises was not without problems—it was controversial, i.e., some states reacted negatively. In both conflicts, the UN was blamed for supporting Western interests.
4. Both the superpowers were, to some extent, involved which makes the crises a part of the Cold War.
5. There were no Soviet combat troops in either of these two conflicts.
6. In both Korea and in Congo there were, apart from the two superpowers, also other countries involved. China and Belgium played very important roles in the conflicts.
7. Both conflicts had a tendency to make the superpowers to position themselves in each region. Asia and Africa became important battlegrounds in the Cold War.

Differences:

1. The Congo Crisis was not only an internal struggle or a Cold War conflict—it was also caused by problems with decolonisation. Korea was more a Cold War conflict and to some extent a conflict between two Korean states.
2. Congo involved a number of factions or groups which made the situation complicated. Congo was more of a Civil War compared to Korea. In 1961, there were four governments who claimed they controlled the country.
3. The crisis in Korea was much more dangerous and had a stronger global impact. There was nothing like China fighting US forces and nuclear threats, in Congo.
4. The origin of the Korean Crisis was an attempt to conquer another state. It was not like that in Congo.
5. The role of the UN differed in Korea and Congo. In Korea, UN forces fought under US command. In Congo, the UN intervention took place largely on the initiative of Dag Hammarskjöld. The UN Charter does not allow intervention in the internal affairs of one member state. But UN forces fought directly in bringing the secession of Katanga to an end (Tshombe).
6. The importance of the Korean War could also be seen from the perspective that it affected US domestic policy, i.e., it helped Eisenhower to win the presidential election—Congo had no such significance.

Conclusion:

Summarise your main points showing the similarities and differences. Emphasise how differently the UN acted and that the Korean War was much more significant.

The War in Indochina

The power vacuum left by the Japanese after WWII led to Ho Chi Minh being able to declare the independence of the People's Republic of Vietnam in 1945. This was opposed by the French who were keen to re-establish their colonies in South-East Asia. In 1946, a full scale war started between the Viet Minh (the Vietnam League for Independence) and the French. When the French left Vietnam in 1954, the war had killed 110,000 French soldiers, which is many more casualties than the Americans suffered in their Vietnam War. They lost 58,000 soldiers. When the French left, the Americans were paying 70% of the French cost for the war.

The late 1950s was a relatively calm period in the area, partly due to the fact that Ho carried out a land reform in the North. In the early 1960s the Viet Cong, the guerrilla movement in the South, intensified its activities. When Kennedy came to power there were 400 US advisers in Vietnam and by the time he was assassinated in 1963, it had increased to 16,000. But it was Johnson who escalated the conflict. After a naval incident in the Gulf of Tonking in 1964 the Congress accepted giving the president the right to *"take all necessary steps, including the use of armed force"*[79] to defend South Vietnam. The President could now escalate the conflict without a formal declaration of war. This 'blank cheque' was used by Johnson and in 1965 there were 180,000 US troops in Vietnam and in 1968 the number had increased to 540,000 men. Johnson also started air bombing the North.

When Nixon came to power in 1968, he realised that US involvement was probably not going to assure victory and he was also worried about the development of the US economy. He started a policy of 'Vietnamisation' to make the South Vietnamese take more responsibility and step by step withdraw US troops. In 1971, there were 157,000 US soldiers in Vietnam and in 1973 a ceasefire was agreed.

If we look at the 1950s and the 1960s, there are two major consequences of the French and the American Vietnam wars (or the Indochina war and the Vietnam war):

International implications of the Indochina and Vietnam War in the 1950s and 1960s:

- The conflict between the French and Viet Minh in Indochina, together with the 'loss' of China and the Korean War, deeply affected US foreign policy. The Viet Minh were supported by China from the early 1950s, and there was a fear that if Vietnam was lost, the rest of South-East Asia would be lost, the Domino Theory. In 1954, the South-East Asian Treaty Organization (**SEATO**) was created by the US, France, Britain, Australia, New Zealand, the Philippines, Thailand and Pakistan, with the **main aim of preventing communist expansion in South-East Asia**.

- The formation of SEATO deeply worried Mao in China and Jiang, the leader of Taiwan, now announced a 'holy war against communism'. This development is probably the reason for China starting to shell some small **islands controlled by Taiwan in 1954 and 1955**. This is referred to as the Taiwan Straits Crisis. During this crisis the US threatened to use nuclear arms against China in line with Eisenhower's policy of 'massive retaliation'. It drew the US and Taiwan closer, signing a **mutual defence pact**. The USSR on the other hand made it clear to Mao that no Soviet support would be given to a Chinese attack on Taiwan. This contributed to the growing **split between China and the USSR**.

Implications in the 1960s:

- When one of the superpowers was involved in a conflict which engaged more than 500,000 soldiers, it had major consequences. The US economy and the dollar suffered severely and it brought an end to the Bretton Woods system, a monetary system where the dollar was placed on the Gold Standard and the most important currencies in the Western World were fluctuating against the dollar. The fact that no victory was achieved, soldiers were killed and the economy suffered made the US and Nixon approach both the USSR and China. The US would not be able to maintain its economic and military superiority if the war was not brought to an end. If the US could not contain China in Asia, and that became more and more clear with the Vietnam War, she had to come to turns with this. A new **policy of détente and linkage** was a policy where the US was prepared to respect Soviet sphere of influences and offer the USSR Western technology,

 Key Point

This conflict will be outlined more in detail in the next part of this guide as it ended in the mid-1970s. It is of vital importance to discuss its consequences if you want to understand this event in a Cold War perspective. But a brief summary must be made when we are discussing the 1950s and the 1960s, in order to get an appropriate overview of this period.

 Key Point

US involvement in Vietnam created a US reluctance to be involved in further military conflicts in the Third World. This was something that the Russians took advantage of in the 1970s. This will be further outlined in the part where we discuss the 1970s.

---

[79] McWilliams, W. C. and Piotrowski, H., *The World Since 1945: A History of International Relations*, p. 200.

if the USSR co-operated in attempts to end the Vietnam War. The late 1960s saw the beginning of détente between the US and the USSR. The Vietnam War was also one reason behind Nixon's visit to China in 1972, the beginning of a US-Chinese rapprochement. A Cold War triangle had been created.

Figure 2.11: Portrait of Chairman Mao at the Tiananmen Gate

The split between the two leading communist states developed in the late 1950s. It had many reasons. Mao was in many ways a **Chinese nationalist** and didn't want China to be just another Russian satellite. There had been problems during the Civil War when Stalin temporarily **supported the Nationalists**. He wanted a strong China to oppose Japan and believed that the Nationalists were the alternative. There were also **ideological reasons** for the split as Mao claimed that a socialist revolution doesn't have to occur in an industrialised society based on industrial workers. Mao emphasised that the Chinese revolution was a peasant-based revolution. Mao also felt that the **terms offered by the USSR in the Sino-Soviet Friendship treaty of 1950** were not favourable to China. The co-operation was more a result of necessity due to the weakness of China after the Civil War and her involvement in the Korean War. During the **Taiwan crises** in 1954–1955, the Russians made it clear that no Russian support could be expected if China attacked Taiwan. After the **Secret Speech** in 1956, relations soon deteriorated. Mao saw Khrushchev's speech as an indirect attack on himself and he didn't support the new policy of **peaceful co-existence**. The USSR was also reluctant to provide Mao with an **atomic bomb**. In 1959, the USSR suddenly withdrew Russian technicians and advisers. The same year there were border disputes and armed clashes between China and India and the USSR remained neutral. There was not one single communist camp under the leadership of Moscow. The importance of personalities has also been emphasised by some historians. Khrushchev and Mao did not get along very well together. It would take many years until this new situation had an effect on the Cold War. In the 1960s during the Cultural Revolution, China went through a period where she was isolated and had no close relation to any superpower. When she decided to end her isolation, she actually turned to the US. This so-called ping-pong diplomacy established a Cold War triangle. More about this will be discussed later.

Cold War Leader 4: Nikita Khrushchev, First Secretary, 1953–1964

When Stalin passed away in 1953, a collective leadership succeeded him. There were immediate positive changes related to the Cold War:

1. An armistice was signed in **Korea** in 1953.

2. In 1954, a peace conference was arranged at **Geneva** to deal with the **Indochina War**, under the chairmanship of the USSR and Britain.

3. In 1955, there was a great power summit in Geneva between the USSR, the US, Britain and France. The leaders met for the first time since Potsdam 1945. The new and positive atmosphere was referred to as '**the spirit of Geneva**'.

4. In 1955, the occupational forces of **Austria** decided to end the occupation and re-establish full independence of the country. This had not been possible in countries like Germany and Korea. Soviet troops were also withdrawn from Finland.

5. Khrushchev started to **reduce the size of the Red Army** unilaterally (without the other side doing it).

6. Khrushchev went to **Yugoslavia** in 1955 to heal the rift between the two states and to show that the USSR could accept the existence of a communist regime not totally controlled by Moscow, a clear break with Stalin's policies.

In 1956, Khrushchev delivered his famous **Secret Speech**. The de-Stalinisation process opened up for new opportunities. Khrushchev declared that he believed in **peaceful co-existence** with the capitalist West and indicated, however vaguely, that a new relation could be established with the satellites in Eastern Europe.

Poland soon announced reforms but Khrushchev was eager to secure that the Poles didn't go too far. In Hungary, however he couldn't control the development and when Imre Nagy announced that his country would allow free elections and perhaps leave the Warsaw Pact, the Red Army invaded Hungary. The crushing of the **Hungarian Uprising** had major consequences:

- It strained the China-USSR relations.
- It brought an end to 'the spirit of Geneva'.
- Eisenhower had talked about a rollback of communism. These words were empty. The US was not prepared to risk a war over Hungary.
- It damaged the reputation of the USSR internationally.

During the **Suez Crisis in 1956**, Khrushchev was given an opportunity to extend Soviet influence to the **Middle East**. Stalin had only armed or given support to countries bordering the USSR. Khrushchev was more adventurous and involved the USSR in the Middle East and **Latin America. This was a departure from Stalin's policies and an escalation of the Cold War.**

Khrushchev also travelled abroad, unlike Stalin, and participated in a number of **summit meetings**. He met both Eisenhower and Kennedy. He left the summit meeting in Paris in anger when Eisenhower refused to apologise for the U2 incident.

In 1958, he put pressure on the Western powers to find a solution to the Berlin and German problems. He gave a six-month ultimatum to find a solution, and if not the USSR would recognise the East German state and hand over the control of Berlin to DDR—a state not recognised by the West. This **Second Berlin Crisis** led nowhere when Khrushchev extended the time limit. The **Berlin Wall** was finally erected in 1961 and in the West it was seen as a symbol of communist repression. But to some extent it stabilised the situation in Germany when East Germans couldn't flee as easy. When the wall had been erected, Khrushchev saw no need for a German peace treaty.

Khrushchev is best known for the **Cuban Missile Crisis.** When he, in 1962, secretly provided Cuba with nuclear weapons he brought the world to the **brink of a nuclear conflict** between the two superpowers. Khrushchev wanted to protect the Cuban revolution because a communist-controlled Cuba would provide the USSR with a springboard to spread communism to underdeveloped countries in Latin America. It would also reduce Soviet nuclear inferiority in relation to the US. When Khrushchev finally agreed to withdraw the missiles, the US had promised not to invade Cuba. It must be noted that this dangerous conflict had a **sobering effect** on the two superpowers. The Hot Line between the Kremlin and the White House was established and in 1963 the Test Ban Treaty was signed, forbidding nuclear testing in the atmosphere.

Khrushchev brought both détente and confrontation to the Cold War. He talked about creating "*many Vietnams*"[80] and addressed Western ambassadors at a reception at the Polish embassy in Moscow in 1956 with "*We will bury you.*"[81] On the other hand, he introduced the concept of peaceful co-existence with the capitalist world. He can be described as very **impulsive,** which clearly contrasted with Stalin.

In conclusion: If we compare this text with the text about Eisenhower, we can conclude that both politicians to some extent contributed to both confrontation but also détente, while Stalin and Truman were more Cold Warriors. If we compare Eisenhower and Khrushchev, it can be argued that Khrushchev was more unpredictable (the Secret Speech and Cuba are two examples).

Cold War Crisis 8: The Prague Spring 1968

If there were signs of a better understanding after the Cuban Crisis, there were also signs of tension and major crisis. The US escalation in Vietnam in 1965 was of major importance. The next crisis would occur in Europe when Czechoslovakia announced a reform policy in 1968. The Soviets had consolidated their power in Eastern Europe between 1945 and 1948 and established a firm control in every country except Yugoslavia. In 1953, when Stalin died, there had been a revolt in Berlin against Soviet control, which was crushed by tanks. After the Secret Speech in 1956, two of the satellites wanted more independence from Moscow. The Poles' desire for more independence was finally accepted because it didn't challenge Soviet power in vital areas. But when the Hungarians announced that they were going to accept free elections and to leave the Warsaw Pact, Russian tanks entered Budapest. In 1960, Albania had also been able to establish independence from Moscow.

It would take 12 years after Hungary until Soviet power was again challenged. Czechoslovakia was the most industrially advanced country within the Eastern Bloc. It had however faced economic difficulties in the 1960s and in 1967 student demonstrations had been brutally suppressed. In January 1968, **Alexander Dubcek** became First Secretary of the Communist Party.

In April 1968, an '**Action Programme**' was announced promising:

- Economic reforms
- Freedom of speech
- A free press

---

[80] Ball, S. J., *The Cold War: An International History 1947-1991*, p. 70.
[81] http://www.quotationspage.com/quotes/Nikita_Khrushchev/ <Accessed 4 January 2016>

- The right to travel abroad and
- Freedom for political parties within the communist controlled national front.

The aim was to create '**socialism with a human face**' but to not question the leading role of the Communist Party, i.e., to not go as far as the Hungarian reformers in 1956. This development alarmed both Moscow and other Warsaw Pact leaders. Several meetings and warnings were given to Dubcek. After a meeting in Warsaw, an open letter was issued from five Warsaw Pact leaders, including the USSR. It warned the Czechs that counter-revolutionaries threatened the existence of socialism in the country: "*…we believe that a decisive rebuff to the forces of anti-communism….in Czechoslovakia is not only your task but ours too.*"[82] Dubcek and the Czech leaders repeatedly assured their loyalty to both socialism and the Warsaw Pact but continued with the reforms. In August 1968, plans were announced that would allow other political parties. New meetings followed because the other communist countries feared:

- that the reforms would lead to a counter revolution, i.e., that Dubcek and the party would not be able to control the development in Czechoslovakia.
- this could in the next step lead to a similar development in other communist countries.

In other words, they feared a new 1956 where Poland announced a new policy and then this soon spread to Hungary where Nagy's policy soon became unacceptable to Moscow. Dubcek repeatedly stated that the Communist Party should maintain its 'leading role' and that Czechoslovakia had no plans to leave the Warsaw Pact.

On 20 August 1968, the five signatories of the Warsaw letter invaded Czechoslovakia. It was met by massive hostility and passive resistance, i.e., no new Hungary. The invasion brought an end to the Prague Spring. It should be noted however that Dubcek was forced into retirement and consequently not executed as Nagy was 12 years earlier.

Impact and Consequences of the Prague Spring

The Prague Spring **only temporarily** halted the process of détente. President Johnson made it clear that no interference from the US was expected and consequently the détente process, which had only partly begun, could continue. **The Vietnam problem**, which might involve Russian co-operation to be solved, was more important. 1968 was the year of the Tet-offensive in Vietnam and to many Americans it became clear that they were fighting a war with heavy casualties which they couldn't win. The US and the Soviet Union had also signed a non-proliferation treaty on 1 July 1968 and both were now planning to begin talks on strategic arms limitation. With a costly war in Vietnam, these talks were very important.

- In November 1968, Brezhnev announced his **Brezhnev Doctrine**: "*When internal and external forces hostile to Socialism attempt to turn the development of any Socialist country in the direction of the capitalist system…(it) becomes not only a problem for the people of that country but also a general problem, the concern of all Socialist countries.*"[83] What the Soviets now announced was that they believed that if one country fell from socialism, all others would do it. This would give the socialist countries the **right to intervene**.
- **China**, who had supported the crushing of the Hungarian Uprising in 1956, condemned the invasion of Czechoslovakia. We can see the beginning of a 'Cold War triangle'.
- The image of the USSR amongst **Euro Communists** was severely damaged.
- As an effect of crushing the reforms in Czechoslovakia, every attempt to reform the command economies in the Eastern Bloc were blocked. The **stagnation** which became obvious in the 1970s had many reasons, but one part of it was that no one dared to propose any reforms after 1968. Gorbachev, at the time a regional politician in the USSR, describes the impact of this in his memoirs. **Consequently the Prague Spring had a major impact in all the communist countries by blocking reforms.**

---

[82] Brown, C. and Mooney P., *Cold War to Détente* (Oxford: Heinemann Educational, 1981) p. 138.
[83] Ibid p. 139.

- In Czechoslovakia, the new leader Gustav Husak introduced a policy of '**normalisation**'. Everyone who could be linked to the Prague Spring was removed or lost their jobs. It created a gulf of bitterness which partly explains why the country exploded in massive demonstrations in 1989 which would lead to the end of communist rule in the country.

Student Activities

We have already stated that 1953–1969 was marked by both confrontation and détente. What was also typical was that the Cold War expanded into new areas. Both the Middle East and The American continent were now involved in the Cold War. If we would make an attempt to divide different events from the period we can see how confrontation and détente were replacing each other. This is partly a simplification, and some other events can be included, but it is possible to conclude that there was both confrontation and détente during this period. Try to fill in the table with the events described below.

Détente	Confrontation
1953 an armistice was signed in Korea	In the US it was the McCarthy years and talk Eisenhower announced his 'New Look'
The new leadership in the USSR started about peaceful co-existence and 'massive retaliation'	
1954 Peace conference in Geneva about Vietnam	1954 SEATO formed, problems in Taiwan

1955 End of occupation of Austria

1955 Germany a full member of NATO and

1955 Summit in Geneva, 'The spirit of Geneva'

1955 The Warsaw Pact formed

1956 The Secret Speech. Talks about 'national roads to socialism' and peaceful co-existence

1956 Problems in Poland and a revolt in Hungary.

1956 The Suez Crisis

1958 Khrushchev's Berlin ultimatum

1959 Khrushchev to the US

1959 Castro to power

1960 the U2 incident and the Paris summit

1961 Berlin Wall and the Bay of Pigs

1962 The Cuban Missile Crisis. After the crisis the USSR started to close 'the missile gap'

1963 The Hot Line, the Test Ban Treaty

1967 The signing of a treaty on demilitarisation of space

1964 The Gulf of Tonkin resolution

1965 US escalation in Vietnam

1968 The Prague Spring

2. Korea, the US, the USSR and China: Superpower Relations (1947–1949)

Exercise 13: Why and with what results did the USSR place missiles in Cuba in 1962?

(An IB-exam question from 2017 would not be asked like this, but the question is a good exercise.)

Why:
1. The USSR wanted to **protect the Cuban revolution**.
2. A communist-controlled Cuba would provide the USSR with a springboard to **spread communism** to underdeveloped countries in Latin America.
3. They could claim that Russia wanted to protect a small state against a superpower. It would strengthen the Russian position in the Third World.
4. At the time the US had 100 intercontinental ballistic missiles (ICBM) and 1,700 intercontinental bombers. The USSR had only 50 ICBM and 150 bombers. An intermediate range missile in Cuba would reach major cities in the US and compensate for the lack of ICBM. In practical terms Khrushchev would **reduce the missile gap** with intermediate missiles in Cuba which would save an enormous amount of money for the USSR and put his country in a better strategic position. The alternative, an expensive build-up of Russian ICBM missiles was very expensive.
5. It would put the USSR in a **bargaining position** towards the US. 'Quid pro quo,' i.e., 'something in return' was a common Cold War strategy. Some kind of solution to the Berlin problem was one possible option.
6. The US had nuclear missiles in **Turkey**. Khrushchev wrote in his memoirs: "*The Americans had surrounded our country with missile bases and threatened us with nuclear weapons, and now they would learn just what it feels like to have enemy missiles pointing at you.*" [84]
7. To show toughness to Khrushchev's critics in China and in the USSR.

What were the results?
1. Account for the **missile crisis** (but notice that it is not a question that is specifically asking for the story of the missiles crisis). It is possible to write a lot here.
2. Account for how the crisis was **resolved** (US pledge not to invade, dismantling of missiles in Cuba and Turkey).
3. In a short-term perspective, it led to a relaxation of great power relations.
4. **The Test Ban Treaty.**
5. The setting up of the **Hot Line**.
6. It contributed to some extent to the **fall of Khrushchev** in 1964.
7. The existence of a communist state in the Caribbean had a **profound effect on US policies in the area**. The Cuban example should not be followed in Latin America. The embargo was not lifted.
8. In a long-term perspective, the USSR decided to **close the missile gap**. It resulted in an extremely costly nuclear build-up in the USSR which probably affected the Russian economy to a very large extent. The missile gap was closed around 1970.

Conclusion: Summarise the main point of the essay. Emphasise that the world has never been as close to a nuclear war as in 1962 during this crisis. Emphasise also that one result of this crisis was a Soviet nuclear build up for the rest of the 1960s as it is a point often ignored.

Exercise 14: 'The Asian development of the Cold War was far more dangerous than European development'. With reference to events from the period 1945–1961, to what extent do you agree with this statement?

(You have to write one part where you show how the development in Asia was dangerous and a second part showing how the development in Europe was dangerous, and then you conclude and show if you agree.)

The Asian development was dangerous in the Cold War:
1. It can be argued that the situation in Asia was more unstable than in Europe. **The Chinese Civil War** restarted in 1945 and ended in 1949. In total, some 4–5 million soldiers were fighting in this war. On the other hand, there was no major foreign military involvement. But this was not the only armed conflict in the area during this period, **The Korean War 1950–1953, the Indochina War started in 1946, the islands between mainland China and Taiwan were bombed in 1954–1955, China occupied Tibet in 1951.** The situation in Europe, except for a few clashes, was more stable.
2. The Korean War was a very dangerous conflict. There were two critical moments in this war. In the late 1950, the UN forces were close to the Yalu river, the border to China. The fact that 300,000 **Chinese soldiers attacked UN forces** at that moment was a major crisis. The second crisis was when MacArthur threatened China with a **nuclear attack** and wanted to widen the war. He was dismissed in April 1951 by President Truman. An attack on China may have triggered a major conflict or perhaps a World War III. MacArthur was able to put a lot of pressure on Truman and told the Congress after his dismissal that he had not been permitted (by Truman) to destroy the enemy. When Truman finally dismissed MacArthur he said it was the most difficult decision he made during his political life. Truman had dropped the A-bomb in 1945.

(Continued)

---

[84] Khrushchev, N., *Khrushchev Remembers*, p. 494.

Exercise 14: 'The Asian development of the Cold War was far more dangerous than European development'. With reference to events from the period 1945–1961, to what extent do you agree with this statement? *(Continued)*

3. There were two major crises in Sino-American relation in the mid-1950s. There are some small **islands in the Taiwan Straits** between Taiwan and China, called Quemoy and Matsu islands. In 1954, the leader in Taiwan threatened China with a 'holy war'. China responded with an artillery bombardment in late 1954 and early 1955. The crisis led to a renewed US pledge to defend Taiwan. When the Chinese conquered another island, Tachen, the US Congress gave Eisenhower a resolution allowing the President to take whatever actions he found necessary. Eisenhower now announced that aggression from the Communists would be met by nuclear arms. In 1958, there were new bombardments and again the **US threatened with the use of nuclear arms.**

4. In **Indochina there was a war** between the Viet Minh and France. Between 1946 and 1954, 110,000 French soldiers were killed. It is difficult to estimate Viet Minh casualties, but it was around 300,000.

The development in Europe was dangerous

1. There were two **crises over Berlin** which were very tense. When the Russians cut off all the land routes to Berlin in 1948, both sides mobilised. It was a critical moment. When the Berlin Wall was erected in 1961 it was a similar situation with troops from both sides facing each other. But it did not lead to an armed conflict between the US and the USSR.

2. The **Hungarian Uprising** was the most violent crisis in Europe between 1945 and 1961. A total of 30,000 Hungarians and 7,000 Russian troops were killed in the uprising. 200,000 Hungarians fled their country. But the US did not try to challenge Soviet authority.

3. The prospect of electoral victories to the Communists in countries like Italy and France was seen as a major danger. Western Europe was considered as very important to the 'free world'.

Conclusion:

The Cold War in Europe was in many ways problematic but it must be concluded that the development in Asia was more dangerous. The war in Korea, where Chinese soldiers attacked the UN/US forces, was a very dangerous conflict. The Taiwan Straits Crises were also alarming.

Exercise 15: Compare and contrast the impact and significance of two Cold War crises each chosen from a different region.

(Here the choice fell on the Suez Crisis 1956 and Cuba 1962.)

Similarities:

1. It can be argued that both crises promoted **Soviet influence in new regions** (Middle East and America). Both crises had also a major importance in spreading the Cold War to new regions.

2. Both crises resulted in increased support to two regional leaders who were seen as symbols against Western influence. Nasser gained a lot of popularity in the Arab and Third World. The same thing can be said about Castro. Of course these men had many enemies but we must remember that this was the period of decolonisation and **many leaders in the Third World saw these two men as role models**.

3. Both crises resulted in the states where the crises took place being strengthened politically. **Nasser** had survived an attempt to overthrow him and with the defeat of France and Britain, and the support from the USSR, he and **Egypt had won a lot politically**. He also secured the control of the Suez Canal. **Castro** had also gained a lot. With the US pledge not to invade Cuba, the immediate threat against his regime was overcome.

4. **To the US both crises were mainly negative.** The Suez Crisis resulted in an embarrassing defeat for three allies. The US had no other option than to oppose the attack, but the outcome of the crisis was highly negative. It opened up the Middle East for the USSR and strengthened Nasser's position enormously. Even though the USSR promised to remove the missiles from Cuba, the crisis resulted in having the US now to accept a communist regime in the Caribbean. A leader who had gained a lot of popularity in the Third World led Cuba. As a result of the crises Khrushchev was strengthened in his belief that the Third World would be of major importance for the continuation of the Cold War. Vietnam lay ahead with support to the North from the USSR.

5. **Both crises contributed to an arms race.** The Middle East was now a Cold War arena and even though Cuba had a sobering effect on both superpowers in a short-term perspective It contributed to a major nuclear military build-up in the USSR. They should close the missile gap.

Differences:

1. It can be argued that the **Cuban Crisis**, where the world stood at the brink of a nuclear war, had a **sobering effect** on the Cold War. The Hot Line and the Test Ban Treaty show this. **The Suez Crisis resulted in the opposite.** The Middle East became a playground where the two superpowers were competing for influence and as an example President Eisenhower announced his **Eisenhower Doctrine** in 1957.

2. **While the Suez Crisis strengthened Khrushchev's position politically, especially in the USSR, the Cuban Crisis resulted in the opposite.** By hardliners, Khrushchev had in the Kremlin been seen as responsible for the problems in Poland and Hungary in 1956. The Suez Crisis, where he firmly supported Nasser, was a success to him. The Cuban Crisis was a disaster to Khrushchev. He had failed with his Virgin Land Policy and provoked the Red Army by reducing its size. The army, and many hardliners, found it extremely humiliating to be forced to remove the missiles after US ultimatums. The Cuban Crisis must be seen as very important for his forced resignation in 1964. In Pravda, he was criticised for being "*hare-brained*" and supporting "*wild schemes, half-baked conclusions and hasty decisions.*[85]"

3. **The UN** had finally a role in the Suez Crisis with its peacekeeping forces. In the Cuban Crisis it played a less significant role.

Conclusion: Summarise your main points. There were both similarities and differences between those two crises.

---

[85] https://www.russianlife.com/stories/online-archive/nikita-khrushchev/ <Accessed 5 January 2017>

3. Détente

Overview

The continuation of the Cold War that will be outlined in this guide is a period of **détente** which took place after the **Vietnam War** in the 1970 and ended with the Soviet invasion of **Afghanistan** in 1979. There are some historians who argue that this relaxation of strain started after the Cuban Missile Crisis. Others argue that it started when the Americans realised that the **economic and military consequences of the Vietnam War** started to threaten the US and when the Russians were finally able to close the **missile gap** and start to discuss with the US from a position of strength. A third factor which affected superpower relations was the development in **China**. In 1969, there were armed conflicts between Chinese and Soviet forces in the Ussuri river at the border between the two communist states. China soon announced an end to isolation during the Cultural Revolution and invited Richard Nixon to Beijing in 1972. The USSR feared a close co-operation between the US and China and reconsider their position in the Cold War triangle.

It was Nixon and his National Security Adviser Henry Kissinger who outlined the US motives for **détente**. By accepting nuclear parity with the Soviets and Soviet spheres of influences, the Russians would support a peace settlement in Vietnam, arms control and co-operate with the US to maintain stability in the Third World. To accept Soviet parity was an acceptance of a **balance of power**. Access to Western technology and investments should also promote Soviet co-operation, hence the idea of '**linkage**'.

There are several important agreements from this period showing a new atmosphere of co-operation. In 1968, **the Nuclear Non-Proliferation Treaty** was signed to prevent a proliferation of nuclear weapons. The Strategic Arms Limitation Talks (or **SALT**) started in 1969 and were finished in 1972 resulting in a **freeze** on intercontinental ballistic missiles, submarine launched ballistic missiles and intercontinental bombers. It was however only a freeze and no reduction. An **Anti-Ballistic Missile Treaty** (ABM) was also signed limiting the development of such systems. SALT II was signed in 1979 but the agreement was never ratified by US Congress. There were many other treaties signed during this period as a result of a better understanding. In 1973, there was a ceasefire in **Vietnam**. In 1975, **The Helsinki Final Act** was signed where the 1945 borders in Europe were recognised as inviolable, pleasing the Soviets. The Western powers were pleased as the agreement stipulated that human rights were universal and that there should be free exchange of ideas and people across Europe.

It is normally considered that this period of détente came to an end in 1979 when the USSR invaded **Afghanistan**, probably the worst mistake made by the Soviets during the Cold War. The US post-Vietnam policies of reluctance to intervene in conflicts abroad enabled the USSR to extend their positions especially in the Third World. Cuban soldiers supported by the USSR were fighting in **Angola and Ethiopia** in the late 1970s. The seeds of the end of détente can be found in this period. It would result in a 'Second Cold War' and it would bring **Ronald Reagan to power**.

The Indochina and Vietnam Wars, 1946–1975

The French and the American involvement in armed conflicts in Indochina lasted from 1946 to 1973. In this text these two conflicts will be referred to as **the Indochina War** and **the Vietnam War** (sometimes called the Second Indochina War). You should be able to put these conflicts in an appropriate Cold War context as a part of your Cold War preparation. The focus of this text will be the international implications and not the wars, even though the main events will be outlined. The most important part of this conflict, from an international and Cold War perspective, is the period after President Johnson's escalation after 1965. This led to new positions in the Cold War triangle and is the reason why you find this conflict in the 'détente period' in the guide.

The Indochina War, 1946–1954

In 1943, Churchill and Roosevelt had signed the **Cairo Declaration** where "*Japan will also be expelled from all other territories which she has taken by violence and greed*" during the war. At **Potsdam** it was confirmed that "*the terms of the Cairo Declaration shall be carried out*" and that these territories should be "*free and independent.*" [86] (ref. see the Potsdam meeting in 1945)

---

[86] www.avalon.law.yale.edu <Accessed 5 January 2017>

French Indochina (Vietnam, Cambodia and Laos) had been a part of the French Empire since the late 19th century. After the **Potsdam** meeting and the sudden Japanese surrender in 1945, it was decided that **Britain should re-occupy the South and Jiang's Nationalists the North**, until the French were able to return. Support had been given to France to return and take control.

- France and the post-war government led by **General De Gaulle** had no intention of embarking on a decolonisation process. **A restoration of France and national prestige after the humiliation during the German occupation** in combination with a fear of a **'domino-reaction' within her colonies** made the French determined to re-impose control.

- During the war, Roosevelt had been inconsistent about the future of Indochina. Finally, in 1945 the US decided to support the return of the French. France was seen as **an important ally in Europe**.

The League for the Independence of Vietnam (**Viet Minh**) had been formed in 1941 to oppose Japanese occupation. It was composed of different groups but led and controlled by the Communists under Ho Chi Minh. Since 1943, they had been fighting the Japanese and liberated parts of the country. **The Chinese Nationalists didn't take firm political control** in the North due to problems in China and in September 1945 Ho could proclaim the foundation of the **Democratic Republic of Vietnam** (DRV) in Hanoi. The French government was not prepared to accept his regime and in 1946 a full-scale war started between the Viet Minh and the French—**the Indochina War** (1946–1954).

Figure 3.1: Ho Chi Minh

Course of Events

- In November 1946, the French attacked Hanoi and Haipong and 6,000 people were killed.

- Ho and the Viet Minh now started a guerrilla war. The size of the Viet Minh in late 1946 was around 80,000 men, poorly equipped compared to the French army which was made up of 115,000 men. The Viet Minh were brilliantly led by General Vo Nguyen Giap. The Indochina War was initially a war of national liberation from colonialism.

- In 1949, the French offered a limited independence, partly due to pressure from the US. **Bao Dai should** remain in power. It was rejected by the Viet Minh as Dai was seen as a **French puppet**. He had previously been a puppet to the Japanese.

- The Viet Minh forces were able to fight a successful war using guerrilla tactics. In 1950, the French suffered a major defeat at Cao Bang. It was in 1949 and 1950 that the **international implications** became more important. In October 1949, Mao came to power in China. In June 1950, just after the outbreak of the Korean War, Chinese military advisers and weapons were sent to Vietnam. In 1950, 79 Chinese officers and military advisers arrived to the North and China delivered 14,000 small arms, 1,700 machine guns and 150 artillery pieces.

- It was also in 1950, when the Korean War started, that Truman and the Americans started to support the French in the Indochina War. From 1950 to 1954, the Americans gradually increased their economic support to the French and in 1954, when France pulled out, the **Americans were paying** more than 70% of France's cost for the war.

- American pressure led to more aggressive French military plans, the so-called Navarre Plan in 1954. But the escalation also led to **domestic opposition in France**. 110,000 Frenchmen were killed in the conflict and it finally convinced the French government that it had to withdraw.

- The Viet Minh victory was accomplished when the French were defeated at the battle of **Dien Bien Phu** in May 1954, after a 50-day siege. In June the French government fell from power and the new Prime Minister, Mendéz-France, pledged to end the war within 30 days or resign.

How Did the Cold War Affect the Great Powers at Geneva?

- The US wanted to exclude France from Vietnam to be able to **fight the Communists** more effectively. Indochina was at this time seen as a **cornerstone** in the struggle against communism in Asia. The US didn't sign the **Final Declaration** because it would be seen as recognition of Red China.

- The USSR also wanted to end the conflict. The new leadership after Stalin wanted to **relax the tension**. In 1954, the Americans wanted to bring West Germany into **NATO** and the Soviets hoped that France would oppose this. In 1955 when Ho visited both Moscow and Beijing, he was promised limited economic help but no military support. The North had to limit their struggle to unify the country in 'diplomatic struggle'.
- China wanted Western powers out of Indochina. She feared an **American intervention**, a new Korea.
- The peace conference in Geneva ended the Indochina War in July. At the Geneva conference the UK, the USSR, France, the US, China and the states of Indochina participated. It was agreed that:

1. Laos and Cambodia should gain independence.

2. There should be a ceasefire in Vietnam and the country was **temporarily divided** at the 17th Parallel pending the general elections which will bring about the unification of Vietnam. Ho's regime in the North was recognised.

3. General elections should be held in July 1956 and then the country should be unified.
   - During the conference Ngo Diem, backed by the US, became Prime Minister in the South. He had every reason to prevent the elections as Ho was expected to win. Diem also decided to do this, backed by the Americans.
   - In 1954, the **SEATO** (the South East Treaty Organization) was set up by the US, France, Britain, Australia, New Zealand, the Philippines, Thailand and Pakistan, in an attempt to prevent the spread of communism in South-East Asia.

The Indochina War had been transformed from a war of decolonisation to a part of the Cold War.

The Vietnam War

- **Diem**, with the support of the US, cancelled the elections that should have been held in 1956.
- Diem was a Catholic leader in a country where 75% of the population were Buddhists. His regime is normally described as corrupt and he lacked support from the population. The reasons for this may have been his reluctance to carry out a genuine land reform and that he was seen by many as an American puppet when he arrived from Paris in 1954. US support was crucial: they soon gave Diem $300 million in assistance.
- The period after Geneva is normally described as relatively calm partly due to the fact that Ho consolidated his regime in the North, implementing a land reform. One million refugees fled to the South and there was no time for organising armed rebellion in the South.
- With the **Sino-Soviet split** in the late 1950s the situation changed. Both China and the USSR wanted to be the leading communist state and influence in Vietnam became important to both of them. In 1959, both China and the USSR decided to **support an armed national liberation struggle** in Vietnam and the North now pledged themselves to a reunification by armed struggle. Khrushchev announced in 1960 that the ultimate victory of communism would be achieved through '**wars of liberation**' in the Third World, and promised help to Vietnam.
- In 1959, the North decided to unify the country by military means if necessary. In **1960**, the guerrillas in the South, **Viet Cong, intensified their activities**. In 1961 alone, 4,000 civil servants were killed by guerrillas in the South. In the same year different groups formed the National Liberation Front (NLF). It was the political arm of the Viet Cong. When Kennedy came to power in early 1961, he inherited 400 military advisers from the Eisenhower administration. When he was assassinated in November 1963, there were 16,000 advisers, but still no real combat troops, except for pilots flying combat missions. Kennedy now had an opportunity to show his 'flexible response' policy, to fight communism with a wide range of weapons. Threatening to use nuclear weapons in the Vietnamese conflict was no use. Military advisers, economic support to the regime and a programme of building 'strategic hamlets' where peasants were supposed to be protected from guerrillas were parts of this policy. The guerrillas however intensified their activities and attacked government buildings and officials. Diem's regime suffered from a lack of genuine support and in 1960 the US ambassador wondered if it was not time to support an 'alternative leadership in Saigon'.

- In November 1963, **Diem was murdered** during a military coup. It would now be military generals who would lead the South, totally dependent on the US. The Americans realised that the absence of a leader in the South with support from the population was one major obstacle to establishing an alternative to Ho in the North. But there was no easy solution to this problem in late 1963.

- In August 1964, the US Congress accepted giving the president the right to "*take all necessary steps, including the use of armed force*"[87] to defend South Vietnam. This was a result of a naval incident in the **Gulf of Tonking**. The result was that Johnson could **escalate** the Vietnam conflict without a formal declaration of war, which has to be made by the Congress. There was an absence of public awareness of the significance of the resolution and why America was suddenly engulfed in a major war in Vietnam. It would backfire when US soldiers were killed and no victory was delivered. Many Congressmen preferred this solution in 1964 when it was an election year.

- In 1965, President Johnson started to escalate the conflict. Vietnam was now without doubt the focus of US Cold War policies. In the meantime, the Sino-Soviet dispute was more tense than ever. But both powers supported the North. After Khrushchev was overthrown in 1964, one of the new leaders, Kosygin, went to Hanoi and made the Soviet support public in 1965. China also gave massive economic and military aid. Troops from the North were trained in China and 50,000 road and rail construction forces from the Chinese army were sent to the North. **This aid was absolutely necessary for the North to fight this war.**

Figure 3.2: Lyndon B Johnson

- Combat troops were sent to Vietnam in 1965. Now the Americans had 180,000 US troops in the country. In 1968, the number had increased to 540,000 men. In 1965, the US started to air bomb the North.

- In 1964, Viet Minh forces started to fight against the Viet Cong in the South.

- **The Tet (lunar new year) offensive** in January 1968 was a **major turning point** which convinced many Americans that the war could not be won. In spite of an enormous superiority in resources and equipment, the guerrillas suddenly attacked Saigon and a hundred other cities. The presidential palace in Saigon, the US Embassy, airports and radio stations were all under attack. The NLF had to take high casualties and 50,000 NLFs were killed, but the psychological impact of the offensive was of major importance.

- The anti-war movement in the US grew in strength. Robert Kennedy, the brother of slain president and a Democrat, announced that he was going to challenge the Democrat Johnson. Johnson now had to fight for his nomination within his own party. In March 1968, Johnson announced that he would not stand for re-election. His social reform programme 'Great Society' had been undermined by the costs of the war and in 1968, 300 US soldiers were killed every week and there was no prospect of victory.

- In 1968, Richard M. **Nixon** was elected US President. He introduced a new policy of **Vietnamisation**. The South Vietnamese army should gradually increase its involvement while the Americans should gradually withdraw. Financial aid should continue. This policy was confirmed in the **Nixon Doctrine** from 1969. Peace talks now started in Paris and the aim was '*peace with honour*'.

---

[87] McWilliams, W. C. and Piotrowski, H., *The World Since 1945: A History of International Relations*, p. 200.

- **The US wanted to end the Vietnam War.** To be able to do that they needed support from both the USSR and China. The US desire to end the Vietnam War with honour and to restore a strong economy made them genuinely try to promote détente. There had not been any comparable and genuine attempt made by the Americans since 1945. The US now offered the Soviets a deal, the **idea of linkage**: The US would recognise the USSR's strategic parity and would not interfere in the Soviet empire and would allow the Soviets to get access to Western technology if the USSR helped the Americans out if Vietnam, an **end of the idea of 'roll-back'**.

  China had gone through the Cultural Revolution and was isolated. The relation with the USSR was more tense than ever and the Americans were fighting a war south of her border. The Warsaw Pact invasion of Czechoslovakia in 1968 and armed border disputes with the Soviets in 1969 alarmed the Chinese. An understanding between the Soviets and the Americans was the worst possible scenario. The rapprochement with the US convinced the Chinese that they did not have to fear a US-Soviet alliance against China and in 1971 China was finally accepted in the UN, replacing Taiwan.

- The Sino-Soviet dispute also affected the USSR. The border disputes in 1969 had the effect of an 'electric shock' in Moscow. **The Soviets feared an invasion of millions of Chinese** radicals. In the early 1970s, the Soviets had finally been able to close the missile gap and had a strong position versus the US and could also avoid a further nuclear build-up. An understanding with the US was more possible than ever. The Soviets feared **an understanding between the US and China**.

- In order to put pressure on the North and to cut off supplies, the war was expanded to **Cambodia in 1969** with air bombardment and later an invasion.

- It was estimated that 400 universities and colleges were temporarily closed down in 1970 due to student strikes.

- In 1971, the US and South Vietnamese forces invaded Laos to support the government against the guerrillas.

- While peace talks dragged on, there was intense air bombing of the North. In 1971, **Nixon** announced that he would visit China the next year.

- On 27 January 1973, **a peace agreement** was finally signed and a cease-fire should come into effect the next day. The **US forces should be withdrawn** and both sides committed themselves to reunification by peaceful means. Before leaving, the Americans supplied the regime in the South with everything they needed to continue the war. As an example the South now acquired the world's fourth biggest air force.

- After the Americans left, the conflict soon restarted but now as a civil war. **In 1975, the North conquered the South** and the conflict was finally brought to an end.

The 1970s resulted in several arms limitation agreements and, which was more sensational, a US-Chinese rapprochement.

How Did the Vietnam War Affect the 1970s?

- The war had been a '**bleeding wound**' for the US. It affected her **economy** and her **prestige abroad**. It is the main explanation for why the US turned to **détente in the 1970s**. It also led to a **reluctance to be involved in armed conflicts in the Third World** on the part of the US. This is shown in the **Nixon Doctrine** from 1969 where Nixon announced that the US should mainly support allies in the Third World and not do the fighting in the future. The idea of '**linkage**' also brought an end to the idea of a '**rollback**' of communism.

- US determination to get out of Vietnam was one reason behind the **rapprochement with China** in the early 1970s. There were other reasons behind this rapprochement like Chinese isolation during the Cultural Revolution and the Sino-Soviet dispute, but the Vietnam War was very significant.

- With a Chinese-US understanding, the USSR feared that if they pushed the US too hard, it would drive the US and China closer together. This was one, but not the only, reason for the **USSR finally supporting détente** in the 1970s.

Author's Tip

As explained earlier, it is not the war that you are supposed to write about. The aim is to analyse the Vietnam War as a part of the Cold War, i.e., to demonstrate the international implications.

- There are historians who argue that the US reluctance to get involved in armed conflicts in the Third World later in the 1970s would enable the Soviets to follow a more aggressive policy there. Soviet and Cuban support in the Civil wars in **Angola and Ethiopia** are two examples. A third example is the Soviet invasion of **Afghanistan** in 1979 which led to 'the Second Cold War' during the **Reagan** era.

In conclusion, it can be said that even though the war had soured relations between the blocs for decades, the Vietnam War actually provided an opportunity for détente in the 1970s. But it must also be emphasised that this was not the only reason for détente. It had deeper roots which can be seen in the description of the Cold War triangle above. More about this will be discussed later.

Figure 3.3: Leonid Ilich Brezhnev

Figure 3.4: Richard Nixon

Figure 3.5: President Nixon meets Mao Tse-tung on 29/02/1972

Why Was There a Period of Détente in the Late 1960s and 1970s?

- The Soviet Union had finally **closed the missile gap**. Now both the US and the USSR had achieved MAD (Mutual Assured Destruction). Brezhnev told the Central Committee in 1972: "*The correlation of forces between the USSR and the US…is now more favourable than ever before.*"[88] The USSR was now anxious to reduce her costs and of course also **reduce the risk of war**. This was especially important because the growth of the Soviet **economy was stagnating**. Gross National Product had grown by 5% annually between 1966 and 1970. In 1971–1975, it was 3.6%. In the late 1970s, it was only 2.2%. The USSR wanted to avoid a continuation of a development of sophisticated and expensive technological nuclear weapons. Nixon's policy of linkage offered opportunities for an increase in **East-West trade** and Western **technology**. Finally, the USSR was alarmed by the **Sino-Soviet split** and the border clashes in 1969.

- The US wanted out of **Vietnam**. The war had eroded the **US economy** and its prestige and threatened her status globally. Arms agreements would not only **reduce the risk of war**, but also bring down the cost of arms development. The US economy had suffered from the Vietnam War and was in recession from 1973. There was also a very strong anti-war movement in the US and Nixon needed an understanding with both the USSR and China to get out of the war. The technological development of new weapons was not only costly but also dangerous. Kissinger believed in an explosion of technology and the number of nuclear weapons, if no arms deal was made.

- China wanted to end her isolation after the Cultural Revolution and she feared the USSR.

Examples of Détente 1968–1979

- **1968 The Non-Proliferation of Nuclear Weapons Treaty.** This early agreement was signed by the US, the USSR and Britain and the aim was to prevent the transfer of nuclear technology to other countries. The two other nuclear countries in the world, China and France, refused to sign.

- **1969 SALT (Strategic Arms Limitation Talks)** negotiations between the US and the USSR started.

- **1971 Nuclear Accidents Agreement** between the US and the USSR was an agreement where both powers promised to increase safeguards against the unauthorised firing of nuclear weapons and to notify the other part if an incident occurred.

- **1972 SALT I** signed by Nixon and Brezhnev. It was an important agreement resulting in a freeze on strategic nuclear weapons. It comprised two parts:
  - **The Interim Agreement on Offensive Arms.** This agreement resulted in a maximum level of ICBM and SLBM but did not place any limits on long-range strategic bombers (ICB). This five-year freeze on levels of ICBM and SLBM was no reduction of the number of weapons but a successful agreement to prevent a further escalation of the arms development. Nothing was said about the number of long-range bombers and the development of MIRVs (multiple independently targeted re-entry vehicles), nuclear weapons with many warheads, where each was capable of being directed to a specific target.
  - **The Anti Ballistic Missile (ABM) Treaty.** ABM is a system with weapons that are able to shoot down enemy missiles. It was now decided that each side should only have two systems with no more than 100 missile launchers each. The idea of limiting this protection was that if one side had a strong protection it might encourage this state to risk a nuclear war.

Did You Know?

'**Strategic nuclear arms**' means long range nuclear weapons and can be used to bomb cities. A missile can be launched from a submarine (SLBM) or from another continent (ICBM). '**Tactical nuclear weapons**' are short range and can be used against enemy forces.

Even though SALT I was only a freeze and no decisions were taken about MIRVs and ICBs, the agreement was an important change in Cold War relations and would result in a continuing process of détente.

The SALT agreement was a recognition of Soviet equality in nuclear weapons. It was also a recognition that a nuclear war would mean the destruction of both, hence a war must be avoided at any cost. This was referred to as **Mutual Assured Destruction**. This was the idea behind the terror balance: fear of nuclear destruction would lead to peace.

---

[88] Ball, S. J., *The Cold War: An International History 1947–1991*, p. 150.

- **1972—The Basic Principles of Relations between the USSR and the US.** This was a formal declaration that both states were committed to peaceful co-existence.
- **1973—The Prevention of Nuclear War Agreement.** This provided for consultation between the two powers in times of crisis.
- **1975—The Helsinki Agreement.** This agreement was signed by all European governments (except for Albania) and the US and Canada. The agreement was a formal recognition of the frontiers in Europe. The main points were:

    1. Respect for sovereignty;
    2. Renunciation of the use of force for settling disputes;
    3. Peaceful settlement of disputes;
    4. Non-intervention in internal affairs;
    5. Respect for human rights;
    6. Territorial integrity of states; and
    7. The inviolability of frontiers.

With this agreement all post-war frontiers in Europe were accepted. The Soviets were pleased because it was an acceptance of the division of Germany and the Soviet sphere of influence.

The signatories also agreed to respect human rights, i.e., the right to travel and freedom of speech. This was considered to be an important achievement by the Western powers.

- **1979 The SALT II agreement.** This agreement limited the number of ICBMs and SLBM to 2,400 each and included a ceiling on the number of MIRVs. The two powers also promised to notify each other on tests. The treaty was signed but never ratified (approved) by the US Congress, mainly due to the Soviet invasion of Afghanistan, but both sides kept the agreement until 1986.
- What is also important to keep in mind is that there were regular **US-Soviet summits** throughout the 1970s which promoted a better understanding:

    1. Moscow 1972: Brezhnev-Nixon
    2. Washington 1973: Brezhnev-Nixon
    3. Moscow 1974: Brezhnev-Nixon
    4. Vladivostok 1974: Brezhnev-Ford
    5. Vienna 1979: Brezhnev-Carter

Ostpolitik

Another development which took place in the centre of Europe in the 1970s was an important part of the détente process: **Willy Brandt's *Ostpolitik*.** West Germany's relation to East Germany had been expressed by Konrad Adenhauer, Chancellor from 1949 to 1963, in the **Hallstein Doctrine** from 1955. West Germany was not prepared to have any diplomatic relations with any state, who recognised the East German state. West Germany also refused to recognise its frontier with Poland and Czechoslovakia from 1945. The West German state had been established after the Berlin blockade and was a result of US support. Consequently she was a reliable ally of the US.

Brandt and his adviser Bahr were forming a new foreign policy. The idea was to overcome the **division of Germany and ease the tension in Central Europe**, rather than fight in the front line with the US in the Cold War. Better relations were needed with the USSR. Bahr said: "*The German question can only be solved with the USSR not against it…the preconditions for reunification are only to be created with the USSR.*"[89] In 1966, Brandt was appointed Foreign Minister in a coalition with the Christian Democrats. In 1967, diplomatic relations were established with Romania, a rejection of the Hallstein Doctrine. In 1969, the

---

[89] Ibid, p. 160.

Social Democrats (SPD) won the elections and formed a government with the liberals (FDP) with Brandt as Chancellor. It was now time for change. The US wanted to get out of Vietnam and West Germany wanted a normalisation with its neighbours in the East, to reduce the tension in Central Europe and the get better relations with 'the Eastern zone'. The USSR was the key to both problems.

- **The Moscow Treaty from 1970** between West Germany and the USSR formally ended WWII and recognised the frontiers and the agreements from the war, i.e., that Poland had been moved to the West at the expense of German territories (the Oder-Neisse line) and the division of Germany.
- **In September 1971, the US, the USSR, Britain and France** signed an agreement recognising each other's rights to Berlin.
- **The East German-West German Basic Treaty from 1972** was a formal recognition of two German states and the links from West Germany to West Berlin were accepted, i.e., no more Berlin Blockade as in 1948. The agreement aimed at increasing commercial, cultural and personal contacts between '**two states within one nation**' as Brandt expressed it.

This process of European détente was further strengthened and confirmed with the signing of **the Helsinki agreement in 1975.**

The Decline of Détente

The ideas of détente and linkage dominated the post-Vietnam War development in the 1970s. But there were several events during this period which would bring the New Right, a coalition between Republicans and neo-conservative Democrats, to power in the US. In 1980 Ronald Reagan was elected US president and his new administration took a much tougher stance against the USSR. Détente was now replaced by the Second Cold War.

> If a 'Second Cold War' started in 1979/80, we must ask ourselves: when was the 'First Cold War'? Well, it must have been from either the Potsdam meeting in 1945 or the declaration of the Truman Doctrine in 1947 to the Missile Crisis in 1962. An alternative to the Missile Crisis as an end to the first period could be the end of the Vietnam War in the early 1970s. That is the 'First Cold War'. There were signs of détente in the mid-1950s, but these promising signs were not enough to change the overall impression of this period as being coined by superpower rivalry.

What Challenged Détente in the 1970s? The Middle East

The Middle East with its oil resources had traditionally been dominated by the West. When Truman announced his Truman Doctrine in 1947, he wanted money not only for Greece, but to Turkey as well. But Stalin didn't really challenge Western interests in the Middle East. It would be different with Khrushchev. From 1955, Nasser's regime in the Middle East received military aid from Czechoslovakia and the USSR which increased the tension in the area. The Baghdad Pact was formed in 1955 and was a Western attempt to contain communism from the Middle East. It was the Suez Crisis in 1956 which definitely made the Middle East an important area in the Cold War struggle. Even if the US was not involved in the Western attack, her two most important allies in Europe were behind it. The Anglo-French attack discredited Western interests in the region and opened up for Soviet influence. In January 1957, Eisenhower launched his '**Eisenhower Doctrine**' and the US Congress gave him the right to provide economic and military assistance to any Middle Eastern country threatened with armed aggression or internal subversion. As a result of this, the US intervened in Lebanon in July 1957. In 1964, a **Soviet Mediterranean fleet** was formed and in 1966 the USSR signed an agreement which gave the Soviets a naval base in Egypt. This was of major strategic importance to the USSR. For the first time, they could really counter US activities in the area. In the Six-Day War in 1967, Egypt, Syria and Jordan were defeated and humiliated by the Israelis. The USSR now started to give massive military aid to Egypt with a complete air defence system and 20,000 military advisers. The USSR became an ally of several Arab countries. US support for Israel of course angered the Arabs.

The Israel-Arab conflict became very tense after the Six-Day War when the Israelis occupied the West Bank and conquered Jerusalem. But it was a delicate act for Marxist-Leninists to co-operate with Muslim states in the Middle East. Brezhnev said: *"Nasser is highly confused on ideological questions… but…of inestimable value to us."*[90] When the Soviets refused to supply Egypt with even more modern offensive military systems and refused to help the Arabs to recapture territories lost in the Six-Day War, Nasser's successor Sadat expelled Soviet military advisers from the country in 1972. This Soviet refusal was due to its concern for the détente process with the US which had started.

In October 1973, Egypt and Syria launched a surprise attack on Israel, the **Yom Kippur War**. The Israelis were taken by surprise while celebrating Yom Kippur, their most important religious festival. The Arab alliance initially made big advances. Both the US and the USSR started with large-scale airlifts with weapons to their allies. The Israelis recovered quickly and launched a large scale counter attack. They invaded Egypt and crossed the Suez Canal and had soon surrounded an entire Egyptian army. The USSR now called for a joint US-Soviet military intervention and threatened to intervene unilaterally if no support was given from the US. Nixon refused and upgraded the alert status of US military forces worldwide. The USSR had to accept a US proposal of a UN peacekeeping force and the Israelis were forced to reluctantly accept a cease fire.

The war was a fiasco for the USSR. Her allies in the region had been defeated and humiliated and it was the US and Henry Kissinger who played a leading role in solving the crisis. In the US, many politicians questioned the intentions of the USSR in the détente process. They had foreknowledge about the attack and neither prevented it nor informed the US. Soviet attempts to extend her influence to new areas previously dominated by the West also had **negative effects on the détente process**. Naval bases around the world were of great strategic importance. The Warsaw Pact had more ships and submarines than NATO but NATO could keep twice as many submarines at sea due to better access to bases. In 1972, the USSR lost her most important base in the Mediterranean and in the Third World. The Yom Kippur War had put strains on superpower relations but too much political prestige had already been invested in the détente process from both sides to let it be destroyed by one international crisis. Brezhnev, who was most bitter, concluded in December 1973: *"Matters would look quite different were it not for this factor of détente….if the current conflict had flared up in a situation of universal, international tension…it might…endangering world peace."*[91]

Africa

In the early 1960s, Khrushchev had declared that the ultimate victory of communism would be achieved through wars of **national-liberation.** During 1970, the Third World went through a period of remarkable turbulence, often rooted indigenous development, regional rivalry but most importantly decolonisation process. Traditionally, the Third World had been dominated by the Western powers but the challenge to this order, once initiated by Khrushchev, would continue and increase. In 1975, the Portuguese colonies **Angola, Mozambique and Guinea-Bissau** were granted independence after a revolution in Portugal in 1974. The USSR was eager to establish close relations with states that could provide the USSR with naval bases. It was of major strategic importance, especially after the loss of Egypt in 1972. In Angola, different guerrilla groups had fought for independence since the 1950s. The MPLA (the Movimento Popular de Libertação de Angola) was supported by the Soviets while the FNLA (Frente Nacional de Libertação de Angola) and the UNITA (the União Nacional para a Independência Total de Angola) were supported by the US, China and South Africa. The Civil War started in February 1975. In 1973, the US Congress had passed a bill, the War Powers Act, restricting the President's ability to send troops to foreign countries without a formal declaration of war. The US post-Vietnam era showed a reluctance to be involved in conflicts in the Third World. When the Soviets provided the MPLA in Angola with

---

[90] Ibid, p. 178.
[91] Ibid, p. 179.

massive military aid, backed by some 17,000 Cuban soldiers, no equivalent US support could be given and in 1976 the MPLA controlled most of the country. The Cuban forces had turned the tide in Angola. In Ethiopia, the regime was supported by the USSR in the war against Somalia in 1977–1978 and again the Cubans sent some 17,000 troops. In 1976, Angola concluded a friendship treaty with the USSR and Mozambique followed in 1977. In the late 1970s, the Soviets had a long list of states in Africa with a pro-Soviet policy: **Angola, Benin, Congo, Ethiopia, Guinea, Guinea-Bissau and Mozambique. Other states had strong links to China**.

The Emergence of the New Right

This development had a major impact on US policies. The emerging New Right, an alliance between Republicans and conservative Democrats, argued that détente was a 'one-way street' allowing the Soviets to extend their influence and that the détente policy had been exploited by the Soviet leadership. It would lead to Reagan and the Second Cold War in the early 1980s and the development in Africa was one important reason for this new policy. The Nixon and Kissinger perception of linkage had involved the idea that the USSR would support US attempts to make the Third World more stable, not a playground for the Cold War. Brezhnev and the USSR rejected this view and saw Western domination of poorer countries as a form of neo-imperialism which had to be opposed.

In the US, President Nixon had been forced to resign in 1974 due to the Watergate scandal. He was replaced by his vice President Gerald Ford. There was no major change in the foreign policy since Henry Kissinger, Nixon's National Security Adviser, had been appointed Secretary of State in 1973. **The policy of détente rested on a US acceptance of Soviet nuclear parity and to respect the Soviet sphere of influence, hence a balance of power. Soviet support for arms agreement, withdrawal from Vietnam and stability in the Third World would be accomplished**. It was not only the Soviet economy which would benefit from a reduction of nuclear development. A traditional reluctance in the US to increase taxes had resulted in budget deficits during the Vietnam War and increased inflation. Together with competition from the Japanese and West German industries, it resulted in the US facing her first balance of trade deficit in the 20th century in 1971. After the Yom Kippur War, the Arab states started to use the oil weapon to put pressure on the Western states over the Israel-Palestinian problem. The increase of oil prices, the Oil crisis, led to an economic recession in the Western world in the mid-1970s. GNP was stagnant, the inflation rate was about 10% per year and unemployment reached 7.5%. Between 1970 and 1980, the US share of global economic output went down from around 38% to 25%. Oil prices quadrupled and the Soviet Union which exported oil, benefited from this. Gerald Ford lost the presidential elections in 1976 to the Democrat Jimmy Carter. **Carter**, a governor from Georgia had a background as an owner of a peanut farm. He was seen as a new fresh alternative, not representing the political establishment linked to the nightmare of the Vietnam War and the Watergate scandal.

Figure 3.6: Jimmy Carter

If Kissinger's détente was linked to a balance of power, Carter's détente should be **linked to *morals***. Carter wanted to bring an end to US support to repressive regimes simply based on the fact that they were anti-Communists. In March 1977, he sent his Secretary of State Cyrus Vance, to Moscow with a proposal to drastically reduce the number of ICBMs and MIRVs. His initiative was rejected by the Soviets. Many felt that détente had brought nothing and politicians were divided over a continuation. Negotiation over a SALT II agreement was going on and domestic pressure forced the US delegation to take a tougher stance. Carter's administration reflected the attitudes in the US in the late 1970s. His two most trusted advisers in foreign policy had very different ideas about foreign policy. **Cyrus Vance** wanted to continue the détente policy. An arms agreement would ease tension and enable the US to cut her defence budget, which was needed for economic reasons. **Zbigniew Brzezinsky** had a Polish background and was Carter's National Security Adviser. As a native Pole he did not trust the Russians and believed that only US strength would make the Soviets agreeable. A renewed nuclear arms race could also ruin the Soviet economy which by now showed clear signs of stagnation. Carter was a newcomer, by many seen as an amateur in foreign policy. The development in Africa put pressure on Carter and soon developments in Afghanistan confirmed the suspicions of the New Right.

Afghanistan

It was the Soviet invasion of Afghanistan in 1979 which finally brought an end to the process of détente. In 1978, a left-wing Afghan group from the People's Democratic Party of Afghanistan (PDPA) overthrew the regime led by Muhammed Daoud. The new regime, led by Muhamed Tarakki, soon signed a friendship treaty with the USSR. A left-wing **reform programme** was introduced including a land reform and emancipating women. These policies **provoked Islamic fundamentalists** and a civil war started. There were also internal problems within the PDPA between two factions, the Khalq and Parcham factions. The civil war escalated in 1979, and so did factional fighting. **In December 1979, the USSR sent 85,000 troops** to Afghanistan in an attempt to establish order and control. The leader of the Parcham faction, Babrak Kamal was installed as President. Again there was widespread resistance against the regime and soon some 100,000 Soviet troops were involved in a war against a highly motivated **Muslim guerrilla**. The guerrilla was provided with funds and weapons by the Americans. It was not until 1988 that Gorbachev announced a gradual withdrawal which was completed in 1989. The civil war continued however and finally brought the Taliban to power.

The US reacted strongly against the invasion. Why?

- Many leading politicians in the US had started to question the détente process and could now argue that this was another example, not only in Africa, where **the Soviets cynically exploited the détente process** to extend their influence to new areas. This put a lot of pressure on President Carter to take strong action.

- In the same year, the pro-American Shah in Iran was deposed in a fundamentalist revolution, denouncing American influence. A radical anti-American fundamentalist revolution in the oil-rich Middle East threatened vital American interest. If the USSR extended her influence in the region, it was another threat. **By opposing the Soviets and supporting the guerrilla in Afghanistan, the US saw an opportunity to side with the Muslim world at a critical moment**. Moscow had thrown a lifeline to the US in a critical region.

To the USSR, Afghanistan Had Far-Reaching Consequences

- In the Muslim world, the USSR now suddenly had a '**third front**'. It was now not only capitalists in the West, and China in the East, who were enemies.

- It brought an **end to the détente** process with the Americans and there was a risk that an expensive nuclear development could start again. It is often said that the war converted Carter to supporting the Brzezinsky hard line policy. Carter said: "*My opinion of the Russians has changed more drastically in the last week than even the previous two and a half years before that.*"[92] Carter now **froze the ratification (approval) of SALT II** (it had been signed in 1979) and placed an **embargo on grain exports** to the USSR and the US decided to **boycott the Olympic Games** in Moscow in 1980. The Persian Gulf was militarised by the US and Carter introduced his **Carter Doctrine**: the Persian Gulf was of vital strategic importance to the US and they would deal directly with an outside force trying to gain control of the region. In 1980, the US also provided **China with military equipment** for the first time. Carter's actions are normally described as a start of the '**Second Cold War**'.

- It can be argued that the war in Afghanistan contributed to the election of Ronald Reagan as US president in 1980. Reagan would describe the USSR as an 'evil empire'.

- The Soviet Union lost influence and support in the Third World and in the Non-Aligned Movement.

- It put a lot of **economic pressure on the Soviet economy** which had already suffered from stagnation.

---

[92] Ibid, p. 185.

- It affected relations with the satellites and China negatively.
- In the Asian republics within the USSR, there was a large Muslim population. It destabilised this part of the Russian empire. Radical Islamist groups gained support.
- The USSR **lost 15,000 soldiers and 37,000 were wounded**. (It has been estimated that 1 million Afghanis died during the war.)
- In 1985, Saudi Arabia increased her oil production fourfold which led to a collapse of the **oil prices**. The USSR lost $19 billions per year which had severe effects on the economy.
- The Soviet block was challenged by Solidarity in Poland. This union was legalised in 1980, the year after the USSR had invaded Afghanistan. In 1981, Solidarity challenged the regime in Poland. It was **impossible for the USSR to invade Poland in 1981**, when they had invaded Afghanistan in 1979. Suslov a leading member in the Politburo said: "*We simply cannot afford another Afghanistan.*"[93]

A final factor challenging the détente process in the late 1970s was the deployment of Soviet **SS-20 missiles**. The Soviets started to deploy a new type of intermediate range missiles in the USSR in 1977. They were targeted on Western Europe and China. These missiles were movable, had a longer range compared to the missiles they replaced and were of the MIRV class, consequently a clear improvement. As a response the US and NATO decided to deploy their **Cruise and Pershing** II missiles in Europe. Cruise missiles flew at low level and were difficult to detect by radar and could be used for surprise attacks. In December 1979, NATO announced that from 1983 there would be 108 Pershings and 464 Tomahawks missiles deployed in Western Europe. The decision alarmed the Soviets as it was seen as a Western attempt to achieve a first strike option against the USSR. It not only alarmed the Soviets, anti-nuclear groups organised protest movements all over Western Europe. The issue about missiles in Europe had a major impact on the population in Western Europe.

Student Activities

The 1970s can be compared to the 1950s. There was both détente and confrontation:

Détente	Confrontation
1968 the Non-Proliferation of Nuclear Weapons Treaty	The Tet offensive
1969 SALT I talks start	The Prague Spring
1970 The Moscow Treaty signed	US troops in Cambodia
1972 Nixon visits China	
SALT I signed	
East and West German Basic Treaty	
1973 US leaves Vietnam	1973 Yom Kippur War
	1973 coup in Chile

> **Key Point**
>
> The reason for including both the Indochina War and the Vietnam War in the 'détente part' is that the Vietnam War ended in 1975 and its outcome is probably the single most important reason for the détente process.

Détente	Confrontation
1975 the Helsinki Agreement	North Vietnam captures Saigon
	Civil War in Angola
1978 Camp David agreement signed	1977 The USSR deploys SS 20 **SS-20** intermediate range weapons in Eastern Europe
	Ethiopian-Somali War
1979 SALT II signed	Islamic Revolution in Iran the USSR in Afghanistan
	NATO announces the deployment of cruise and Pershing missiles

3. Détente

Exercise 16: Discuss how the Vietnam War affected the Cold War.

(Note that this is asking for the Vietnam War. Show that you know the distinction between the Indochina War and the 'American' Vietnam War.)

- There is no definite starting point for this conflict. But start with Diem and how elections were cancelled. The formation of **SEATO** caused problems in the region and was probably one reason for the **Taiwan crises** in 1955 and 1956. Vietnam did not have a major impact on Cold War relations in the mid-1950s. Both the USSR and China wanted to achieve a peaceful unification of Vietnam in the late 1950.
- There was an escalation in 1960 when the North decided to unify the country with arms if necessary. Both the USSR and China decided to support the North, anxious to maintain good relations with an important ally in times of Sino-Soviet disputes. This help in the **early 1960** must be described as **limited**.
- **The Kennedy administration never questioned the strategic importance of Vietnam**, hence they believed in the Domino Theory. But with limited fighting the US advisers were increased from 400 to 16,000 men. It is a significant increase but no combat troops were sent and the escalation cannot be compared to Johnson's.
- From 1965, **Johnson** started to escalate the US involvement by sending combat troops and starting air attacks on the North. As a response to this the USSR and China initiated with massive military aid. The Vietnam War was by now the **main trouble spot in the Cold War**.
- **The Vietnam War undermined the American position globally**. The Bretton Woods system—the leading role of the dollar in the world economy—collapsed. The US soon suffered from inflation caused by the war and as a consequence faced her first balance of trade deficit in the 20th century in 1971. Worldwide the US was seen as an aggressor and lost support especially in the Third World. US credibility as a 'champion of freedom' in the struggle against communism also suffered. If the US should be able to continue her leading role as a defender of Western liberalism, the war had to be brought to an end. The Vietnam War led the Americans to **reconsider her Cold War strategy**, to support détente. You could say that this was the first genuine US attempt to accomplish a détente process during the Cold War. But notice that the détente process was also due to Soviet nuclear parity and the Sino-Soviet split.
- With détente, '**rollback**' of communism was abandoned and the balance of power, an acceptance of communist sphere of influences, was established. The US needed the support of both the USSR and China to get out of the war. China was finally accepted into the United Nations in 1971 and opened up after the Cultural Revolution. The US desire to end the conflict resulted in **better relations with both the USSR and China**. The Cold War in the 1970s saw new relationships and the Vietnam War was one reason for this.
- **US reluctance to get involved in a new conflict in the Third World** in the 1970s made the US more cautious. According to some historians and the New Right, this led to the Soviets to trying to extend their influence in Africa especially, but also Afghanistan.

Conclusion: It was from the mid-1960s that the Vietnam War had a major impact on the Cold War and in the 1970s it was one major reason for the détente process. It also led to US reluctance to get involved in new conflicts.

Exercise 17: Discuss why there was a period of détente in the 1970.

(Explain why it started and what happened.)

a) Why was there a détente process?
- **The Americans** needed to end the Vietnam War because it undermined their position both globally and domestically. US credibility to be able to fight communism, support in the Third World, the US economy and support for the president, all suffered from the war. The Americans realised that they needed support from both the USSR and China to accomplish their goal of ending the war.
- **The USSR** had finally closed the missile gap in the early 1970s. The cost had been astronomical. The stagnation of the Soviet economy started in the early 1970s and Soviet leaders realised that they had to slow down military expenditure. They were also attracted by the possibility of getting access to Western technology, the US idea of linkage. The Soviets also feared the Chinese after border disputes in 1969. They realised that if they did not respond to American proposals, an understanding between the US and China could be a result.
- **China** was going through a volatile period during the Cultural Revolution. After the Warsaw Pact invasion of Czechoslovakia and the border disputes with the USSR they feared a Soviet attack. China was very isolated during the Cultural Revolution and the industry had suffered from this isolation and political purges.

By turning to her enemy, China could gain both economically and strategically.

- In **West Germany**, the Social Democrats and Willy Brandt wanted to establish better relations with the Soviet Union and her satellites. The idea was to overcome the division of Germany and

(Continued)

Exercise 17: Discuss why there was a period of détente in the 1970. *(Continued)*

ease the tension in Central Europe, rather than fight in the front line with the US in the Cold War. Better relations were needed with the USSR.
- Important achievements in détente (read more about each point in the text):
- The Moscow Treaty from 1970 between West Germany and the USSR
- 1971 The Nuclear Accidents Agreement between the US and the USSR.
- 1972 SALT I signed by Nixon and Brezhnev.
- 1972 The East German-West German Basic Treaty.
- 1972 Biological Weapons Convention signed by 126 countries.
- 1973 Ceasefire in Vietnam and the American withdrawal.
- 1973 The Prevention of Nuclear War Agreement signed by the US and the USSR.
- 1975 The Helsinki Agreement signed by all European governments except Albania.
- 1979 SALT II signed. It went further than SALT I but was never ratified (approved) by the US Congress due to the war in Afghanistan. Both sides kept the agreement until 1986.

Exercise 18: Discuss why détente was brought to an end in the late 1970

- **The Yom Kippur War** in 1972. The USSR had known about the attack but not warned the US. The Soviets were frustrated over the fact that Nixon's decision to place US troops on strategic alert had made it impossible to give crucial help to her Arab ally which then faced another humiliating defeat.
- The Soviets tried to extend their influence in the Third World in the 1970s. However, Soviet influence in this part of the world was limited compared to US influence. Strategically, the **USSR needed naval bases** in other parts of the world to be able to keep ships and submarines at sea. The Warsaw Pact outnumbered NATO as regards to the number of ships but could not take advantage of this as they didn't have access to naval bases, hence they were inferior to NATO which had bases in the Third World. Soviet expansion in **the Middle East and in Africa** can partly be seen against this background and was viewed with alarm in the US.
- In 1975, **North Vietnam conquered the South**.
- In Africa, the Soviets gained allies. In **Angola and Ethiopia, pro-Soviet regimes** were established after armed conflicts where massive Soviet aid and Cuban troops played decisive roles. There were pro-Soviet regimes in **Angola, Benin, Congo, Ethiopia, Guinea, Guinea-Bissau and Mozambique.** Other states had strong links to China. The USSR also established naval bases in countries in the Third World.
- In 1979, the USSR invaded **Afghanistan** and installed Babrak Kamal as president. The same year the pro-American **Shah in Iran** was deposed in a fundamentalist revolution, denouncing American influence. A radical anti-American fundamentalist revolution in the oil-rich Middle East threatened vital American interests.
- **In Europe, right-wing dictatorships fell from power in Portugal and Greece in 1974, and in Spain in 1975.** In both France and Italy, the communist parties attracted substantial support. All these states except for Spain were NATO members and it was viewed with alarm in the US.
- The 'New Right' in the US concluded that the **Soviets cynically exploited US reluctance to intervene in the Third World after the Vietnam War**. A new US attitude could be seen during the Carter administration after the invasion of Afghanistan, and even more clearly when Reagan came to power in 1980. This view blames the USSR and her aggressive foreign policy in the Third World particularly for the Second Cold War.
- There is an alternative explanation focusing upon the US and the 'New Right' and **US domestic policy**. Fred Halliday represents this view. In his *The Making of the Second Cold War* he argues that the domestic development in the US was the driving force. In the 1970s, the south and west in the US became more important economically and politically. Most of the military industries were concentrated in these areas and the electorate is normally more conservative here. The recession after the Vietnam War and the oil crisis in combination with the détente policy, had made the US militarily weak. Congress was dominated by the New Right and there were many conservative Congressmen with links to the military industrial complex. It has been estimated that 7 million people in the US were directly employed by the armament industry in the 1970s and politicians representing these groups had political reasons for discrediting the détente policy. It is partly an oversimplification to focus purely upon Soviet aggression. The US intervened in different ways in the 1970s. The coup in Chile in 1973 is one example. **It was the emergence of a new political right which was the driving force behind the process of ending détente, and not so much Soviet activity.**

4. The Coming of the Second Cold War and the Collapse of the USSR

Overview

The invasion of Afghanistan was of major importance in ending the détente process. Carter came under domestic pressure and in 1981 Ronald **Reagan** was elected US president. Reagan decided to increase the strength of the US army and put the Soviets under a 'systematic challenge'. In 1983, he introduced the idea of a new defence system, the Strategic Defence Initiative (SDI). The Soviets were facing major problems. The war in Afghanistan and Reagan's systematic challenge all led to the **Second Cold War**. In the USSR, the economy was stagnating and the old leadership had no solution to the problem. Between 1982 and 1985, three Soviet leaders passed away: Brezhnev, Andropov and Chernenko. This brought a young and dynamic leader to power in the USSR in 1985: Michael **Gorbachev**. He soon introduced far-reaching reforms both domestically and internationally. The reform process went however out of control and in 1991 the Soviet Union collapsed.

The Background: Economic Stagnation during Brezhnev but an Increase of Military Spending

The Brezhnev era is very important as a background to the problems in the early 1980s in the USSR. Brezhnev came to power after the fall of Khrushchev in 1964. After a period of collective leadership like Malenkov and Khrushchev, he soon emerged as the real leader of the Soviet Union. A long-term consequence of the Cuban Missile Crisis was the Soviet decision to **achieve nuclear parity** with the US. This was achieved in the early 1970s but the cost was **astronomical**. The military competition with the US and her NATO allies put a lot of strain on the Soviet economy. **GNP in the Soviet Union in the 1970s was less than half of the US's GNP.** The border disputes with China caused alarm in the Soviet Union. In the 1970s, the USSR kept 44 army divisions on the border to China while they had only 31 divisions in Europe. Consequently, the Sino-Soviet dispute resulted in the majority of the Soviet army, totalling 3.7 million men, protecting a border next to a communist state. In the 1970s, signs of stagnation in the economy were beginning. **The GNP growth had been around 10% annually in the 1950s. It was 7% in the 1960s and fell to 5% in the 1970s. In the early 1980s, the growth was around 3%.** The ageing Soviet leadership didn't realise that the Soviet command economy needed far-reaching reforms. In spite of the détente process in the 1970s, defence spending actually increased. **Many signals** indicated that the Soviet Union needed a new policy with reforms, but they were **ignored by Brezhnev**. The fall of economic growth in combination with increased defence spending and military assistance to the Third World undermined the economy. Involvement in the Third World was dramatically increased: the USSR provided both Syria and Egypt with new arms after the Yom Kippur War in 1973. Cuban troops were transported to Africa in 1977 and military aid was given to both Angola and Ethiopia, naval bases were built in Africa, support was given to Vietnam in 1978–1979 in a conflict with China, troops were sent to Afghanistan in 1979, in the early 1980 there were 25,000 military advisers in Cuba, Syria and Vietnam. It continued after Brezhnev with support to North Korea in 1984, and Nicaragua and Libya in 1985. **Brezhnev's ignorance of economic realities is probably one important reason for the collapse of the Soviet Union in the late 1980s.**

Carter's policies

Carter who came to power in the US in 1977, conducted a foreign policy with two faces. His early years showed **commitment to détente and far-reaching proposals for arms reduction**. Détente should be linked to morality and the US should no longer support repressive regimes just because they were anti-Communists. Between 1978 and 1979, Carter cancelled the development of neutron bombs and signed START II. His later years are however normally described as the beginning of the Second Cold War, after the Soviet invasion of Afghanistan. This pattern of dualism was reflected in his two most important foreign policy advisers: **Cyrus Vance** was the new Secretary of State and believed in a continuation of détente and a new SALT agreement. He was opposed by **Zbigniew Brzezinsky**, the National Security Adviser. Brzezinsky, a native Pole, distrusted the Soviets and believed that it was only

US strength that would make the Russians co-operate. Kissinger's old balance of power was rejected by Brzezinsky. The US should establish military superiority which was the only way to force the Soviets to change their policies. Brzezinsky stated: "*I don't consider nuclear superiority to be politically meaningless.... strategic superiority can influence political behaviour. It can induce some countries to act in a fashion that sometimes can be described as a "Finlandization"*"[94] (i.e., to indirectly control a country through military superiority). He also believed that an expensive arms race would destabilise the Soviet economy. There were experts in the US who believed that the stagnating economy in the USSR in combination with policies in the Third World and military defence spending within the Soviet Union, were now bringing the country close to a collapse. Carter who was inexperienced in foreign policy followed Vance's line before Afghanistan but was converted to Brzezinsky's tougher stand after Afghanistan. Carter achieved some notable successes. In 1977, the **Camp David Accords** were signed between Egypt and Israel. Israel returned Sinai to Egypt and Egypt was the first Arab state to recognise Israel. The Soviets had been excluded from the agreement. Relations were also improved with China and in 1979, Mao's successor Deng Xiaoping visited the US. Full diplomatic relations were established between the US and China in 1979. START II was also signed in 1979 but would soon be rejected by the Americans when the Second Cold War started.

1979: A Turning Point

1979 was a turning point and marked the beginning of the Second Cold War. The growing strength of the **New Right** in American politics in combination with the international development resulted in an enormous political pressure on President Carter. The hearings in the US Senate for ratification (approval) of the SALT II agreement resulted in a vigorous attack on the President's foreign policy. The SALT agreement was referred to by one Senator as "*appeasement in its purest form.*"[95] In January 1979, the pro-American Shah of Iran fled his country and **Ayatollah Khomeini came to power** in an Islamic fundamentalist revolution, strongly opposing Western influence and especially the US. In November, the US embassy in Tehran was attacked and 53 Americans were held hostage for more than a year. The Iranian crisis led to oil prices tripling. In March, a left-wing revolutionary movement seized power in the Caribbean island of **Grenada**. In July, the Sandinistas were finally able to seize power in **Nicaragua** and in **El Salvador** reformist military officers seized power. The USSR was not involved in the Nicaraguan revolution but Cuban advisers were there, playing a limited role. It was also announced that the US had discovered Soviet combat troops in Cuba. The troops had been there for years. When the Soviets invaded **Afghanistan** in December the same year, the US feared that the USSR was now extending its position in a very sensitive region: the oil-rich Middle East. It was only years after Soviet and Cuban involvement in Africa and the USSR had now established close relationships with several African states. The development in Afghanistan made Carter finally support the Brzezinsky line leading to the Second Cold War. The Soviets disliked what they considered as Carter's zig-zag policies.

Key Point

Notice that the view about the Second Cold War was a US response to an increase in communist activities globally, has been challenged by Fred Halliday. He is arguing that the emergence of the New Right in the US was the driving force behind the Second Cold War. Most historians do however support the view that Soviets actions internationally, and especially in Afghanistan, led to the Second Cold War.

How did the US and Carter respond to this development? He declared in December 1979, when the Soviets invaded Afghanistan: "*My opinion of the Russians has changed more drastically in the last week than even the previous two and a half years before that.*"[96] **The defence budget was dramatically increased**. Carter's two last budgets increased military spending from $174 billion to $200 billion. Reagan, who came to power in 1981 (he was elected in November 1980), increased it with an additional $32.6 billion in 1982 to $232.6 billion, 13% in one year. It brought an end to 'détente with morale' and reintroduced the attitudes and the language of previous periods. In January 1980, Carter froze the ratification (approval) of SALT II and stopped US grain exports to the USSR. The Moscow Olympics in 1980 was boycotted. In January 1980, Carter announced "*any attempt by any outside force to gain control of the Persian Gulf region will be regarded as an assault on the vital interests of the United States of America, and such an assault will be repelled by any means necessary, including military force,*"[97] better known as **the Carter Doctrine**. A Rapid Deployment Force was set up to deal with crises in the region.

---

[94] Ball, S. J., *The Cold War: An International History 1947–1991*, p. 176.
[95] Ibid, p. 177.
[96] Ibid, p. 185.
[97] Ibid, p. 186.

Ronald Reagan and his Systematic Challenge

The Reagan administration was more than willing to continue Carter's tough stance. The Carter administration had been attacked by Reagan. In 1981, he said: "*So far détente has been a one way street which the Soviet Union had used to pursue its own aims…(and) reserve the right to commit any crime, to lie, to cheat…when you do business with them—even in détente—keep that in mind.*"[98] Even though the US economy suffered from a recession, the 1982 military budget was increased by 13%. The USSR were to be exposed to a '**systematic challenge**' by the US. New weapons were to be developed which would be difficult to counter for the Soviets. New weapons would make Soviet weapons obsolete (out of date) which would put pressure on the Soviet economy. The Reagan administration started the largest peacetime military build-up in US history. Between 1981 and 1988, military spending went from $117 billion per year to $290 billion.

Figure 4.1: Ronald Reagan

Since 1977, the Soviets had been deploying SS-20 intermediate-range weapons in Eastern Europe. It was a typical Cold War strategy where one side tried to compensate for what was seen as offensive moves from the other side. The Soviets saw it as a response to US deployment of Thor and Jupiter missiles earlier (see the post-revisionist view and the 'security dilemma'). In 1979, the US and NATO announced their '**dual track**' decision: new cruise and ballistic missiles would be deployed in Europe from 1983 if the Soviet Union did not dismantle their SS-20s. The new Western missiles, **Pershing 2 and Cruise**, were a new generation of nuclear weapons which were both faster and more difficult to detect and very difficult to counter. They could be launched from mobile missile carriers. In the USSR, it was seen as a major escalation. The Chief of the General Staff in the USSR, Nikolay Ogarkov, stated: the US is "*taking matters to a point of keeping the world on the 'brink of war.*"[99]

In the early 1980s, the Soviets faced a major challenge in Poland. Problems with the economy had resulted in the creation of an independent trade union **Solidarity**. In 1980, the Polish government recognised the union's right to exist in the Gdansk accords. The Soviet government was critical and stated that… "*the agreement…signifies the legalisation of the anti-socialist opposition.*"[100] Preparations for an invasion were made but the Soviet leadership preferred the Poles sorted out their own problem. In 1981, the government declared martial law in Poland in an attempt to crush Solidarity. It led to a political crisis and the US responded with economic and trade sanctions on both Poland and the USSR.

The deployment of new nuclear weapons in Europe led to major demonstrations in Western Europe. In the USSR, the leadership realised that this would put a lot of pressure on the European NATO members. In Geneva, there were talks between the Americans and the Soviets, **the Intermediate Nuclear Forces talks (INF)**, and the European governments in the West wanted an agreement where the Soviets would remove their SS-20s because then there would be no need for Pershing and Cruise missiles in Europe, which would satisfy the **peace movement**. There were also talks about a reduction of strategic weapons, the **Strategic Arms Reduction Talks (START)**. Germany was the key country. Brandt had been succeeded by Helmut Schmidt. He was faced by a difficult situation as an ally to the US: the grass roots of his party and many prominent leaders like Brandt and Bahr opposed the deployment of new missiles in Germany. Bahr stated: "*humanity is going insane…*"[101]

---

[98] Williamson, D., *Europe and the Cold War 1945–91*, p. 171.
[99] Ball, S. J., *The Cold War: An International History 1947–1991*, p. 190.
[100] Ibid, p. 196.
[101] Ibid, p. 212.

In 1983, Reagan announced his **Strategic Defence Initiative (SDI)** better known as the '**Star Wars**' project. The aim was to develop a totally new and expensive technology, a **shield** protecting the US from **space**. The SDI missiles were part of a defensive system which would destroy Soviet missiles before reaching the US by forming an **impenetrable shield. Few scientists took it seriously** in 1983 and it was seen as science fiction, but it was **difficult to totally ignore**. If the Americans poured money into an expensive research programme, it was possible that the SDI-development in the future would lead to a technological breakthrough, which would bring the Americans ahead of the Soviets. The SDI project played a major role in arms talks in the 1980s. It was a part of '**the systematic challenge**' of the USSR. The same year Reagan gave a speech which now must be described as 'famous', to the National Association of Evangelical Christians. The Soviet Union was described as an '**evil empire**': "*Let us be aware that, while [the Soviet leaders] preach the supremacy of the state, declare its omnipotence over individual man, and predict its eventual domination of all peoples on the earth, they are the focus of evil in the modern world. So, in your discussions of the nuclear freeze proposals, I urge you to beware the temptation of pride—the temptation of blithely declaring yourselves above it all and label both sides equally at fault, to ignore the facts of history and the aggressive impulses of an **evil empire**, to simply call the arms race a giant misunderstanding and thereby remove yourself from the struggle between right and wrong and good and evil.*"[102]

Reagan's anti-communist rhetoric was very controversial in the early 1980s. But he was actually right when he described the depth of the internal weaknesses in the Soviet Union. In a famous speech to the British parliament in 1982, he declared that the USSR was in the midst of a great revolutionary crisis and that the dimensions of this failure were astounding. It would however take some more years until this became really clear.

In November 1983, NATO started the deployment of the Pershings and the Cruise missiles. The USSR responded by pulling out from the Intermediate Nuclear Forces (INF) talks and START negotiations. The Second Cold War had reached its lowest point. It was the worst year in the Cold War since the Cuban Missile Crisis in 1962.

It was argued that the difference between Cold War I and Cold War II was that in the West the Soviet empire in the 1980s was not seen as an ideological threat any longer. The appeal of Soviet communism had been lost in the Prague Spring of 1968. The fear of the Soviets in the 1980s was purely militarily.

Soviet Problems

The situation in the early 1980s was even more complicated by internal problems in the USSR. In 1982, the ageing Brezhnev died and was succeeded by Yuriy **Andropov. Brezhnev** had not realised the need for reforms and to reduce the defence spending. The war in Afghanistan and support for the regimes in Cuba, Vietnam, Ethiopia and many others required enormous sums of money. The USSR suffered from a 'global over-stretching'. Andropov had serious health problems and was under medical treatment for most of his time in power. When Andropov passed away, after only two years he was succeeded by another veteran, Konstantin Chernenko. He passed away after only one year in power in March 1985. When Gorbachev was elected General Secretary in 1985, there were many problems to solve:

- The economic growth of the Soviet economy had been going down since the late 1950s.
- The Soviet Union spent 40% of their state budget on the armed forces.
- The gap between the GNP of the USSR and the US was growing steadily and had been doing so since 1958.
- The Soviet society was lagging behind in the development of new technology, especially within computing. It was estimated that Soviet scientific computers were slower than their American counterparts by a factor of 20.
- Infant mortality was rising, the birth-rate was declining and average male life expectancy had gone down from 66 years in the 1960s, to only 60 in 1986.
- Revenues from the oil industry were going down.
- In Poland, the situation was tense with the challenge from Solidarity.

---

[102] http://americanrhetoric.com/speeches/ronaldreaganevilempire.htm <Accessed 5 January 2017>

- The war in Afghanistan didn't go well and discredited the USSR in the Third World and in the Middle East.
- Brezhnev's ambitions in the Third World had faced several setbacks, most notably Egypt and Iraq, but also in Africa. The annual cost for supporting Cuba, Vietnam, Ethiopia and Afghanistan alone was estimated to $40 billion.
- China was still challenging the USSR as an alternative leader of the socialist camp.
- In Western Europe, Soviet communism was denounced by 'euro-communists'.
- Reagan was following a policy of 'systematic challenge' of the 'evil empire' and his Star War project worried leaders in the Kremlin.

Gorbachev and the Fall of Communism

Figure 4.2: Mikhail Gorbachev   *Figure 4.3:* Eduard Shevardnadze

The fall of the USSR is one of the most important events in the 20th century. The empire ceased to exist and the satellites in Eastern Europe were free from Soviet control. The Soviet involvement in Afghanistan also came to an end and a number of new states emerged from the Soviet empire. The collapse of the Soviet empire also brought an end to the Cold War—it is therefore necessary to explain this development as a part of the Cold War.

Michael Gorbachev was elected General Secretary at the age of 54 after Chernenko passed away in March 1985. Gorbachev was the youngest member of the politburo and the first Soviet leader to be born in the Soviet Union and not in Tsarist Russia. Old hardliners and former Stalinists like Brezhnev, Andropov and Chernenko had now been replaced by an open-minded optimist and reformer.

Gorbachev introduced a number of breathtaking reforms both domestically and internationally. He described it as "*a complete renewal of all aspects of Soviet life, economic, social, political and moral.*"[103] It must be noticed that Gorbachev initially **was a Leninist** who made attempts to reform the system in order to make it survive.

Gorbachev's plan for reconstruction contained two main points:

1. **Cooperation with the West to end the Cold War in order to reduce the costs of the arms race.**

2. A reconstruction of the Soviet empire. The key words were:
   - *glasnost* ('openness')
   - *perestroika* ('restructuring')
   - *demokratizatsiya* ('democratization')

---

[103] Bell, P. M. H. and and Gilbert, M., *The World Since 1945: An International History*, p. 357.

Student Activities

Main Events during the Gorbachev Era (with Emphasis on the Cold War)

1985

Gorbachev made his first visit to the West, France, as Soviet leader. He proposed that the superpowers should reduce their strategic weapons by 50%. From 1985 to 1988, Gorbachev and Reagan met annually in four different summits. The first took place in **Geneva** in 1985. No major agreements were made except for the fact that they agreed to meet again. There had been no summits for five years so the meeting was important in establishing personal relations.

In 1985, Saudi Arabia increased their oil production fourfold, and as a result **oil prices collapsed**. The USSR lost $20 billion per year. According to Yegor Gaidar, Prime Minister of Russia after the collapse of the USSR, Gorbachev disregarded the problem and started to **borrow money from abroad**. In 1989, when the economy stalled completely, the USSR had to negotiate with Western powers to get new money. It is also worth noting that in 1985 Gorbachev introduced an anti-alcohol campaign, which perhaps was wise from a health perspective, but this together with the collapse of the oil prices, **eroded the tax base** of the country.

1986

At the 27th Party Congress, Gorbachev announced that he believed that far-reaching economic reforms were needed and that the war in Afghanistan was a 'bleeding wound'. The famous scientist and dissident Andrei **Sakharov** was invited to return to Moscow by Gorbachev in December 1986 after six years of internal exile in Gorky. It signalled a new era.

The second summit meeting between Gorbachev and Reagan in **Reykjavik,** Iceland, was an astonishing conference. Gorbachev announced that he was prepared to **withdraw** his **SS-20 missiles** from Europe, if the US withdrew their Pershing and cruise missiles, i.e., an acceptance of Reagan's 'zero-option' solution. It had until now been rejected by the USSR. He also proposed a **50% reduction of all long-range missiles**. In return, Gorbachev wanted the Americans to call off the Star Wars project (**SDI**) but Reagan refused to abandon his project. Gorbachev then shocked the Americans by proposing **the abolition of all nuclear weapons** within 10 years. Reagan's commitment to the SDI resulted in no agreement being made.

Figure 4.4: Ronald Reagan and Mikhail Gorbachev

1987

The Washington Treaty (or **INF Treaty**) was signed. All missiles based on land in Europe and Asia, with a range of between 500 to 5,500 kilometres should be destroyed within three years. A dispute which had lasted over 10 years, involving most of the allies of the two superpowers, had finally been brought to an end.

1988

The same year an agreement between the superpowers was made in Geneva on the ending of the war in **Afghanistan**. Later this year Gorbachev announced that Soviet armed forces would be **reduced by 500,000 soldiers**, without any demands on US reductions (a unilateral reduction). He also announced a gradual withdrawal of troops

1989

from the GDR (East Germany), Czechoslovakia and Hungary. Gorbachev announced that the USSR would no longer interfere in the internal affairs of the satellites, i.e., the **Brezhnev Doctrine was dead**.

Elections in the USSR to a new supreme legislative body called the Congress of People's Deputies. Contested elections were introduced resulting in **non-Communists being able to be elected**. The majority was, however, still in the hands of the Communist Party. The dissident Andrej Sacharov was elected and he criticised the Communist Party when meetings in the Congress were broadcast on television. It had an enormous impact in the USSR.

In the early 1989, round-table talks in Poland led to free elections being scheduled to June the same year. In this first free election in a communist state since the 1940s, Solidarity won 99 out of 100 seats in the Senate. Poland was the first country in the Eastern Bloc to elect a non-communist Prime Minister. In May, Hungary announced that the Iron Curtain would be opened. It was a test of Gorbachev's willingness to abandon the Brehznev doctrine. This year communist rule was brought to an end in the satellites: **Poland, Hungary, GDR, Bulgaria and Romania**, without the USSR intervening. The withdrawal of Soviet troops from Afghanistan was completed. **The Cold War had been brought to an end**.

'Gorbymania', enthusiasm for Gorbachev, swept around the world but in the USSR communist hardliners saw it as a betrayal of the Soviet Union and the sacrifices its people had made during WWII.

1990

In 1990, Gorbachev was elected to a new office: president of the USSR. To Gorbachev, this was a way of creating his own political platform independent of the Communist Party. In March, the Congress had removed article 6 in the constitution, i.e., the Communist Party had no longer a political monopoly. The economy was now in a critical situation. **The GNP went down by 4% in 1990 and 15% in 1991**. There were severe shortages of basic food supplies, i.e., meat and sugar. Communist hardliners were criticizing Gorbachev <u>and</u> **nationalism in the Baltic States and Georgia posed an enormous problem** to Gorbachev who had committed himself to democratic solutions. In the Congress of People's Deputies **Yeltsin** had been offered a new platform criticizing the president. Gorbachev's solution to the mounting nationalist problems was a new **Union Treaty** giving the republics within the Soviet Union far more autonomy. But it didn't seem to satisfy some republics and by the end of the year many hardliners were given key positions in the Soviet government. Due to this the foreign minister **Eduard Shevardnadze resigned** dramatically in December claiming that 'Dictatorship was coming'.

1991

In January 1991, local branches of the KGB and armed forces worked together to seize the TV tower in **Vilnius in Lithuania**, most likely without any foreknowledge of Gorbachev. **Fourteen civilians were killed.** This disastrous clash made a new Union Treaty even more important to Gorbachev.

Boris Yeltsin was elected president of Russia in June 1991 and the question of Russia's willingness to sign a new Union Treaty became a key question. Without a Russian membership in the union, the Soviet Union was dead.

In August, just before a new Union Treaty should have been signed, communist hardliners made an attempted **coup**. Yeltsin took the leadership in Moscow against the coup, and it collapsed.

The coup was seen as a collapse of the old system, which Gorbachev to some extent was seen as a part of. **Yeltsin's authority gained from the coup, while Gorbachev was more or less in the hands of the Russian President.**

> **Key Point**
>
>
>
> With the collapse of the Soviet Empire, the Cold War came to an end. One of the 'enemies' did no longer exist and the republics emerging from the empire were weak and non-communist. It was a sudden and dramatic change. Gorbachev as an individual is probably the most important individual contributing to this development.

In December the leaders from Russia, Ukraine and Belarus declared that the **USSR no longer existed** and founded the **Commonwealth of Independent States** (CIS). Later the same month it was extended and 11 former republics joined the CIS.

On 25 **December, Gorbachev had to resign**. Without a Soviet Union, Gorbachev had no political platform. On 31 December, the USSR formally ceased to exist. Yeltsin was the new leader in Russia.

Why did Soviet communism collapse?

This question is interesting to discuss for a number of reasons. The collapse of the empire influenced a lot of countries. It is also interesting to discuss from a Cold War perspective. Some have argued that it was Reagan's policies which caused the collapse, i.e., that it can be seen as a part of his Cold War policies. Others have argued that this was caused by internal reasons, hence a development that shall not primarily be linked to the Cold War.

A. External pressure:

1. Military reasons

- It is interesting to notice that the stagnation of the Soviet economy goes back to the 1960s. In 1958, the difference between the US and Soviet GNP was at its narrowest and after that the gap constantly grew wider. This was the time when the space race and the development of intercontinental ballistic missiles started. As a result of the Cuban Missile Crisis, the Soviets decided to **close the missile gap**. The costs were astronomical: Soviet authorities had indicated that military spending was around 20%. In the spring of 1987, Gorbachev revealed that the real cost was **40% of the state budget**. The US spent 4–6%.

- The critical question to be asked is if we should see this cost as a result of external pressure, i.e., an adequate response to pressure from the US or as an inadequate response to a situation where communist leaders raised up in a system preaching the message of an inevitable clash with the capitalist world, ignored all sense of reality (if so, it's not external pressure).

- In the 1970s, the USSR had to keep 44 army divisions on the Chinese border, due to the Sino-Soviet split, and they only had 31 divisions in Europe.

- The annual cost for supporting Cuba, Vietnam, Ethiopia and Afghanistan alone was estimated to be US $40 billion. The USSR suffered from a 'global over-stretching'.

- The war in **Afghanistan** was of major importance. Edward Shevardnadze, Gorbachev's foreign minister, said that the decision to leave Afghanistan was the first and most difficult step. Everything else flowed from that. The war in Afghanistan also made it impossible to take actions in Poland against Solidarity.

McCauley writes: "*It* (the USSR) *had to devote about two-thirds of its scientists and about one-third of its economy to its military efforts.*"[104] It is not likely that any state can afford this in a long run. But we cannot find evidence for a substantial military build-up during the Gorbachev years or as a response to Reagan's policies. So from a short-term perspective it is difficult to claim that military spending caused a sudden collapse.

2. Nationalism

Glasnost or openness soon led to the abolition of censorship. It became evident that the republics within the **Soviet Union and the satellites in Eastern Europe** were not satisfied with decentralised power and democracy without independence. They wanted real independence. Freedom of speech released decades of bitterness over Stalin's repression and terror. In 1988, Gorbachev abandoned the **Brezhnev doctrine** and allowed the satellites to determine their own internal affairs. Nationalist feelings led to Soviet control of Eastern Europe coming to an end in the autumn of 1989. It also led to a number of republics within the Soviet Union becoming independent states.

---

[104] McCauley, M., *Russia, America and the Cold War: 1949–1991*, 2nd ed. (Harlow: Pearson Education Ltd, 2004) p. 118.

3. Influences from the outside world weakening the Soviet system

The Soviet empire was influenced from the outside in different ways.

- The Russian population was attracted by Western habits and **consumer goods** which contrasted to the shortages and the queues in the Soviet Union. The Soviet system in the 1980s was eroded by Western influence and consumer goods just as the Tsarist system had once been eroded by liberal and socialist ideas.
- There were also spiritual influences like **Pope John Paul II** among Catholics in Eastern Europe and especially in Poland. When he visited Krakow in 1979—million Poles were there to welcome him. Gaddis writes that "*he began a process by which communism…would come to an end.*"[105]
- The influence of **Islam** became important in Soviet republics in Central Asia especially when the conflict in Afghanistan started. The Iranian revolution brought Khomeini to power in 1978–1979 and even though there were different schools of thought in Islam, both the revolution in Iran and the war in Afghanistan were fertile grounds for radical Islamist groups, gaining more support in Central Asia.

4. The price of oil collapses

In December 1985, Saudi Arabia decided to alter its oil policy drastically. In six months, oil production in Saudi Arabia increased fourfold which led to a collapse of oil prices. The Soviet Union lost $20 billion per year. The reason for the new policy was that the Saudis feared that the Soviet invasion of Afghanistan was a first step to gain control of the oil fields in the Middle East. The historian Richard Pipes, an advisor to President Reagan in the 1980s, has claimed that the US did what they could to keep oil prices low as a part of their policy of weakening the Soviet Union. The leaders in the USSR now faced a difficult problem because oil money was needed to pay for imports of grain to the USSR.

5. Solidarity in Poland

In 1980, the Polish regime recognised that a union, not controlled by the government, could exist as a legal entity. Ten million Poles joined this union, **Solidarity**. It soon led to that Solidarity challenged the regime politically and in December 1981 the Polish government decided to introduce martial laws and ban Solidarity. An independent union organising millions of workers was sensational and posed a major challenge to the whole Eastern Bloc. The war in Afghanistan made it impossible for the Soviet army to intervene. Suslov a leading member in the Politburo said "*We simply cannot afford another Afghanistan.*"[106] When Gorbachev introduced his reforms, it affected the satellites in Eastern Europe. In 1988, there were massive strikes in Poland and the government made an agreement with Solidarity to end the strikes and to sit down in round-table talks. In February 1989, a decision was made to allow free elections in Poland. In the elections in June, Solidarity won 99 of 100 seats in the Senate and Poland got a non-communist Prime Minister. Solidarity had a major importance in breaking down communist control in the Eastern Bloc.

6. Growing economies in the developing world undermined Lenin's ideas about imperialism

Developments in the Third World further eroded support for the Soviet system. Countries that accepted Western investments and market economy had the fastest growing economies while countries with a socialist orientation were facing serious economic problems. Lenin's ideas about colonialism and imperialism were abandoned by economists even in the USSR.

---

[105] Gaddis, J. L., *The Cold War* (London: Penguin, 2007) p. 193.
[106] Sebestyen, V., *Revolution 1989: The Fall of the Soviet Empire*, p. 58.

B. Was the collapse of the Soviet system due to internal reasons?

1. Sixty years of communist rule

The effects of more than 60 years of communist rule had far reaching consequences. The agricultural sector never recovered from Stalin's collectivisation and 20 years of Stalinist terror had a profound effect on the Soviet society for generations. Decades of planned economy, during which communist leaders could ignore the reality of economic life had enormous consequences. Brehznev's rule is a good example of this where 40% of the state budget was used for military purposes in peace time. Gorbachev inherited a nation with serious structural weaknesses.

2. Planned economy did not generate growth

Was the collapse due to the economic system of the USSR, i.e., a **planned economy**? A planned economy means that a large proportion of the economy is owned and controlled by the state. Thousands of state planners or bureaucrats decided what to produce, when it should be produced and at what price. It has been described as a rigid command economy. In 1990, the USSR register one of its greatest grain harvests ever, but 40% of the harvest rotted or was eaten by insects . The same problems existed within the industrial sector. The ***nomenklatura, the old elite***, obstructed systematic reforms and new initiatives. Crockatt writes: "*…the new forces within the Soviet society encountered resistance from the old political structures and values.*"[107] McCauley concludes that "*only a market economy generates rising prosperity over decades.*"[108]

3. Gorbachev made mistakes

Most historians agree that the reforms opened a floodgate which led to a collapse. Did he reform this iron-system too much too soon? Crockatt writes… "*Once given rein, the direction of the newly released force of public opinion could not necessarily be controlled.*"[109]

- **The economy was transformed**

The **Law on Cooperatives** in 1987 permitted private ownership of businesses in the service, manufacturing and foreign trade sectors. Workers were allowed to leave collective farms. Between 1985 and 1988, 13,000 producing cooperatives were formed and 300,000 family-owned businesses. 50% of the service sector was suddenly in private hands.

The **Enterprise Law** transferred decision making from the central ministries to the enterprises. Managers in state-owned companies were now given much more power.

The **Law on Joint Ventures** allowed foreign ownership of companies and Crockatt describes the effects as 'explosive'.

Goldman argues "*shock therapy might have worked in a country where there were producers ready and waiting for the optimum market conditions.*"[110] When Gorbachev now reformed from above, there was no effective system for capital investment, credit, fiscal and monetary controls, i.e., institutions and administration necessary to organise a market economy.

Political changes

In 1988, Gorbachev announced in the UN that every nation had the right to choose its own government, i.e., a **rejection of the Brezhnev doctrine**. It didn't take long until both republics within the USSR, like the Baltic States, and the satellites in Eastern Europe demanded real independence: "*Nationalism within the Soviet republics could hardly have been given voice had it not been for glasnost.*"[111] There were 15 republics and more than 120 ethnic groups within the USSR and Gorbachev assumed that they would remain loyal if they were offered democracy. In late 1989, communism collapsed in Eastern Europe and the impression was that it had Gorbachev's tacit support.

---

[107] Crockatt, R., *The Fifty Years War*, p. 74.
[108] McCauley, M., *Russia, America and the Cold War: 1949-1991*, p. 115.
[109] Crockatt, R., *The Fifty Years War*, p. 344.
[110] Ibid, p. 350.
[111] Ibid, p. 346.

4. Lack of timing

The liberalisation coincided with an economic crisis where state incomes from reducing production of alcohol went down due, to Gorbachev's policies and, even more important, there was a fall in world **oil prices**. So the political reform programme was introduced in a severe economic crisis. If Lenin had once 'timed' the October revolution, Gorbachev did not time the right moment for this drastic transformation.

Soviet economic growth 1986–1991 (%)

Year	1986	1987	1988	1989	1990	1991
Economic growth (%)	2.3	1.6	4.4	2.4	–4.0	–15.0

Gorbachev writes in his memoirs: "*I thought we had a system that could be improved. Instead I learned that we had a system that needed to be replaced.*"[112] It is, however, possible to argue that the collapse of the Soviet system, i.e., the end of the Cold War, was due to both external and internal factors.

5. The conflict with Yeltsin

Yeltsin and Gorbachev had been enemies ever since Yeltsin had been dismissed from the politburo in 1987. **The Congress of People's Deputies offered him an unexpected opportunity to come back**. In 1991 when he was elected **president** of Russia, he became a driving force in the process of **keeping Russia out of the union**. Without Russia there could be no Soviet Union. When finally the CIS was formed, the USSR ceased to exist and this deprived Gorbachev his platform. Is it possible to argue that animosity between two leaders might cause the fall of an empire? Margret Thatcher writes: "*If the two of them had been able to sink their differences […] the reforms might have been renewed.*"[113] Yeltsin writes: '*But why hide it—the motivations for many of my actions were embedded in our conflict, which had arisen in earnest just prior to the central committee plenum in 1987 that led to my being ousted from the politburo.*"[114]

Historiography

Many historians emphasise that the collapse of the Soviet system was due to an **internal collapse**. Bell writes: "*The essential point still seems to be that they contributed to a drama which started within the Soviet Union.*" Dobrynin, the Soviet Ambassador in Washington, concludes: "*The fate of the Soviet Union was decided inside our country.*"[115] Shevardnadze, the Foreign Minister, agrees and points out that Soviet Russia had once survived WWII. "*Neither Hitler or Reagan could do it,*"[116] he said, talking about breaking up the Soviet Union from the outside.

The **key** issue is to determine to what extent this internal collapse was affected by **external factors**. You will find a wide range of explanations. Kennan, the father of Truman's containment policy in 1947, writes: "*The suggestion that any Administration had the power to influence decisively the course of a tremendous domestic political upheaval in another great country on the other side of the globe is **simply childish***" and that the "*Republican Party leadership won the Cold War is intrinsically silly.*"[117] The historian Richard Pipes, also an adviser to Reagan, found the statement astonishing and quoted Kennan in his famous Mr X article of 1947: "*It is entirely possible for the US to influence by its actions the international development, both within Russia, and throughout the international Communist movement.*"[118] The idea behind Kennan's containment policy had once been based on the assumption that containment would "*encourage an internal implosion in the Soviet Union.*" Those supporting the view of the importance of external pressure emphasise the importance of Reagan's 'systematic challenge'. But there are few historians who explicitly claim that it was Reagan who made the Soviet system collapse.

---

[112] Bell, P. M. H. and Gilbert, M., *The World Since 1945: An International History*, p. 357.
[113] Thatcher, M., *The Downing Street Years* (London: Harper Press, 2011) p. 803.
[114] Yeltsin, B., *The Struggle for Russia* (New York: Crown, 1994) p. 16.
[115] Bell, P. M. H. and Gilbert, M., *The World Since 1945: An International History*, pp. 387-388.
[116] Bell, P. M. H. and Gilbert, M., *The World Since 1945: An International History*, p. 387.
[117] *New York Times*, 28 October 1992
[118] *New York Times*, 6 November 1992

Crockatt writes: "*The Soviet economy was not on the point of collapse when Gorbachev came to power. The catastrophic decline in the late 1980s was a direct result of Gorbachev's policies.*"[119] But he makes a further distinction between 'failures of the system' and Gorbachev's policies. Hence he is making a distinction between the two main points if we want to discuss 'internal reasons': "*…the collapse would not have taken place* (a collapse as a result of Gorbachev's policies) *had not serious structural weaknesses existed.*" Gorbachev wanted to save socialism but would not use force to do so. Gaddis concludes that he could not achieve one without abandoning the other and that his goals were incompatible, hence Gorbachev made important mistakes.

It is, however, possible to find a **combination** of these two interpretations. External pressure affected the USSR but there were also problems within the empire, which led to the collapse. McCauley concludes that "*monocausal answers are no longer acceptable.*"[120] Bell believes that internal factors were more important than external factors, but he accepts that both are of importance: "***the Soviet Union collapsed primarily through internal failures, exacerbated but not created by external pressure***."[121]

Cold War Leader 5: Ronald Reagan US President, 1981–1989

1981

Ronald Reagan came to power in 1981. It was after the Soviet Union had invaded Afghanistan and the new President had announced a tough stance in his campaign for presidency. In 1981, he said: "*So far détente has been a one way street which the Soviet Union had used to pursue its own aims…(and) reserve the right to commit any crime, to lie, to cheat…when you do business with them-even in détente-keep that in mind.*"[122] Even though the US economy suffered from a recession, the 1982 military budget was increased by 13%. The USSR should be exposed to a '**systematic challenge**'. New weapons should be developed which would be difficult to counter for the Soviets. New weapons would make Soviet weapons obsolete (out of date) which would put pressure on the Soviet economy. The Reagan administration started the largest peacetime military build-up in US history. Between 1981 and 1988, military spending went from $117 billion per year to $290 billion.

In 1977, the USSR started to deploy SS-20 intermediate range weapons in Eastern Europe. The Soviets saw this as a response to activities from the US and NATO. NATO responded by announcing the deployment of Pershing 2 and Cruise missiles in Western Europe. It led to years of discussions and anti-war demonstrations in Western Europe. The Western Alliance started this deployment in 1983 despite the protests. The USSR responded by calling off the Strategic Arms Reduction Talks (START) the same year.

In 1983, Reagan announced his **Strategic Defense Initiative (SDI)** better known as the '**Star Wars**' project. The aim was to develop a totally new and expensive technology, a **shield** protecting the US in **space**. The SDI project played a major role in arms talks in the 1980s. It was a part of '**the systematic challenge**' of the USSR.

In October 1983, Reagan ordered US forces to invade Grenada, where a 1979 *coup d'état* had established a Marxist-Leninist government. It was the first military operation conducted by US forces since the Vietnam War, and it resulted in a US victory, but 19 US soldiers were killed and 116 wounded.

The same year, Reagan described the USSR as an '**evil empire**' in a famous speech. The year 1983 represents the lowest point in what is normally described as the 'Second Cold War.'

The years 1981–1985, Reagan's first four year in office, were problematic from another point of view: the Soviet leadership suffered from health problems. Between 1982 and 1985, three General Secretaries passed away: Brezhnev, Andropov, and Chernenko. This fact made a constructive dialogue with summit meetings very difficult to organise and Reagan's first four years in office must be characterised as years of confrontation and no constructive talks.

---

[119] Crockatt R., *The Fifty Years War*, p. 341.
[120] McCauley, M., *Russia, America and the Cold War*, p. 4.
[121] Bell, P. M. H. and Gilbert, M., *The World Since 1945: An International History*, p. 388.
[122] Williamson, D., *Europe and the Cold War 1945-91*, p. 171.

1985

This year represents an opening in the relations between the two superpowers when Gorbachev came to power. Gorbachev wanted a constructive dialogue because he realised that the Soviet economy could not bear the costs for the army. Reagan on the other hand genuinely feared a nuclear showdown.

1986

The second summit meeting between Gorbachev and Reagan in **Reykjavik**, Iceland, was an astonishing conference. Gorbachev announced that he was prepared to **withdraw his SS-20 missiles** from Europe, if the US withdrew their Pershing and cruise missiles, i.e., an acceptance of Reagan's 'zero-option' solution. Until now it had been rejected by the USSR. He also proposed a **50% reduction of all long-range missiles**. In return, Gorbachev wanted the Americans to call off the Star Wars project (**SDI**) but Reagan refused to abandon his project. Gorbachev then shocked the Americans by proposing **the abolition of all nuclear weapons** within 10 years. Reagan's commitment to the SDI resulted in no agreement being made. But the meeting had shown that far-reaching agreements could be made.

In 1986, it became known that funds from arms deals with Iran had been secretly used to finance Contras in Nicaragua, fighting the left-wing government in the country. It violated US laws and Reagan claimed that he was unaware of the operations. This scandal severely affected the popularity of the President in the US.

1987: The Washington Treaty (or **INF Treaty**) was signed. All missiles based on land in Europe and Asia, with a range of between 500 to 5,500 kilometres should be destroyed within three years. A dispute which had lasted over 10 years, involving most of the allies of the two superpowers, had finally been brought to an end.

1988: The same year an agreement between the superpowers was made in Geneva on the ending of the war in **Afghanistan**. Later this year Gorbachev announced that Soviet armed forces should be **reduced by 500,000 soldiers**, without any demands on US reductions (a unilateral reduction). He also announced a gradual withdrawal of troops from the GDR (East Germany), Czechoslovakia and Hungary. Gorbachev announced that the USSR would no longer interfere in the internal affairs of the satellites, i.e., the **Brezhnev Doctrine was dead**.

When Reagan visited Moscow for the fourth summit in 1988, a journalist asked the president if he still considered the Soviet Union the evil empire. "*No*," he replied, "*I was talking about another time, another era.*"[123]

In conclusion: Reagan had resigned when communism collapsed in Eastern Europe in 1989 and when the USSR collapsed in 1991. Many have argued that his policies, a substantial increase of military expenditures, caused the fall of the Soviet Empire. **But it must be emphasised that the Soviet Union did not accelerate military spending after President Reagan's military build-up started.** Reagan, a fierce anti-communist, **must be credited for building a constructive dialogue when Gorbachev came to power.** Reagan's vice president George Bush was much more reluctant to see Gorbachev as a man of peace, during the eight Reagan years. Gorbachev and Reagan ended a conflict which had lasted for more than 40 years.

There are historians who argue that it was Reagan's Systematic Challenge which finally caused the fall of the empire. This has been contradicted by those who argue that the USSR did not respond with a military build-up, during the first Reagan years. The USSR had already used 40% of their state budget for military needs during the Brezhnev era. Most tend to argue that the fall of the empire was mainly due to internal weaknesses of the Soviet system.

Cold War Leader 6: Mikhail Gorbachev Leader of the USSR, 1985–1991

1985: The fall of the USSR is one of the most important events in the 20th century. The empire ceased to exist and the satellites in Eastern Europe were free from Soviet control. The Soviet involvement in Afghanistan also came to an end and a number of new states emerged from the Soviet empire.

---

[123] Bell, P. M. H. and Gilbert, M., *The World Since 1945: An International History*, p. 367.

The collapse of the Soviet empire also brought an end to the Cold War—it is therefore necessary to explain this development as a part of the Cold War.

Michael Gorbachev was elected General Secretary at the age of 54. He introduced a number of breathtaking reforms both domestically and internationally. It must be noticed that Gorbachev initially was a Leninist who made attempts to reform the system in order to make it survive.

Gorbachev's plan for reconstruction contained two main points:

1. Cooperation with the West to end the Cold War in order to reduce the costs of the arms race.

2. A reconstruction of the Soviet empire. The key words were:
   - *glasnost* ('openness')
   - *perestroika* ('restructuring')
   - *demokratizatsiya* ('democratization')

Main events during the Gorbachev era (with emphasis on the Cold War):

1985: Gorbachev made his first visit to the West, France, as Soviet leader. He proposed that the superpowers should reduce their strategic weapons by 50%. Gorbachev and Reagan met annually in four different summits. The first took place in **Geneva** in 1985. No major agreements were made except for the fact that they agreed to meet again. There had been no summits for five years so the meeting was important in establishing personal relations.

1986: At the 27th Party Congress, Gorbachev announced that he believed that far-reaching economic reforms were needed and that the war in Afghanistan was a 'bleeding wound'.

The second summit meeting between Gorbachev and Reagan in **Reykjavik,** Iceland, was an astonishing conference. Gorbachev announced that he was prepared to **withdraw** his **SS-20 missiles** from Europe, if the US withdrew their Pershing and cruise missiles i.e. an acceptance of Reagan's 'zero-option' solution. It had until now been rejected by the USSR. He also proposed a **50% reduction of all long-range missiles**. In return Gorbachev wanted the Americans to call off the Star Wars project (**SDI**) but Reagan refused to abandon his project. Gorbachev then shocked the Americans by proposing **the abolition of all nuclear weapons** within ten years. Reagan's commitment to the SDI resulted in no agreement being made.

1987: The Washington Treaty (or **INF Treaty**) was signed. All missiles based on land in Europe and Asia, with a range of between 500 to 5500 kilometres should be destroyed within three years. A dispute which had lasted over ten years, involving most of the allies of the two superpowers, had finally been brought to an end.

1988: The same year an agreement between the superpowers was made in Geneva on the ending of the war in **Afghanistan**. Later this year Gorbachev announced that Soviet armed forces should be **reduced by 500 000 soldiers**, without any demands on US reductions (a unilateral reduction). He also announced a gradual withdrawal of troops from the GDR (East Germany), Czechoslovakia and Hungary. Gorbachev announced that the USSR would no longer interfere in the internal affairs of the satellites i.e. the **Brezhnev Doctrine was dead**.

1989: In early 1989, round-table talks in Poland led to free elections being scheduled to June the same year. In this first free election in a communist state since the 1940s, Solidarity won 99 out of 100 seats in the Senate. Poland was the first country in the Eastern Bloc to get a non-communist Prime Minister. In May Hungary announced that the Iron Curtain would be opened. It was a test of Gorbachev's willingness to abandon the Brehznev doctrine. This year communist rule was brought to an end in the satellites: **Poland, Hungary, GDR, Bulgaria and Romania,** without the USSR intervening. The withdrawal of Soviet troops from Afghanistan was completed. **The Cold War had been brought to an end.**

'Gorbymania', enthusiasm for Gorbachev, swept around the world but in the USSR communist hardliners saw it as a betrayal of the Soviet Union and the sacrifices its people had made during WWII.

1990: In 1990, Gorbachev was elected to a new office: president of the USSR. To Gorbachev this was a way of creating his own political platform independent of the Communist Party. In March the Congress had removed article 6 in the constitution i.e. the Communist Party no longer had a political monopoly. The economy was now in a critical situation. **The GNP went down by 4% in 1990 and 15% in 1991.** There were severe shortages of basic food supplies, i.e., meat and sugar. Communist hardliners were criticizing Gorbachev and **nationalism in the Baltic States and Georgia posed an enormous problem** to Gorbachev who had committed himself to democratic solutions. In the Congress of People's Deputies **Yeltsin** had been offered a new platform criticizing the president. Gorbachev's solution to the mounting nationalist problems was a new **Union Treaty** giving the republics within the Soviet Union far more autonomy. But it didn't seem to satisfy some republics and by the end of the year many hardliners were given key positions in the Soviet government. Due to this, foreign minister **Eduard Shevardnadze resigned** dramatically in December claiming that 'Dictatorship is coming'.

When the two German states were allowed to merge in 1990, the USSR accepted that the West German state could also be a member of NATO. The USSR supported UN decisions in the Gulf War, i.e., supported the Americans in this conflict, hence showing that the Cold War was over.

1991: In January 1991, local branches of the KGB and armed forces worked together to seize the TV tower in **Vilnius in Lithuania**, most likely without any foreknowledge of Gorbachev. **14 civilians were killed.** This disastrous clash made a new Union Treaty even more important to Gorbachev.

Boris Yeltsin was elected president of Russia in June 1991 and the question of Russia's willingness to sign a new Union Treaty became a key question. Without a Russian membership in the union, the Soviet Union was dead.

In August, just before a new Union Treaty were to be signed, communist hardliners made an attempted **coup**. Yeltsin took the leadership in Moscow against the coup, and it collapsed.

The coup was seen as a collapse of the old system, which Gorbachev to some extent was seen as a part of. **Yeltsin's authority gained from the coup, while Gorbachev was more or less in the hands of the Russian president.**

In December, the leaders from Russia, Ukraine and Belarus declared that the **USSR no longer existed** and founded the **Commonwealth of Independent States** (CIS). Later the same month it was extended and eleven former republics joined the CIS.

On **25 December Gorbachev had to resign**. Without a Soviet Union, Gorbachev had no political platform. On 31 December, the USSR formally ceased to exist. Yeltsin was the new leader in Russia.

In conclusion: Gorbachev wanted to reform the Soviet system in order to make it survive. For different reasons this failed and the empire collapsed. The war in Afghanistan was brought to an end, Soviet control of Eastern Europe ended and the USSR ceased to exist. **The Cold War had been brought to an end**. Gorbachev witnessed this process without using violence. **He is probably the most important individual in bringing an end to the Cold War.**

4. The Coming of the Second Cold War and the Collapse of the USSR

Exercise 19: To what extent did military expenditure lead to the collapse of the USSR?

(Discuss the importance of military expenditure and compare this with other reasons.)

Yes, military expenditure caused the collapse of the Soviet system:

1. Write about the size of GNP in the USSR and how much was used for military needs (40% of the state budget). It is also a good point to compare Soviet GNP with GNP of US/allies.
2. Write about how the Soviets used resources for closing the missile gap after the Cuban Missile Crisis. A large proportion of her scientists were used for military needs.
3. Show how the Soviet economy began to stagnate when they embarked on the policy of closing the missile gap.
4. Show how engagements in other countries especially in the Third World consumed resources. The war in Afghanistan and the conflict with China put additional strain on the economy.

There were other reasons which led to the collapse:

1. Planned economy did not generate sufficient growth. This command economy lay behind the stagnation in that state planners did not promote new techniques and methods. It is not a coincidence that the Soviet system did not realise the importance of computer technology and just continued to plan for 'heavy industry'.
2. Gorbachev introduced too much too soon. After decades of repressive policies he suddenly allowed freedom of speech, Glasnost. There had also been decades of state control of the economy and when private companies were eventually allowed they had to co-exist with state planners who opposed Gorbachev's policies. Different nationalities within the Soviet Union used Glasnost to express their unwillingness to be Soviet republics, which led to a disintegration. By trying to control alcohol consumption the state lost revenues. Together with a collapse in international oil prices this led to a collapse of the Soviet economy. This sudden collapse was not expected by most experts and the reason for it is that Gorbachev introduced too many reforms within too short a time period.
3. There was strong support for nationalism both in the satellites in Eastern Europe and in some Soviet Republics.
4. Brezhnev must bear responsibility for not reforming the economy during the stagnation years.
5. Reagan's systematic challenge didn't cause a sudden collapse of the Soviet system. But you can argue that Reagan's increase in military spending, the SDI, support for the guerrillas in Afghanistan, etc., convinced Gorbachev that far-reaching reforms were needed and that an understanding with the West was necessary. Reagan's policy is one important explanation of Gorbachev's reforms which led to the disintegration of the Soviet system.

   Remember, Tocqueville had once expressed the danger of reforming a bad government.

6. The Soviet system was eroded step by step by outside ideas about Western consumption, culture and religion. Finally, there was a lack of support for the system, even within the USSR.
7. The development in Poland with Solidarity had a major impact in the satellites. Poland was the first country to elect a non-communist Prime Minister in 1989. This year the communist systems collapsed in all the satellites.

Historiography: Most historians support the view that the reasons for the collapse are a combination between different factors. However, there is a tendency to emphasise causes from within the system. McCauley writes that monocausal answers are no longer acceptable.

Conclusion: As has been written earlier, there are a wide range of explanations and there will be many 'schools of interpretation' trying to emphasise different points. We support McCauley's view that it is a combination between different causes. In your answer try to emphasise what you think are the most important reasons.

Exercise 20: To what extent did external pressure lead to the collapse of the Soviet system?

(An open question in Paper 2 would not be phrased like this. But this question, open or not, could be asked in Paper 3 as well.)

Yes, external pressure made the Soviet Union collapse:

1. Write about the Soviet attempts to close the missile gap from the early 1960s and link it to the stagnation of the Soviet economy.
2. Write about the size of the GNP in the Soviet Union compared to the GNP of the US and her allies.
3. Write that a large proportion of GNP was used for military reasons. It is a strong argument to claim that this must have affected the Soviet economy in a negative way.
4. Write about Reagan's systematic challenge and his SDI project which put additional strains on the Soviet economy.
5. The Sino-Soviet split made the Soviet Union place large proportion of her army to guard the border with China.
6. The war in Afghanistan was a military, political and economic disaster.
7. The impact of Western consumption and spiritual influences from the new Polish Pope and Islam in Central Asia eroded the support for the Soviet regime.

(Continued)

8. Strong nationalist feelings in the satellites challenged Soviet authority. In Poland, the Solidarity movement challenged Soviet authority.

No, internal reasons led to the collapse:

1. Write about the Soviet command economy which didn't generate growth comparable to the growth of the market economies. The *Nomenklatura* also obstructed a modernisation of the Soviet system.
2. Brezhnev ignored the need for reforms in the 1970s.
3. Repressive policies from the regime had alienated a large proportion of the population. This was especially important in the Baltic Republics where many people wanted independence.
4. Gorbachev reformed too much too soon. It was difficult, if not impossible to allow freedom of speech, market economy and free elections in a society without any democratic tradition. He opened a floodgate of reforms in a situation where there was strong external pressure and where oil prices had more or less collapsed. He was tested in many areas. Let's look at one to exemplify his problems: How do you combine Glasnost or openness, Baltic nationalism and Gorbachev's desire to strengthen the Soviet system? Gorbachev's détente also led to the USSR being deprived of her 'outside enemy'. This outside enemy had partly united the country and justified economic hardship. The enemy had now disappeared but the economy collapsed. Few understood this.
5. There was a lot of nationalism in Soviet republics.

Conclusion: We support a combination between internal and external factors.

Exercise 21: To what extent was Gorbachev responsible for the collapse of the Soviet system?

Yes: In 1985, Gorbachev became General Secretary of the Communist Party, i.e., the leader of the USSR. For 70 years the Communist Party had organised a rigid system where freedom of speech, the right to organise political parties, etc. had not existed. It was also a planned economy, i.e., private enterprises were not allowed. Within a couple of years he had announced:

1. In 1986, foreign policy versus the capitalists was fundamentally changed. Genuine co-operation and coexistence with the capitalist states was desirable. The 'outside enemy' had for years been a justification for economic hardship.
2. In 1988, censorship and the Brezhnev Doctrine were abolished. In the same year private enterprises were allowed.
3. In 1989, there were elections to the Congress of People's Deputies where voters were allowed to cross out names of candidates. Twenty per cent of the delegates were not elected. It was a significant step towards free elections in the USSR. In Eastern Europe, the communist regimes collapsed with tacit support from Gorbachev. Hungary and Poland were the first to allow free elections which gave power to non-communist parties.
4. In 1990, the directing role of the Communist Party was brought to an end by a change in the constitution.
5. Far-reaching economic reforms were introduced in 1987 and 1988 which contributed to the collapse.

Gorbachev allowed a free debate, private companies, ended the Communist Party's monopoly of power, the satellites to choose their own governments and made peace with the outside enemy—after 70 years of iron rule. It was probably almost beyond imagination to most Soviet citizens. The difficulties were expected: the *nomenklatura* didn't want to co-operate in the destruction of their power. Nationalism was strong in many republics and in the satellites. It can be argued that it was too much too soon and that Gorbachev must bear responsibility for the collapse.

Crockatt writes that the Soviet economy was not on the point of collapse when Gorbachev came to power and that the decline in the late 1980s was a direct result of Gorbachev's policies.

No, it was not Gorbachev who caused the collapse:

1. The Soviet system was doomed even without Gorbachev. Evidence for this is the stagnation of the economy which can be traced back to the 1960s.
2. No genuine attempts to reform the economy were made during the Brezhnev years.
3. The basic problem was that planned economy didn't generate sufficient growth over a longer period.
4. This internal weakness was exacerbated by external pressure (military expenditure, nationalism, the war in Afghanistan and Reagan' systematic challenge).
5. Repressive policies had alienated large proportions of the population. Support for the regime had also been eroded by the impact of Western consumption and spiritual influences from the Catholic Pope and Islam. This was a long process which we cannot blame Gorbachev for.

Conclusion: The problems which Gorbachev faced were to some extent caused by long-term events and that the system had been suffering from internal weaknesses for a long time. Gorbachev's attempts to reform this system resulted in additional problems and contributed to the collapse because he had unleashed forces he couldn't control.

Exercise 22: Examine the importance of détente in ending the Cold War.

(The arguments to be used are presented in two parts to show you the points more clearly.)

First of all you have to discuss the term détente, i.e., lessening of tension between the superpowers. Détente was introduced with Khrushchev and Eisenhower in the late 1950s. This does however not explain the end of the Cold War. Détente from the perspective of ending the Cold War does become more relevant if we discuss détente in the 1970 and détente with Gorbachev and Reagan.

Yes, détente contributed to the end of the Cold War:

1. Discuss the détente process in the 1970s: the SALT-agreements, the Helsinki Accords and Ostpolitik. Right wingers in the US thought that the real outcome of this process was that the Soviets were able to expand their influence and the failure of the détente process is one explanation to the advent of Reagan and the Second Cold War (Halliday has questioned this view in his writings, see the end of détente). A lasting result from this period of détente was probably that personal contacts were established which would have some significance in the 1980s.

2. Détente with Gorbachev and Reagan: there are many examples of major events and agreements which finally brought the Cold War to an end: the annual summit meetings, the new foreign policy of the Soviet Union versus capitalist states from 1986, withdrawal from Afghanistan, the INF Treaty from 1987, the rejection of the Brezhnev doctrine in 1988, Soviet troops withdrawn from Eastern Europe and the unification of the German states. These agreements were accomplished by two politicians, who must be recognised for their achievements: Reagan was committed to fight communism but was flexible enough to make agreements with this 'evil empire'. It was Gorbachev who was the driving force in this process and his initiatives had a major importance in ending the Cold War peacefully.

No, it was not détente which ended the Cold War:

1. Détente was necessary for the Soviet Union and Gorbachev if the reform process should succeed. What was it that forced Gorbachev to enter a policy of détente?

2. The cost for the Cold War was unbearable to the Soviet Union. The correlation between military expenditures and the stagnation can be seen from the 1960s.

3. Another problem was that planned economy didn't generate sufficient growth and that the Soviet GNP could not compete with the US's GNP. Détente was needed. These internal factors resulted in that an understanding with the West became necessary.

4. Reagan's 'systematic challenge' made an agreement with the West even more important.

5. The Chernobyl accident, the war in Afghanistan and a collapse of oil prices, made an arms agreement with the West even more important. Détente was needed.

Conclusion: Internal problems in the USSR made it necessary for Gorbachev to reduce military costs, if he should succeed with his *perestroika*. Problems in the USSR and external pressure made détente necessary, and détente led to the end of the Cold War.

5. Germany, China, Vietnam and Cuba during the Cold War

Finally, we will summarise how the Cold War affected four countries: Germany, China, Vietnam and Cuba. The examples are chosen from different IB regions. It is very useful in exams to be able to discuss one or two countries from a Cold War perspective. Most of the points that will be outlined below have already been discussed in the guide.

How was Germany affected by the Cold War?

1945–1950: With the defeat of Germany, the most powerful state in continental Europe didn't exist politically and militarily. There was a power vacuum in the centre of Europe. Strategically, this **power vacuum** was of enormous importance for the Cold War.

A number of war-time conferences, ending with Yalta and Potsdam, formed an agreement where Germany should be divided into **zones of occupation**. An **Allied Control Council** where each occupational country had veto power should govern the country. A Western zone in the eastern zone, i.e., Berlin, was a part of the solution. The **Berlin problem** became one of the most difficult problems in the Cold War because it opened up the Iron Curtain. Approximately 200,000 people fled each year between 1945 and 1961, until the Berlin Wall was erected. No final agreement was made over reparations and the Soviets were left to take what they could in their zone.

Co-operation between the occupational forces never worked. As early as 1946, there were signs of a political and economic division of Germany. Soon there were plans to form an independent German state in the West. **Byrnes's Stuttgart Speech** in 1946 is one example of this. When a currency reform in the Western zones was announced in 1948, Stalin decided to cut off all land routes to Berlin. The **Berlin Airlift** was the first real crisis in Europe after the war.

In 1947, the US had announced the Marshall Aid Programme. It had a major impact on both West Germany and Western Europe and led to massive industrial growth with a GNP growth in Europe of around 15–25% annually. Financial stability returned. Politically, the development in 1947 was a **major turning point**. It was now clear that the US would play an active world role and it is hardly surprising that **Stalin now tightened his grip in Eastern Europe**.

In 1949, NATO was formed, partly as a result of the **Berlin Crisis**. The same year a **West German and an East German state** were proclaimed.

1950–1960: From 1950, the Americans saw the rearmament of Germany as a keystone in their European Cold War policy. The question of allowing Germany to be a full member of NATO, the creation of a German army, remained a major issue between the superpowers. Stalin feared this development and in 1952 proposed that Germany should be a united, neutral country. This was rejected by the West.

In 1953, when Stalin had passed away, there was an **uprising** against the communist regime in East Germany. It was crushed by the Russians with troops and tanks.

In 1954, formal restrictions for not allowing a German army were removed and West **Germany became a member of NATO in 1955**. The same year the **Warsaw Pact** was formed and **East Germany** became a member of this pact. From 1955, the two German states were rearmed.

In 1955, the Foreign Minister in West Germany, Walter Hallstein, laid down his **Hallstein Doctrine**: West Germany refused to recognise East Germany and would break off diplomatic relations with any government acknowledging East Germany.

In 1958, Khrushchev declared his first **Berlin ultimatum**: he demanded that all foreign occupation troops must leave Berlin within six months. If not, the USSR would unilaterally hand over the control of Berlin to East Germany. This would force the Western powers to deal with a regime they had not, and could not, recognise (see the **Hallstein Doctrine**). The deadline passed without anything happening. Khrushchev had been invited to the US and didn't want to press his point.

1960–1970: The migration from East Germany threatened the existence of the East German state. In August 1961, the **Berlin Wall was erected**. In October, the situation was very tense and tanks from both sides faced each other for 16 hours at Checkpoint Charlie. But the erection of the wall led to Berlin becoming less problematic from a superpower perspective, the gap was closed.

In 1966, the Social Democrat Willy Brandt was appointed Foreign Minister in West Germany. In 1967, diplomatic relations were established with Romania, a rejection of the Hallstein Doctrine. It was the beginning of the 'German détente' process: **Ostpolitik**. Brandt became Chancellor in 1969 and he embarked on a more independent role versus the US, his Ostpolitik.

1970–1980: In 1970, the **Treaty of Moscow** was signed between West Germany and the USSR. The existing frontiers in Europe should be respected, i.e., an acceptance that Germany had been moved 300 kilometres to the West. The border with Poland, the Oder-Neisse line, was fully recognised by West Germany and Poland in the **Treaty of Warsaw** in 1970. In the **Four-Power-Agreement**, the occupational powers of Germany recognised their joint rights to Berlin. **The East German-West German Basic Treaty from 1972** was a formal recognition of two German states and the links from West Germany to West Berlin were accepted. The Helsinki agreement from 1975 also recognised the existing borders in Europe.

In 1977, the Soviets started to deploy their new **medium range missiles, SS-20s**, in central Europe. They could not reach the US but could target her allies in Europe, such as Germany. After long negotiations, the US and her allies in Europe started to deploy Pershing missiles in Western Europe. It led to public protests in many countries including West Germany. Brandt openly sided with the anti-war movement and it led to a major split in German society.

1980–1990: The opposition to the deployment of Pershing II missiles in Europe led to a mass **peace movement** and a **split** of the Social Democratic Party in West Germany. The Western powers wanted the USSR to withdraw their SS-20s, if the deployment of Pershings was cancelled. West Germany became a very important **mediator** between the US and the USSR. Chancellor Schmidt concluded: the Federal Republic gained worldwide importance never achieved before.

The German Chancellor Schmidt concluded that unrest and fear in the world and in Europe affected and endangered German-German cooperation: there were problems in Afghanistan, Africa and, next to Germany, Poland. If problems earlier in Germany had affected the Cold War, it was global problems in the late 1980s problems that affected the détente process in Germany.

The Social Democrats lost the elections in 1983 and the new Christian Democrat government led by Chancellor Kohl accepted the missiles. Kohl did his best to preserve good relations with the USSR and continue rapprochement. How important was this missile crisis in a Cold War perspective? The historian Ball concludes that the most serious threat to the Western alliance came with the Euromissile crisis of 1979–1983.

In the autumn of 1989, the communist regime in **East Germany collapsed**. During the night of 9–10 November, the Berlin Wall was knocked down. It had tacit support from Gorbachev.

In March 1990, there were free elections in East Germany. The Communist Party got 16% support, while the Social Democrats got 22% and the Christian Democrats 48% of the votes. In July in a meeting with Chancellor Kohl, Gorbachev accepted a German unification. In the **Two plus Four agreement**, the four occupational powers and the two German states accepted a **re-unification** which took place on 3 October 1990. Germany was allowed to join NATO after an agreement between the US and the USSR. Was this the real end of the Cold War?

How was China affected by the Cold War?

1945–1949: Between 1945 and 1949, the Civil War restarted between the Nationalists and the Communists. It didn't become a major Cold War event. The US initially provided the Nationalists with weapons but sent no combat troops. The importance of China was clear: it became one of five permanent members of the Security Council in the UN—represented however by the Nationalist government.

In 1949, the People's Republic of China was proclaimed.

1950–1960: In 1950, the **Sino-Soviet Friendship Treaty** was signed, and China was now considered by the West as a part of the 'Russian Bloc'. But Mao was never Stalin's client. Mao described China as a part of a 'vast intermediate zone', meaning that China did not belong to the USSR or the US. But China needed Soviet help which led to 'the leaning to one side' period in China. Mao realised that Soviet help was needed for the reconstruction of China and to conquer Taiwan.

Late in 1950, the Chinese decided to intervene in the **Korean War**. That the Chinese actively and successfully fought the Americans in Korea, 1950–1953 had major implications. The Americans now implemented their NSC-68 plan which led to a major **global** military build-up. China gained prestige in the Third World but was now isolated diplomatically and closely tied to the USSR. The war also led to firm commitments from the US to **Taiwan** and the French in **Indochina**. The Chinese stood behind the Viet Minh in **Vietnam** from the early 1950s. It is probable that without this Chinese support the Viet Minh had not been able to fight foreign intervention as successfully as they did.

China was seen by the Americans as a driving force behind both the Korean War and the Indochina War. The development in the region led to the formation of SEATO in 1954.

There were two major crises in Sino-American relation in the mid-1950s. There are some small **islands in the Taiwan Straits** between Taiwan and China, called Quemoy and Matsu islands. In 1954, the leader in Taiwan threatened China with a 'holy war'. China responded with an artillery bombardment in late 1954 and early 1955. The crisis led to a renewed US pledge to defend Taiwan. When the Chinese conquered another island, Tachen, the US Congress passed a resolution allowing Eisenhower to take whatever actions he found necessary. Eisenhower announced that aggression from the Communists would be met by nuclear arms. In 1958, there were new bombardments and again the **US threatened with the use of nuclear arms.**

In 1959, the USSR decided to pull out of an agreement where they had promised to provide China with nuclear technology. This process had taken two years and Mao reacted strongly. The nuclear issue was one of the reasons for the Sino-Soviet split.

Late 1950s–1970: The Great Leap Forward and the Cultural Revolution represent a period in Chinese history were she was **isolated** and was **opposing both the US and the USSR**. In 1964, they exploded their first atomic bomb and probably the most likely target was the USSR.

1970–1980: The **rapprochement to the US** in 1971 had major **Cold War implications**, from a Chinese perspective only comparable with the Korean War. That China was turning to the US sent **shock waves through the USSR**. A deep understanding between China and the US would totally isolate the USSR. It made the Soviets fully embark on the **détente** policy with the US. China was now accepted in the UN and there was Chinese support for bringing an end to the Vietnam War.

In 1972, **Nixon visited China**. In a joint declaration the Chinese stated that there was only one legal Chinese government and that Taiwan was one of its provinces. The US acknowledged that there was only **one China** and that they ultimately would withdraw their forces from Taiwan.

In the late 1970s, **Deng** had become the real leader of China. In 1978, the US broke off diplomatic relations with Taiwan and ended their defence agreement. China promised not to use force to unite the country. **The US gave full diplomatic recognition to China from 1 January 1979**. The Chinese thought that the US would control the USSR so it would not turn on China. This development angered the USSR and led to complications in the SALT II negotiations. Sino-American cooperation was seen as a danger in the USSR. In the 1970s, the Soviets had more troops guarding the Chinese border than they had in Europe. The Sino-Soviet split had major implications in the 1970s and 1980s. China and the US supported the FNLA in Angola while the Soviets supported the MPLA. In 1978, Vietnam invaded Cambodia. The USSR supported Vietnam while Cambodia was supported by China. China even attacked Vietnam. The triangular relationship between the three great powers of the Cold War continued under Deng in the early 1980s.

1980–1990: In the 1980s, China embarked on her policy of **modernisation** under the leadership of Deng and maintained **good relations with the US**. China and the US shared intelligence on the USSR and the US also started to export military equipment to China in 1980. The Reagan administration continued this policy. When the Soviet system started to deteriorate in the mid-1980s, the **USSR was no longer seen as an immediate threat**. Diplomatic relations were established at senior level and relations improved. In 1989, Gorbachev went to Beijing in an attempt to end the Sino-Soviet split. The visit took place amid mounting student demonstrations for democracy (which led to the massacre at Tienanmen square) but Gorbachev concluded that their relationship had reached a 'new stage'. China found her way out of the Cold War during the period of détente in the late 1980s while the USSR finally disintegrated.

How was Vietnam affected by the Cold War?

1945–1950: The start of the conflict in Indochina after 1945 was mainly the issue of **decolonisation**. The power vacuum left by the Japanese after WWII led to Ho Chi Minh being able to declare the independence of the People's Republic of Vietnam in 1945. This was opposed by the French who were keen to re-establish their colonies in South-East Asia. In 1946, a full-scale war started between the Viet Minh (the Vietnam League for Independence) and the French. The US was initially reluctant to support the French in Indochina but realised that cooperation with the French in Europe was very important after the war—hence support was given to them in Asia. With the advent of communist control of China, this country became involved in Vietnam. China was not prepared to accept a US ally south of her border so Vietnam was a part of the Cold War as early as in the 1940s.

1950–1960: The NSC-68 report in January 1950 advocated a substantial US military build-up. The Korean War had not started but recommendations in the report were affected by the development in Asia. China had been 'lost' to communism and a full-scale war had raged in Vietnam since 1946. With the start of the Korean War in June 1950, the US started to support the French in Vietnam.

China increased its support for the North in the 1950s. The Chinese feared the US would intervene. At the time of the Geneva agreement, the **US paid for more than 70%** of France's cost, showing the importance of the conflict. Stalin was more reluctant to support Ho in the war against the French. Khrushchev wrote that Stalin 'treated Ho insultingly' when he visited the USSR in 1950.

When **SEATO** was formed in 1954 one of the main aims was to prevent the spread of communism in South-East Asia. **Vietnam was now seen by the Americans as a key country in the region**. The region provided the Japanese with important markets and strategically it was of major importance, hence the idea of the **Domino Theory**. If Vietnam was lost there would be a chain reaction throughout Asia.

Both the USSR and China favoured a settlement over Vietnam at Geneva in 1954. China didn't want to risk US intervention on its southern borders. Vietnam was temporarily partitioned at the 17th parallel, and under the terms of the Geneva Accords, elections were to be held in 1956 to establish a unified government. Diem came to power in the South with US support. He soon cancelled the promised elections. The French left after Geneva and was replaced by the US. But the late 1950s was a calm period when the Communists were consolidating their control in the North.

No priority was given to the Vietnam question from the communist camp in the late 1950s. If Vietnam should be united it had to be through peaceful means. In the USSR, Khrushchev had introduced his policy of peaceful co-existence and China feared a US intervention.

In 1959, the North decided to unify the country by military means if necessary. In **1960**, the guerrilla in the South, the **Viet Cong, intensified its activities**. Kennedy responded by increasing US economic aid and military advisers from 400 to 16,000 men in 1963.

1960–1970: In the early 1960s, Khrushchev declared that the victory of socialism would be achieved through **wars of national liberation** in the Third World. Both the USSR and China now supported the North in its struggle and it was seen as a threat by the US. This was one reason for Kennedy's '**flexible response**' policy and Vietnam became a testing ground for flexible response. But Kennedy didn't escalate the conflict. When he was assassinated in 1963 there were around 16,000 US advisors in the country. Diem was also killed the same year in a coup d'état when some generals seized power. The US had foreknowledge about the coup. South Vietnam went through a very turbulent period where different generals led the country.

When Johnson started **to escalate the conflict in 1965**, Vietnam became the **centre of Cold War** struggle in the world. In 1967, there were more than 500,000 US soldiers (and from many other nations as well) in Vietnam but no victory was delivered. It deeply affected the US economy and jeopardised her international role in the struggle against communism. To Vietnam this war was a disaster with more than half a million foreign combat troops and extensive air bombing.

As a response to the escalation, both **the USSR and China promised military aid** in 1964 and 1965. Due to the Sino-Soviet split there were no co-ordinated actions. These undertakings were of a massive nature. In the late 1960s, China had 50,000 road and rail construction forces and anti-aircraft divisions in Vietnam. The Vietnam War led to a drastic increase of military installations in China.

1970s: The failures in Vietnam led to a new US foreign policy. Nixon introduced his 'Vietnamisation' of the war and his Nixon Doctrine. There should be a gradual withdrawal and the army of the South should fight the war. The US needed to get out of Vietnam and Nixon realised that it was necessary to establish good relations with both the USSR and China. The new policy of **linkage and détente** had other reasons than only Vietnam, but this conflict was probably the single most important reason behind détente and it totally changed the Cold War. The US now abandoned her policy of a **communist 'rollback'** and believed in a 'modus vivendi', i.e., a balance of power with the Soviets and China. The Sino-Soviet split showed that the communist world was no longer seen as one, monolithic, power where everything was led from Moscow. The Cold War Triangle had been established and the Vietnam War and the US desire to get out of this war 'with honour', had been an important part in this process. The US left Vietnam in 1973 and in 1975 the regime in the North conquered the South.

No country in the world has suffered as much as Vietnam from the Cold War. The war of decolonisation which started in 1946, soon developed into a Cold War conflict. **The country was at war for about 40 years fighting for its independence in a Cold War context.** But it didn't end with this. There were regional conflicts after 1975 resulting in a war against China in 1979. The casualties are difficult to estimate. Around 110,000 French soldiers died in the Indochina War. 58,000 US soldier died in the Vietnam War. The number of victims from Vietnam is very difficult to estimate but figures of more than 3–4 million have been mentioned by some. Even if it were fewer than this, the price in human suffering to the Vietnamese population is beyond imagination.

How was Cuba affected by the Cold War?

Castro seized power in Cuba in late 1959. In 1960, he declared himself a Marxist-Leninist. After that, the Cuban revolution became **a key area in the Cold War**. A communist state in the Caribbean was very difficult for the Americans to accept. When industries were nationalised in 1960, the US responded with a trade embargo and the same year Cuba signed a trade agreement with the USSR.

When Kennedy was elected US president, he inherited a plan from the CIA to attack Cuba with the help of Cuban exiles. The US trained the exiles, financed the operation and provided necessary equipment. The idea was that an attack would spur a spontaneous revolt in Cuba. When the plan was implemented at the **Bay of Pigs on 17 April 1961**, everything went wrong and the exiles were easily defeated by the Cuban army. It was a fiasco and Cuba became an obsession with Kennedy. There was no doubt that Kennedy still wanted to overthrow the Cuban regime. Only three days after the Bay of Pigs he gave Castro a warning that the US government would not hesitate in meeting its primary obligations, the security of the nation. The trade embargo was maintained, the CIA continued with sabotage actions and there was strong political and military pressure from the US.

It was in this situation that Khrushchev decided to offer medium range nuclear missiles to Cuba. There were many reasons for this, but the main reason was to protect Cuba against a second invasion. The Soviet leader also believed in 'many Vietnams' and Cuba could be a very important springboard for this in America. Medium range missiles on Cuba would also compensate for Soviet nuclear inferiority in terms of intercontinental nuclear missiles. **When the US found out about the missiles, it led to a 13-day crisis where the world stood at the brink of a nuclear Armageddon.** The solution was that the USSR would bring back the missiles if the US promised to not invade Cuba. Castro was left out from the negotiations.

But the US perception of a Cuba being a communist threat against US domination in the region was not solved with this. **The trade embargo was not lifted.**

Did the Americans have any reason to fear Castro? Castro, with the support of the USSR, wanted to inspire other countries in **Latin America** to turn to communism. He had ideological reason for this but it would also end Cuba's isolation in the region. There were revolutionary groups in Latin America receiving both training and weapons from Cuba. The most well known is Castro's friend and ex-minister Che Guevara. Both **Che Guevara** and Castro hoped to inspire '**many Vietnams**', a small nation fighting a non-conventional war against the Americans, but now in Latin America. In 1965, Che left Cuba to support a revolutionary group in Bolivia but was captured and shot in 1967. The attempts to spread the revolution in Latin America didn't succeed but these Cuban-inspired attempts worried the US.

The US trade embargo made Castro more or less totally dependent on Soviet aid. Consequently he was loyal to the USSR and supported the Warsaw Pact's invasion of Czechoslovakia in 1968. Castro was also an internationalist and the decolonisation process in Africa gave him an opportunity to show this commitment. In 1974, there was a revolution in Portugal. The year after, Portuguese colonies were granted independence, i.e., Mozambique, Guinea-Bissau and Angola. In **Angola** a bitter civil war started between the MPLA, FNLA and UNITA. These organisations were backed by several foreign states and MPLA was backed by the USSR. The FNLA was backed by the US, i.e., decolonisation became a part of the Cold War. To Castro, the decolonisation and a struggle for national liberation from foreign control, was a 'known experience'. Cuba intervened militarily and sent **17,000 Cuban troops** who were shipped by the Russians to support the MPLA in the civil war in Angola. The MPLA seized power in Angola and signed a friendship treaty with the USSR in 1976. Mozambique did the same the following year. In 1977, Castro again sent about **17,000 combat troops** to another conflict in Africa: the Ethiopian government wanted to expel Somalia from the Ogaden region. **Ethiopia** soon became a pro-Russian state.

Castro's involvement in the decolonisation process and his support for world revolution kept the conflict with the US alive. No possible détente with the US was in sight. But by supporting her Soviet ally in further globalisation of the Cold War in the Third World, Cuba would strengthen her bonds with the Russians upon whose support the **Cuban economy was so dependent**.

Castro was deeply involved in questions about a 'New economic order' in the 1970s. The Non-Aligned Movement became a tool for Castro's dedication to this question. It was problematic to the organisation that a close ally to the USSR was so active. Cuba was the only Latin-American country to join the organisation and served as its chair from 1979 to 1982.

In **1979**, a revolution broke out in Nicaragua in Central America. The Sandinistas, a coalition of Marxists, other radicals, and liberals, overthrew Anastasio Somoza after a guerrilla war. Somoza was considered as a corrupt leader even by President Carter in the US and close to a human disaster. There was much international support for the new regime which received substantial aid from many countries in Western Europe but soon also 2,500 advisors from Cuba. The aim of the new regime was to create a mixed economy and social and economic justice. The Carter administration also gave some aid in the beginning. With the advent of Reagan as President in January 1981, the situation changed and the US started to support the Contras, a right-wing group fighting the regime in Nicaragua. In 1983, the US invaded the small Caribbean island of **Grenada,** to overthrow a left-wing regime. Reagan claimed that the regime was turning the island into a '**Soviet-Cuban colony**'. There were both Cuban and North Korean advisers in Grenada who were overwhelmed by the Americans. When the Grenada invasion took place, the regime in Nicaragua urged the regime in Havana to recall its advisers in Nicaragua. It was believed that the Cuban presence might trigger a US invasion of Nicaragua; hence, the few Cubans had a major impact.

The developments in Nicaragua and Grenada are important events from a Cold War perspective. But Cuban activities in these two conflicts were of **minor importance**. The very fact that attention was paid to Cuba in these conflicts shows the importance of Cuba in Cold War relations.

6. The Nuclear Arms Race and the Major Arms Agreement

In 1945, the Americans exploded the first atomic bomb, and were followed by the Soviets in 1949. Soon, both superpowers developed hydrogen bombs. The next step was to develop ballistic missiles in the late 1950s. These missiles were soon installed on submarines. In the 1970s, individual missiles were equipped with multiple warheads. The 1970s also saw the development of anti-missile systems. Cruise missiles were created to fly low and hit their targets. Arms development is important and the main events and arms agreements will now be summarised:

What were the main events in the arms race 1945–1991?

1945 — **The first atomic bombs** were used against the Japanese cities of Hiroshima and Nagasaki. It ended WWII and, according to some, started the Cold War.

1949 — **The USSR** exploded their first bomb.

1952 — The US exploded their first **hydrogen bomb** and the year after the Russians did the same. In **1952, Britain** exploded their first atomic bomb.

1957 — The USSR shocked the Americans by launching an **ICBM and a satellite into the space**. The Americans followed months after.

1960 — First **submarines** equipped with nuclear missiles. They could remain submerged for two months.

1960 — France became a nuclear power.

1964 — **The Test Ban Treaty**, signed by the US and the USSR, prohibited nuclear tests in the atmosphere, in outer space and under water.

After the Cuban Missile Crisis, the Soviets decided to **close the missile gap** and to attain parity with the US, which they achieved in the early 1970s.

1964 — **The Chinese** exploded their first atomic bomb.

1968 — **The Non-Proliferation of Nuclear Weapons Treaty** signed by the US, the USSR and Britain. Nuclear technology should not be transferred to other countries. France and China did not sign.

1972 — **SALT I** signed. It comprised two treaties:

The Anti-Ballistic Missile Treaty (ABM). The number of ABM systems was limited to two each as it was considered that an effective anti-ballistic system could make one aggressor more tempted to start an attack (the ABM system would defend the aggressor).

The Interim Agreement on Offensive Arms. There should be a five-year freeze on levels of ICMBs and SLBMs. There were no limits on strategic long-range bombers or MIRVs (Multiple Independently targetable Re-entry Vehicles).

The SALT agreement was a recognition of Soviet nuclear equality. It was also a recognition that a nuclear war would mean the destruction of both, hence a war must by avoided at any cost. This was referred to as **Mutual Assured Destruction**. This was the idea behind the terror balance: fear of nuclear destruction would lead to peace.

1979

SALT II. This agreement went further than SALT I. It limited the number of ICBMs and SLBMs to 2,400 each and included a ceiling on the number of MIRVs. It was not ratified by the US Congress due to the invasion of Afghanistan but both governments kept to the agreement until 1986.

1970s: There was a new arms race in the 1970s. In 1977, the USSR started to deploy SS-20 intermediate-range weapons in Eastern Europe. The Soviets saw this as a response to activities from the US and NATO. NATO responded by deploying Pershing 2 and Cruise missiles in Western Europe. It led to years of discussions and anti-war demonstrations in Western Europe. The Western Alliance started this deployment in 1983 despite the protests.

1982

START, Strategic Arms Reduction Talks started while the dispute on medium range missiles was going on. The USSR called it off in 1983 when the first US Pershings were deployed in Europe.

1983

Reagan launches his SDI project. After 1985 Gorbachev was prepared to make far-reaching reductions of nuclear arms if Reagan gave up his SDI project—which he refused.

1987

The Washington Treaty (or **INF Treaty**) finally ended the dispute about intermediate missiles which had been a controversy for 10 years. All missiles based on land in Europe and Asia with a range of between 500 and 5,500 kilometres should be destroyed within three years. It was the first nuclear treaty ever to reduce, and not only limit, the number of missiles. It led to **the elimination of one category of weapons** and also a detailed programme for verification of weapon destruction by inspectors. We should emphasise that it only reduced the total nuclear arsenal by 5%.

1991

The signing of the START I Treaty which reduced the number of Soviet long-range nuclear warheads from 11,012 to 6,163 and US warheads from 12,646 to 8,556. The Cold War was now fading away. In 1991, the same year, the Warsaw Pact was dissolved. Gorbachev resigned on 25 December and the Soviet Union ceased to exist on 31 December 1991.

Notice: START I was followed by START II in 1993 which reduced the number of warheads to 3,000–3,500 on each side, by one-third. These two treaties resulted in substantial reductions of long-range nuclear weapons. When one adds the INF agreement from 1987 abolishing all medium-range missiles, the two sides achieved a lot. SALT I and II didn't reduce the number of weapons. It only put a ceiling on the maximum number of weapons.

Finally let's summarise the development of the number of long-range nuclear weapons. The arms race didn't end with the Soviets reaching parity in the early 1970s. Nor is it possible to trace the economic collapse of the USSR in the 1980s in these figures (notice that no figures exist for START I from 1991):

		1964	1968	1970	1972	1980	1990
US	ICBM	834	1,054	1,054	1,054	1,039	990
	SLBM	416	656	656	656	576	624
USSR	ICBM	200	800	1,300	1,527	1,330	1,710
	SLBM	120	130	280	560	937	930

Source: Brown Mooney Cold War to Détente.

Further Reading

One source that represents the **orthodox view** is Arthur M. **Schlesinger** Jr's *Origins of the Cold War, Foreign Affairs 46* (1967). A useful book covering the whole Cold War written by a leading **revisionist** is **Walter LaFeber**'s *America, Russia and the Cold War 1945–2002*. This book can also be used as a course book. **Post-revisionism** can be represented by **John Lewis Gaddis** in *The United States and the Origins of the Cold War*. His *We Now Know—Rethinking the Cold War* (1997) is an analysis of the Cold War from its origins to the Cuban Missile Crisis and it includes new archival evidence from the Soviet bloc. His view on Stalin must be described as historiographically 'orthodox'.

Martin **McCauley** has written books explaining both the origins and the end of the Cold War which include many useful primary documents: *Origins of the Cold War 1941–1949* and *Russia, America and the Cold War*.

Other possible course books covering the whole period are: *The World since 1945: An International History* by P. M. H. **Bell** which is a very well written book about the Cold War. A similar book with the same title is *The World Since 1945: A History of International Relations* by C. **McWilliams** and H. **Piotrowski**. *The Cold War: An International History 1947–1991* by S. J. **Ball** is a very good and useful source with many first-hand accounts from key individuals from the Cold War. Richard **Crockatt**'s book *The Fifty Years War* is a very well written account about the Cold War. There are many references to scholars who have investigated different Cold War issues. It is a very good source if you want to get information about where to find different in-depth studies for Internal Assessment or Extended Essays. David **Williamson** has written a textbook for A-level use, *Europe and the Cold War 1945–1991*.

If you want to find documents from the Cold War, J. **Hanimäki** and O. A. **Westad**'s *The Cold War: A History in Documents and Eyewitness Accounts* is a very useful source. There are also many useful internet sources: The **Avalon project** at Yale Law Schools has published a number of documents in history and diplomacy and we strongly recommend http://www.yale.edu/lawweb/avalon/avalon.htm. A very interesting source is the '**America Rhetoric**' site where you can both read and listen to many speeches made by American decision makers (http://americanrhetoric.com/). **The Cold War International History Bulletin (CWIHP) at Woodrow Wilson International Center for Scholars** provides you with hundreds of documents and in-depth articles from archives and scholars discussing Cold War history. You can find it at **www.cwihp.si.edu/**. It is a very useful source for Internal Assessment and Extended Essays.

There are always conflicts that attract more attention than others. The Cuban Missile Crisis is one. An absolutely outstanding source analysing this conflict is **Lebow** and **Stein**'s *We All Lost the Cold War* and another very special source showing the unique conversations in the ExComm is *The Kennedy Tapes: Inside the White House during the Cuban Missile Crisis* by Ernest **Zelikow** and Philip **May**.

There are accounts written by key decision makers during the Cold War which are very interesting, despite their obvious limitations concerning objectivity. **Khrushchev**'s memoirs 'Khrushchev Remembers' is a very common source in Paper 1 and fascinating to read. Michael **Gorbachev**'s 'Memoirs' is another interesting source. A comparable source is Henry **Kissinger**'s *American Foreign Policy*. Robert **Kennedy**'s *Thirteen Days* gives us his story about the Cuban Crisis. There are almost unlimited sources written by key decision makers: Brezezinski, Bush, Carter, Churchill, Dobrynin, Ford, Kennan, Nixon, Reagan, Sadat, Shultz and Thatcher all wrote their political 'story'.

Finally, the best and most useful television documentary is **CNN**'s *The Cold War*.

NOTES

NOTES

NOTES

NOTES

NOTES

IBDP REVISION COURSES

Summary

Who are they for?
Students about to take their final IBDP exams (May or November)

Locations include:
Oxford, UK
Rome, Italy
Brussels, Belgium
Dubai, UAE
Adelaide, Sydney & Melbourne, AUS
Munich, Germany

Duration
2.5 days per subject
Students can take multiple subjects

The most successful IB revision courses worldwide

Highly-experienced IB teachers and examiners

Every class is tailored to the needs of that particular group of students

---

Features

- Classes grouped by grade (UK)
- Exam skills and techniques – typical traps identified
- Exam practice
- Pre-course online questionnaire to identify problem areas
- Small groups of 8–10 students
- 24-hour pastoral care.

Revising for the final IB exams without expert guidance is tough. Students attending OSC Revision Courses get more work done in a shorter time than they could possibly have imagined.

With a different teacher, who is confident in their subject and uses their experience and expertise to explain new approaches and exam techniques, students rapidly improve their understanding. OSC's teaching team consists of examiners and teachers with years of experience – they have the knowledge and skills students need to get top grades.

The size of our Oxford course gives some particular advantages to students. With over 1,000 students and 300 classes, we can group students by grade – enabling them to go at a pace that suits them.

Students work hard, make friends and leave OSC feeling invigorated and confident about their final exams.

We understand the needs of IBDP students – our decades of experience, hand-picked teachers and intense atmosphere can improve your grades.

> "I got 40 points overall, two points up from my prediction of 38, and up 7 points from what I had been scoring in my mocks over the years, before coming to OSC. Thank you so much for all your help!"
>
> OSC Student

Please note that locations and course features are subject to change - please check our website for up-to-date details.

Find out more: osc-ib.com/revision +44 (0)1865 512802

MID IBDP SUMMER PROGRAMMES

Summary

Who is it for?
For students entering their final year of the IB Diploma Programme

Locations include:
Harvard and MIT, USA
Cambridge, UK

Duration
Min. 1 week, max. 6 weeks
1 or 2 IB subjects per week

- Improve confidence and grades
- Highly-experienced IB teachers and examiners
- Tailored classes to meet students' needs
- Wide range of available subjects
- Safe accommodation and 24-hour pastoral care

Features

- Morning teaching in chosen IB subject
- 2nd IB subject afternoon classes
- IB Skills afternoon classes
- One-to-one Extended Essay Advice, Private Tuition and University Guidance options
- Small classes
- Daily homework
- Unique IB university fair
- Class reports for parents
- Full social programme.

By the end of their first year, students understand the stimulating and challenging nature of the IB Diploma.

They also know that the second year is crucial in securing the required grades to get into their dream college or university.

This course helps students to avoid a 'summer dip' by using their time effectively. With highly-experienced IB teachers, we consolidate a student's year one learning, close knowledge gaps, and introduce some year two material.

In a relaxed environment, students develop academically through practice revision and review. They are taught new skills, techniques, and perspectives – giving a real boost to their grades. This gives students an enormous amount of confidence and drive for their second year.

> "The whole experience was incredible. The university setting was inspiring, the friends I made, and the teaching was first-class. I feel so much more confident in myself and in my subject."
>
> OSC Student

Please note that locations and course features are subject to change - please check our website for up-to-date details.

Find out more:  osc-ib.com/mid   +44 (0)1865 512802